Time Out

1000
things to do in New York

timeout.com

Published by Time Out Guides Ltd, a wholly owned subsidiary of Time Out Group Ltd.
Time Out and the Time Out logo are trademarks of Time Out Group Ltd.

© **Time Out Group Ltd 2008**

10 9 8 7 6 5 4 3 2 1

This edition first published in Great Britain in 2008 by Ebury Publishing
A Random House Group Company
20 Vauxhall Bridge Road, London SW1V 2SA

Random House Australia Pty Limited 20 Alfred Street, Milsons Point, Sydney, New South Wales 2061, Australia
Random House New Zealand Limited 18 Poland Road, Glenfield, Auckland 10, New Zealand
Random House South Africa (Pty) Limited Isle of Houghton, Corner Boundary, Road & Carse O'Gowrie,
Houghton 2198, South Africa

Random House UK Limited Reg. No. 954009

Distributed in USA by Publishers Group West
1700 Fourth Street, Berkeley, California 94710

Distributed in Canada by Publishers Group Canada
250A Carlton Street, Toronto, Ontario M5A 2L1

For further distribution details, see www.timeout.com

ISBN: 978-1-84670-085-9

A CIP catalogue record for this book is available from the British Library

Printed and bound by Firmengruppe APPL, aprinta druck, Wemding, Germany

The Random House Group Limited supports The Forest Stewardship Council (FSC), the leading international forest
certification organisation. All our titles that are printed on Greenpeace approved FSC certified paper carry the FSC
logo. Our paper procurement policy can be found at http://www.rbooks.co.uk/environment.

Time Out carbon-offsets all its flights with Trees for Cities (www.treesforcities.org).

Time Out Guides Limited
Universal House
251 Tottenham Court Road
London W1T 7AB
Tel + 44 (0)20 7813 3000
Fax + 44 (0)20 7813 6001
Email guides@timeout.com
www.timeout.com

Contributors Timothy Benzie, Cristina Black, Simon Coppock, Adam Feldman, Gabriella Gershenson, Richard Koss, Tom Lamont, Kate Lowenstein, Lee Magill, Jon McGrath, Katharine Rust, Drew Toal, Ben Walters, and contributors to *Time Out New York* and Time Out guides.

Interviews by Katharine Rust.

The Editor would like to thank the following for suggestions and assistance: Elizabeth Barr, Jane Borden, Sophie Freidman, Dustin Goot, Courtenay Kendall, Clare Lambe, Abigail Lelliott, Lisa Levinson, Ally Millar, Keith Mulvihill, Jay Muhlin, Christina Theisen, Nicole Tourtelot, Emily Weiner, Mike Wolf, Helen Yun.

Front and back cover by Sarina Finkelstein, Jeff Gurwin, Michael Kirby, Jonathan Perugia, Ben Rosenzweig, Alys Tomlinson and Time Out NY.

Photography by pages 3, 5 (top right, bottom left), 39, 65, 121, 138, 164, 170/171, 200, 247, 272, 296, 297, 307 Jonathan Perugia; pages 5 (top left), 7 (bottom left), 9 (middle), 22, 23, 30/31, 45, 53, 55, 76, 13, 101, 106, 107, 113, 146/147, 153, 154, 155, 163, 167, 180, 208, 212, 214, 224, 237, 266, 267, 275, 277, 285, 287, 299, 303 Ben Rosenzweig; pages 5 (top & bottom middle), 7 (left), 9 (bottom), 34, 64, 67, 86, 87, 105, 118, 127, 173, 182/183, 190/191, 201, 230/231, 246, 250/251, 252, 262, 282, 288, 294, 302 Alys Tomlinson; pages 5 (bottom right), 7 (top right), 43, 56, 57, 70, 71, 81, 82, 83, 85, 90/91, 95, 110/111, 116, 117, 130/131, 150/151, 157, 158/159, 188, 199, 204, 210/211, 219, 220, 221, 244, 261, 263, 273, 286, 308 Michael Kirby; pages 7 (bottom middle), 21, 50/51, 79, 124, 165, 193, 233, 243, 259, 290/291, 293, 300 Jeff Gurwin; pages 9 (top), 13, 234/235 Fumie Suzuki; pages 10/11 Jael Marschner; pages 5, 128, 178, 197, 270/271 Time Out NY; page 27 Ben Goldstein; page 28 D Finnin/AMNH; page 33 Ming Tang-Evans; pages 61, 203 Sarina Finkelstein; pages 74/75 Carol Taveras; pages 84, 255 Talia Simhi; page 89 Kathy King; pages 94, 205, 209, 217, 256 Cinzia Reale-Castello; page 97 Don Pollard; page 122 Heloise Bergman; pages 136, 148, 175 Jodie Love; page 149 Paul Brissman; page 189 Katelacey.com; page 202 Nami Sung; page 223 Alexander Milligan; page 238 Mr Bullitt; page 239 Scott McDermott; page 248 Ralph Modica; page 257 Roxana Marriquin; pages 264, 265 Vincent Amasse; pages 276, 278 Beth Levendis.
The following images were provided by the featured establishment/artists: pages 29, 69, 169, 195, 215, 222, 241.

Illustrations Ian Keltie – www.keltiecochrane.com.

Contents

About the guide

Telephone numbers

All phone numbers listed in this guide assume that you are calling from within New York. From elsewhere in the US, dial 1 followed by the listed number. From abroad, dial your international access code, then 1 for the US, followed by the listed number.

Disclaimer

While every effort has been made to ensure the accuracy of information within this guide, the publishers cannot accept responsibility for any errors it may contain. Businesses can change their arrangements at any time so, before you go out of your way, we strongly advise you to phone ahead to check opening times, prices and other particulars.

Advertisers

The recommendations in *1000 Things to do in New York* are based on the experiences of Time Out journalists. No payment or PR invitation of any kind has secured inclusion or influenced content. The editors select which venues and activities are listed in this guide, and the list of 1,000 was compiled before any advertising space was sold. Advertising has no effect on editorial content.

Let us know what you think

Did we miss anything? We welcome tips for 'things' you consider we should include in future editions and take note of your criticism of our choices. You can email us at guides@timeout.com.

THIS IS
YOUR NEW YORK™

Introduction

Despite the rigid street grid, New York ain't an orderly city. Chock-full and frenetic, fascinating and frustrating in equal measure, it defies easy arrangement: Spend a day clambering rocks surrounded by skyscrapers, viewing Vermeers in the morning and waterfalls in the afternoon, eating foie gras for brunch and bagels at midnight—*then* try to put this motley city into some kind of order.

We haven't tried. Instead, our suggestions for 1,000 things to do in New York—sourced from *Time Out New York*'s peerless team of city experts, rabid Gothamites every one— come at you without arbitrary pigeon-holing, as a flurry of ideas and tips and suggestions, the better to inspire you to activity on a quiet Sunday or a for gaping hour in the afternoon.

This guide does not categorize, alphabetize or rank; number one does not represent the city's best, nor 1,000 its worst (though there is a handy thematic index on *p315* for those who crave some kind of arrangement). What we love is the awesome aggregation of sights, tastes, events and activities within the five boroughs, and this book is an ode to our favorites: From waterfalls in Brooklyn to puppet shows in Central Park, Czech food in Queens to milk and cookies in Chelsea, ice-cream floats made with stout to margaritas made with pork rind, youthful yoga classes for carpet-crawlers to napkin-sketching classes for bar-crawlers. We'll reveal where to play outdoor chess and indoor golf, sing-a-long at a piano bar or sit in silence at a church recital, take a load off in a Chinese massage parlor or expand your mind in a black-lit library. Want more? How about the town's tastiest grilled cheese, fanciest public toilets, naughtiest statues, liveliest kids' theaters, finest fries, prettiest blocks, kitchiest photo booths and most-perfect pizzas. Hey— we'll even tell you what *not* to do.

Our 1,000 things may not exhaust New York's varied offerings; that might not be possible. But these are our unmissables—and we dare you to work through them all.

Tom Lamont, Editor

1

Top the Rock to admire the Empire State

We love the Empire State Building. We do. But as an observation point, the Top of the Rock deck beats it hands down. How so? Easy: The 360-degree viewing platform atop the Rockefeller Center tower (30 Rockefeller Plaza between 49th and 50th Sts) doesn't just offer a brilliant panorama of the city, it offers a brilliant panorama that includes the ESB—rising out of Manhattan in all its glory. Case closed.

2 Enjoy Sunday music at the Frick

Not content with being home to one of the best fine art holdings in the world, the Frick Collection puts on a stellar concert series on intermittent Sunday afternoons. With its glass dome and elegant wallpaper, the Music Room evokes the 19th-century salon that robber baron Henry Clay Frick doubtless intended—a sublime setting for chamber music. Cheap deal alert: If you'd rather skip the $25 ticket price, you can listen in from the Garden Court.

Frick Collection *1 E 70th St between Madison and Fifth Aves (212-547-0715/shopfrick.org/concerts/tickets).*

3 See a trial at the Criminal Courts

Forget *Judge Judy*, we're talking real perps hoping to avoid real jail time. Each of the courts is open to the public on weekdays from 9am to 5pm, with your best bet for legal drama the Criminal Courts. Even if you can't slip into a trial, you can at least observe legal eagles and their clients, or observe the pleas at the Arraignment Court (until 1am).

Criminal Courts Building & Manhattan Detention Complex *100 Centre St between Leonard and White Sts.*

4 Party at P.S.1

Summer's not officially here until the Warm Up music series, an orgiastic block party, begins at the end of June. These Saturday late-afternoon/early-evening hoedowns take place weekly in the courtyard of Long Island City's P.S.1 Contemporary Art Center. The party, which has featured such luminaries as the Scissor Sisters and DJ Harvey, has evolved from its humble beginnings to stupendous heights, with more than 4,000 up-for-it party people regularly packing the concrete courtyard.

P.S.1 Contemporary Art Center *22-25 Jackson Ave at 46th Ave, Long Island City (718-784-2084/ps1.org).*

5 Go bouldering in Central Park

At the north end of Central Park, just west of Harlem Meer, is a mysterious dark rock, about ten feet tall. Its wrinkled face is marked not only by the hand of nature—responsible for the glacial fractures, the faint bloom of moss—but also by the hand of humans. Smudges of white chalk form what at first appears to be a random pattern, an indecipherable but perhaps important message.

The chalk marks the places where "boulderers" (climbers without ropes) have clung to the unforgiving rock, their sinews stretched and muscles bulging as they search for trails along its face. Such routes are called "problems" in the parlance of the sport, which requires nothing more than climbing shoes, a bag of powdered chalk, and the desire to shred one's fingertips. Boulderers are an obsessive bunch, and they put a high value on rocks like this one, where they can work their minds and muscles to the max while never getting more than ten feet off the ground. Ironic it is, then, that this particular piece of Manhattan schist is called Worthless Boulder.

Worthless has a colorful history. Back in the 1980s, boulderers dubbed it Rap Rock and named its problems after Run-DMC songs and bands like Public Enemy. Until the early 2000s, junkies and hookers used to favor the spot, which was clogged with foliage and sprinkled with broken glass. Once, a corpse was found lying behind Worthless's silent bulk. But by building alliances with the park authorities, the city's tight-knit climbing community cleaned up the area. Today, it's clear of brush and debris. A fresh carpet of wood chips cushions the ground beneath the most technically challenging problem on the face, now tagged as Mean Green.

For information on climbing in the park (Rat Rock, near Heckscher Playground, is another favorite locale), call the Central Park Conservancy at 212-348-4867 or visit climbnyc.com.

Nicky's

6
Order a banh mi at Nicky's

Good *banh mi* is a marvel of contrasting flavors and textures, brilliant ingredients combined into a simple sandwich: salty pork pâté, sweet pickled carrots, thick cuts of cool cucumber, and cilantro on a mayo-slathered, toasted baguette. Ninh Van Dang made exceptional *banh mi* at An Dong, his famous Sunset Park shop, and his fans are thrilled that the restaurant was reincarnated (albeit in slightly altered form) as this East Village spot.

The family has expanded the sandwich line-up, adding chicken, pork chops, and portobello to the original roster of pork pâté and sardine. Ultimately, though, there's no reason (short of being vegetarian or Kosher) to order anything but the classic: A $5 sandwich that's crunchy, tangy and supremely addictive.

Nicky's Vietnamese *150 E 2nd St between Aves A and B (212-388-1088).*

7
Look for the clipboard guy outside the AMC

Hard-core cinéastes stand outside AMC Loews Lincoln Square 13 weekend evenings and keep their eyes peeled for a dude with a clipboard. He's from Movie View, a marketing company that holds test screenings waaaay in advance. Late last year, we were offered same-day tickets—for as many friends as we wanted—to a rough cut of *Baby Mama*, a comedy starring Tina Fey released the following April. To register without stalking anyone, go online to screeningsexchange.com, or call 877-842-9247, and sign up for e-mail invites.

8
Sip a beer on the Staten Island Ferry

The gratis trip on the Staten Island Ferry is like a 30-minute booze cruise sans entry price and stale soundtrack. Kick back with $3 beers (served from 8am to 4am) on one of the wooden benches while cruising at 16 knots past Lady Liberty and Ellis Island.

9-17 *Get to know the other Fifth Avenue*

Think of Manhattan's Fifth Avenue, and you'll most likely picture museums, fur coats and a whole lot of tourists. But for a cross section of New York life, you need to stroll Brooklyn's Fifth Avenue from beginning to end: Eastern European, Mexican, Middle Eastern, Italian—the neighborhoods blend seamlessly together, yet each remains distinct.

Start to explore from Pacific St station. From there you can go Irish at O'Connor's (39 Fifth Ave between Bergen and Dean Sts, 718-783-9721), a landmark bar that's been pouring cheap pints since 1931. Then wander down the tree-lined avenue past disparate storefronts—a sleek yoga center next to an old-school shop selling Jesus figurines—until you reach Apropos Café (186 Fifth Ave between DeGraw and Sackett Sts, 718-230-7605). This elegant little café and wine bar serves potent iced coffee ($2) made with roasted Danesi beans. When you hit J.J. Byrne Memorial Park on 3rd Street, head in and visit the Old Stone House (718-768-3195), a replica of the Dutch domicile occupied by the British during the Revolutionary War's key Battle of Brooklyn.

Keep going, and just past the Prospect Expressway, you'll find Eagle Provisions (628 Fifth Ave at 18th St, 718-499-0026), a nod to the neighborhood's pocket of Eastern Europeans. Hanging kielbasa and a room full of cheap international brews are reminiscent of Beerfest—the first time that's ever been a good thing. Green-Wood Cemetery (500 25th St, 718-768-7300) is worth an in-depth tour by itself, but just the dramatic entrance at 25th Street will entrance with its magical Gothic archway laden with birds' nests. Make do with a detour up a few steep steps to Artemesia Path, which overlooks stunning mausoleums. At 41st Street, climb the hilly staircase up to Sunset Park, one of Brooklyn's highest points, and look beyond the commercial chaos for calming views of the East River.

After that, there's a slew of Mexican restaurants along the stretch at 58th Street. Refuel at authentic Cinco Estrellas (5724 Fifth Ave at 57th St, 718-492-1212), where you can plop down in a pink booth and listen to upbeat Spanish music while locals sit on barstools with Coronas. A big plate of chilaquiles ($6.95) comes with a spicy salsa verde and smoky refried beans. Then, around 68th Street, you'll notice storefronts adorned with Arabic letters, women with their hair shrouded in scarves, and hookah pipes beckoning from the windows. At Lebanese-owned Sweet Delights (6818 Fifth Ave between Bay Ridge Ave and 68th St, 718-491-5885), snare boxes of baklava and Saudi Arabian dates, or freshly baked, walnut-filled maamoul cookies from one of the trays.

Come 95th Street, Fifth Avenue unites with Fourth and you're almost at the Verrazano Bridge. Cross the Belt Parkway to the Shore Parkway Promenade and you'll get a spectacular view of New York Bay. Or, if you're tired from the hike, rest on the grass at John Paul Jones Park (between Shore Rd and 101st St), named for the American patriot born and raised in... Scotland.

Recharged and feeling smugly cosmopolitan, it's time to feel all New Yorker again: steady yourself and get ready to board the R at 95th.

Green-Wood Cemetery

Dance Polish in Greenpoint

The nexus of Greenpoint's burgeoning indie-rock scene, Warsaw at the Polish National Home (261 Driggs Ave at Eckford St, Greenpoint, Brooklyn, 718-387-0505, warsaw concerts.com) presents live acts such as the New Pornographers and TV on the Radio. On occasional Saturday nights, the high-ceilinged 1914 hall reverts back to its original (and still daytime) identity as the Polish National Home, hosting Polish dance parties with plenty of canned Frankie Yankovic. No matter who's in attendance, $3.50 Jack and Cokes and $5 noshes (pierogi, kielbasa and cheese blintzes) are available.

Expand their little minds at two children's museums

Worried the youngster's not getting enough mental stimulation? Head to the Children's Museum of Manhattan (212 W 83rd St between Amsterdam Avenue and Broadway, 212-721-1234, cmom.org, admission free-$9) and plug them into the Inventor Center. Here computer-savvy kids can take any idea they dream up—a flying bike, a talking robot—and design it on-screen using digital imaging. Once they're convinced the world could be a brilliant place, take them to the Brooklyn Children's Museum (145 Brooklyn Ave at St Marks Ave, Crown Heights, Brooklyn, 718-735-4400, brooklynkids.org, admission $5) and show them that it already is. Founded in 1899 as the world's first museum designed for kids and refurbed this year, BCM was due to reopen (at the time of writing) in Spring 2008. If your offspring can't find something of interest among the 20,000 or so artefacts—prehistoric fossils, international toys—it's probably time to give up and hand 'em back to the carer.

Get a bit of woopie at Baked

Sweet freaks could die happy after a single mouth-stretching bite of this two-hands-necessary take on the classic woopie pie ($2.50). Soft cake envelopes a thick dollop of creamy filling. Oh boy.

Baked *359 Van Brunt St between Dikeman and Wolcott Sts, Red Hook, Brooklyn (718-222-0345).*

Keep your cool at the Village Vanguard

Still going strong after more than 70 years, the Village Vanguard (178 Seventh Ave at Perry St, 212-255-4037, villagevanguard.com) is one of New York's real jazz meccas. Coltrane, Miles, Dizzy and Bill Evans have all grooved in this former speakeasy, whose photo-lined walls testify to the spot's hallowed history. Big names—old and new—continue to fill the lineup at this basement joint, and the 16-piece Vanguard Jazz Orchestra has been the Monday night regular for almost 40 years. Reservations are a must and it's cash only at the bar.

Delve into the Anthology Film Archives

Led by the indefatigable Jonas Mekas, this East Village treasure, which opened in 1970 and moved here in 1979, is a mandatory destination for all lovers of—and newbies looking to explore—avant-garde film and video. There are two movie theaters for screenings, as well as a library and gallery space to ensure all angles are covered.

Anthology Film Archives *32 Second Ave at 2nd St (212-505-5181/anthologyfilmarchives.org).*

23

Run up the Empire State

King Kong may have preferred clambering up the exterior, but every February hundreds of runners take to the 40-foot wide stairs of the Empire State Building for one of the city's more strenuous races, the ESB Run Up. From the bottom to the observation deck on the 86th floor, participants cover 1576 steps—an altitude of 1050ft. While the record is nine minutes and 33 seconds, most runners straggle up several minutes later. Their reward: The view from the tallest skyscraper in the city. And an elevator ride back down. Applications to run can be made online with the New York Road Runners (nyrr.org).

24 *Get the real island vibe*

Even though Manhattan is an island, it doesn't much feel like one. Maybe it's because humans have managed to pile so much concrete, glass and steel on to such a narrow little strip of land that any sense of natural topography is all but lost. Still, anyone looking for an escape may be surprised to learn that another island, one offering gentle ocean breezes and many picturesque 19th-century homes, lies within easy reach.

In 1637, so the story goes, a Dutchman "paid" the native Lenape tribe who were living on the island two axe heads, some beads and a few nails for full ownership of the tiny island. In 1664, the British put a dampener on any plans the Dutch might have had when they took over New Amsterdam and renamed it New York, eventually taking over official ownership of the island, changing the name from Nutten Island (named for its wealth of nut trees) to Governors Island.

The island's strategic location, smack-bang in the middle of New York Harbor, cemented its future as a military outpost, and for more than 200 years it was strictly off limits to the public. All that changed in the mid 1990s, when the United States Coast Guard decided to give up the high cost of island life and decamp. The island sat in limbo for several years while New Yorkers bandied plans about. In summer 2008, the island will, for the second year, be welcoming visitors from June until September.

Just a five-minute ferry ride from Manhattan (catch it from the Battery Maritime Building, Slip No.7, directly east of the Staten Island Ferry terminal), the 172-acre isle still retains a significant chunk of its military-era construction, including Fort Jay, started in 1776, and Castle Williams, completed in 1812 and for years used as a prison. The 22-acre area containing the forts and historical residences is now a national landmark, meaning that plans for casinos or expensive high-rise condos are—thankfully—out of the question. Today, the island is jointly run by the city, the state and the National Park Service.

"Each year we're hoping to further expand the activities available," explains Leslie Koch, president of the Governors Island Preservation & Education Corporation. So far, island activities include biking and a summer-long concert series on Saturday afternoons at Colonel's Row. The National Parks Service also organises free historical walking tours, during which you'll learn about the former Army base's checkered past. Governors Island has been a site for everything from 17th-century transvestites and Civil War internments to President Reagan's famous lunch summit with Mikhail Gorbachev in 1988.

The short walk from the ferry terminal to the charming historic grounds is like stepping into a time machine that whisks you back to 1950s smalltown America, an Ivy League campus and a Revolutionary War battleground all at the same time. It has the almost surreal atmosphere of an abandoned film studio's back lot: turn one corner and you're on the set of *Pleasantville*, turn another and you're in *The Shawshank Redemption*. The script for Governors Island's third century is just waiting to be written.

Governors Island *212-825-3045/www.nps.gov/gois*

---

25 *Eat at Daniel, the chefs' favorite restaurant*

Last year we asked 40 top chefs (anonymous, but you'd know them all) what was the best restaurant in New York. Daniel Boulud's Upper East Side restaurant Daniel scored the most votes. You can tell from revolving door off Park Avenue and the grandiose interior, with neoclassical columns and velvet seats: This is fine dining. The cuisine is rooted in French technique with au courant flourishes like fusion elements and an emphasis on local produce. You can expect the likes of cooked pluots, a smart acidic counterpoint to seared foie gras, or Vermont veal cooked three ways (crisp sweetbreads, rare tenderloin, braised cheeks) on the $105 three-course prix fixe or $175 six-course prix fixe. The pastry chef's creations—perhaps a frothy vacherin, dotted with potently flavored peaks of lemon meringue and raspberry marshmallow—are whimsical and delicious.

Daniel *60 E 65th St between Madison and Park Aves (212-288-0033).*

Got the balls?

Hipster? Mommy? Old-timer? Everybody's got the bocce bug.
Kate Lowenstein *rolls up for a game.*

New York hipsters are finally learning for themselves what the old men of Italy, France, the former Yugoslavia and Queens could have told them ages ago: Bocce—a close sibling of pétanque, boçanje and bowls—is an excellent way to pass a few hours. Or a lifetime, as the case may be for those European seniors.

Upon stepping into Floyd (131 Atlantic Ave between Clinton and Henry Sts, Cobble Hill, Brooklyn, 718-858-5810), the cozily ramshackle neighborhood bar that introduced bocce to the twenty- and thirtysomething set when it opened in 2004, I was greeted warmly by a crowd of strangers battling out the end of a three-month-long tournament. It took about 15 seconds to understand the blessedly simple game (and this is coming from someone who needs to be reminded of the rules every time she plays horseshoes): Two teams compete to get their balls (made of plastic or metal) as close as possible to a smaller ball, called a pallino. Said to have its roots in a diversion popular during

the Roman Empire, this ancient game requires a minimum of skill to take part—and hence is accessible even to uncoordinated souls who can't make it through a round of darts without missing the corkboard altogether.

"There are two camps of bocce players," announces Matt, a beer-wielding member of team Kiss My Pallino. "Half of us are here to drink and have fun, and the other half is very serious about the game. Those are the people in the matching shirts." A quick schmooze with the uniformed players was enough to make me question Matt's prejudice: Everyone, it seems, was there to drink and have fun, and while those in identical shirts possibly showed a little more team spirit, the whole thing was clearly more about drinking, flirting and generally making merry than anything else. Floyd makes an appropriate backdrop: Mismatched fraying couches, a twanging country music soundtrack (or whatever the jukebox is playing) and an extensive whiskey bar is good for a homey,

Floyd

cheerful afternoon and evening—even if your team is losing. Which is what Matt's team did (losing, that is, to the uniformless team Watch Your Balls), but not before a suspenseful moment involving a tape measure to determine the final score.

Bocce at Floyd is played on a 40-foot-long, red clay court whose pockmarks the old-hand players have memorized. When I visited, the tournament was in its tenth season—long enough for team Boccelism (the subject of much bathroom-wall commentary) to have won four

> *"Playing bocce was clearly more about making merry than anything else."*

times, according to player Chris Mooney of the Coffee Flats Terrors, which has won twice. While winning clearly isn't a priority for every team—victors are rewarded with $200 and a four-hour stint in a limo with a clown—most partake in the trash talk and swagger.

One such cocky group is the Bourbon Balls, whose only female member, Christine "I'm kind of like Smurfette" Nimock, explains that being a woman counts neither for her nor against her in the game. "The ratio is probably about 70 to 30, men to women," she says, "and the women are either as good or better." (So much for that nasty rumor about our faulty spatial reasoning abilities.) When asked about the recently opened bar Union Hall (702 Union St between Fifth and Sixth Aves, Park Slope, Brooklyn, 718-638-4400), which is under the same ownership as Floyd, Nimock sneers. "The people who play bocce there are trendy," she says, "but not good-trendy. They're the kind of people who had to move to Park Slope because it's the only neighborhood they'd ever heard of outside of Manhattan." Ouch.

With its furniture upholstery intact, a handful of fireplaces, and a menu that includes elaborate salads called the James E Walker and the Jerome F Peck (taken from an old photo of a group of shriners in the back of the bar), we wondered if by "trendy" Smurfette might have just meant "less scruffy." The Union Hall crowd

may be hoodie-under-blazer to Floyd's baseball-cap-and-t-shirt, but you'd have to be looking pretty hard to make that distinction. And who's looking when there are two 40-foot-length har-tru bocce courts to ogle instead? After putting my name on a list and waiting my turn, I had a go at the sport (can we call it that and pretend we're getting exercise?), playing against a friendly couple who were more than happy to share some of the finer points of the game with me (when to put backspin on the ball, for example, and how hitting the opponent's orbs out of the way is called "spocking"). They then wasted no time in beating me at it. Despite my losses, I found the civility of the game and satisfying thwack of the balls addictive.

"I got the idea for a bocce court in Florida, of all places," laughs Jim Carden, who (along with Andy Templar) owns both Floyd and Union Hall. "It was in a clearing in the woods out in the boondocks, and to get to it you had to take Sewer Line Road. But what I loved about it was that there were Cubans, Puerto Ricans, Floridians, punk rockers and us—the tourists—all playing together. It struck me as a trans-cultural phenomenon that would work well in Brooklyn." And indeed it has worked well, though the Cobble Hill and Park Slope crowds aren't as diverse as the Sewer Line Road one.

For those not interested in knocking balls with trendsters—or young people at all, for that matter—there's always the Istria Sport Club (28-09 Astoria Blvd between 28th and 29th Sts, Astoria, Queens, 718-728-3181). When my friends and I entered the two-level restaurant and asked to play bocce, the host looked at us like we were aliens asking for a handout. That was either because we were the only native English-speakers in the sea of Istrian families eating and watching soccer on the massive TV screen, or because it was the dead of winter and the court was outside. In any case, after some unintelligible whispering and pointing, the owner graciously got out the balls and led us to the back patio, where the 80-foot, packed sand court made us feel like hot tub regulars plopped into an Olympic pool. Happily, the game was just as pleasurable in its larger iteration (there's something great about being able to put a little oomph into your toss, actually), and we had a Yugoslavian bocce champion advising us along the way ("bocce is good for your body," he said solemnly). Cheap drinks (generous helpings of beer and wine are $3 each) and passable food (we liked the fuzi, ownmade Istrian noodles, $10) sealed the deal: This is the place to come if you're looking for the bocce but not the scene.

Those who aren't intrepid enough to find Park Slope or Astoria (goodness knows what Smurfette would say about you) will be glad to know that there's also indoor bocce to be found in Manhattan. At Il Vagabondo (351 E 62nd between First and Second Aves, 212-832-9221), once a local hangout for Northern Italian immigrants, diners eat at checkered tablecloths beside a 100-year-old, 60-foot clay court. The food here is unmemorable (expect little beyond spaghetti with meat sauce, $13), and the wine not nearly as cheap as in Astoria ($8 for a glass—they are paying Manhattan rent prices for that court, after all), but the kindly waiters will smile and clue you in on the game if you couldn't possibly pass as a regular.

Because of its central location, Il Vagabondo bridges the divide between yuppie players and Old World pros. Otherwise, the latter tend to hold court outdoors—a warm day yields games everywhere from the Washington Square arch to Bath Beach Park, Brooklyn—while the former stay close to the jukebox and Schlitz supply. But our guess is that it won't be long before the more youthful pallino chasers catch onto the highlight of the year for the older community: The annual bocce tournament, held every September in Juniper Park, Queens. The winners get to ride on a float in the Columbus Day parade—and call themselves the best bocce team in New York City. And what trash-talking whippersnapper wouldn't like that?

Union Hall

30-37 *Spend the weekend surfing, without leaving Gotham*

While New York will never be mistaken for a premier surfing destination, that doesn't mean you can't find some gnarly waves here, brah. The problem is that what most city-dwellers know about surfing comes from Point Break. Fortunately, you don't have to go to the South Pacific to experience surfing: There are plenty of tubes right here.

First things first—hop on the LIRR ($6.75 each way from Penn Station, off-peak) to Long Beach. After disembarking, cross West Park Avenue to Bi-Wise Drugs (26 W Park Ave, 516-432-7131) to purchase a beach day pass ($10) before dropping your stuff off at Jackson by the Beach Hotel (405 E Broadway, 516-431-3700; from $120), one of the few places in town to spend the night. It has a Serra-esque Minimalist thing going on, and the televisions date from the days of Frankie and Annette, but it's conveniently situated near the ocean and downtown.

Catch the N33 bus and head to West Beech Street, where you can rent a bike at Buddy's Bikes Etc (907 W Beech St, 516-431-0804; $25 per day) and cruise around the bar- and restaurant-laden west end of Long Beach. After you return your rental, cross the street to The Beach House (906 W Beech St, no phone), an open-air bar that has live music and tasty crab cakes ($14). Later, turn to The Inn (943 W Beech St, 516-432-9220) for an evening of sweaty dance-and-grope.

Next morning, head just a few blocks to The Coffee Nut Café (250 E Park Ave, 516-897-6616), where the wide variety of java flavors ($1.65-$2.75) will help you recover from your long, sordid night. Unless you traffic in board shorts, stock up on beach gear at Unsound Surf (359 E Park Ave, 516-889-1112, unsoundsurf.com) and sign up for lessons with Elliot Zuckerman of Surf2Live Surfing School (516-432-9211, surf2live.com; from $65). "Listen, you're the quarterback jock. It's all balance and coordination. How hard can it be?" Well, Keanu, as it turns out, pretty hard. The group lessons at Long Beach are about 90 minutes long, and Zuckerman's staff—all young and tan—teach you how to stand up properly. Later, they give you push-starts into waves so you're not just floundering around on your board. Plus, the school provides all of the equipment. After being disabused of the idea that you'll be a natural at surfing, grab a bite to eat at Corbin & Reynolds (20 W Park Ave, 516-431-4600). Clean yourself up first, though; burgers run about $10.

Continue your surf odyssey in Far Rockaway, a ten-minute cab ride from Long Beach, although the two wave-heavy beaches there have a tendency to get crowded on the weekends (go early in the morning). Also, most locals don't take kindly to neophytes who get in the way. ("This is where you tell me all about how locals rule, and yuppie insects like me shouldn't be surfing your break.") Those who want to stay on the path of Keanu should consider taking the first few surf trips with a friend who actually knows what he or she is doing. This will help prevent disaster, whether it's in the form of a bad wipeout or just getting your ass kicked for being stupid. Overcrowded surf beaches can bring out the worst in people. If you're unsure where to go or how to comport yourself, ask around at The Rockaway Beach Surf Shop (177 Beach 116th St, 718-474-9345).

Late morning, head back to the city and strike the right note by hitting up Bondi Road (153 Rivington St between Clinton and Suffolk Sts, 212-253-5311), a bar named after that most famous of Sydney beaches. It has a $15 all-you-can-drink brunch, which will put you into an appropriate state of mind for the coma-inducing Lomi Lomi Hawaiian Luau Massage at Just Calm Down (32 W 22nd St between Fifth and Sixth Aves, 212-337-0032; $175 for 60mins). While Keanu didn't get a rubdown, your fatigued muscles will appreciate the traditional pushing and pulling motions delivered to your back, care of Hawaii-native Kawai Anakalea.

38 Love the ukulele

A four-day pluckapalooza in early April, the NY Uke Fest (nyukefest.com) at the Theater for the New City (155 First Ave between 9th and 10th Sts, 212-352-3101) draws ukulele aficionados with performances, jam sessions, workshops and vendors offering new, used and rare instruments. The ukulele was invented in Hawaii in the 1880s (the name means "jumping flea" in Hawaiian, a reference to the nimble fingers of a skilled player), but has seen a recent resurgence from a New York-centric "ukulele underground," whose numbers include Stephin Merritt, the Hazzards and the Moonlighters. No word yet on any air ukulele performances.

39

Dedicate a seat to someone at the Film Forum

With its premier programming and rich repertory offerings (ranging from Hitchcock to Ousmane Sembene), this West Village theater is a veritable cine-oasis. But don't stop at buying a ticket. "One of the benefits of donating to Film Forum at a 'higher level' is getting to dedicate a seat plaque to yourself or anyone you desire," says programmer Mike Maggiore.

"Two of my favorite seat plaques are located next to each other," says Maggiore. The seats, B and C in row 18 of the second theatre, were donated by Frances McDormand and Joel Coen. They read: "Through the generosity of Karl Mundt" (the name of John Goodman's insurance salesman-cum-psycho in *Barton Fink*) and "In loving memory of Doris Crane" (the name of McDormand's boozy, bingo-obsessed murder victim in *The Man Who Wasn't There*). Who will you dedicate yours to?
Film Forum *209 W Houston St between Sixth Ave and Varick St (212-627-2035/filmforum.org).*

40 Catch Barbara Carroll at the Oak Room

Barbara Carroll's sublime weekly cabaret brunch at the historic Algonquin Hotel has become the stuff of jazz legend. The cool, light swing of her piano playing is matched by her effortless elegance. Carroll is in her 80s, so that's seven decades of musicianship you're listening to, distilled into the quintessence of Manhattan chic.
The Oak Room *Algonquin Hotel, 59 W 44th St between Fifth and Sixth Aves (212-419-9331/ algonquinhotel.com).*

41 Take nookie seriously at the Museum of Sex

Despite the subject matter, don't expect too much titillation at this museum (admission $13.50-$14.50). Instead, you'll find presentations of historical documents and items—many of which were too risqué to be made public in their own time—that explore prostitution, burlesque, birth control, obscenity and fetishism. More fun is the extensive collection of pornography that forms the Ralph Whittington Collection: Gathered by a retired Library of Congress curator, it features thousands of items, including hundreds of 8mm films and videos, as well as blow-up dolls and other erotic paraphernalia.
Museum of Sex *233 Fifth Ave at 27th St (212-689-6337/mosex.org).*

42 See a horserace at the most urban track in America

Belmont can keep its airs and graces, the rough-and-ready Aqueduct (110-00 Rockaway Blvd at 110th St, Jamaica, Queens, 718-641-4700, nyra.com) is the only track we know of with a subway station. And seeing the race here beats the hell out of any OTB parlor. This is where men who like racing come. If you fancy joining them, The Wood Memorial (a test run in spring for promising three-year-olds) is the key event each year. Otherwise, races run Oct-May, Wed-Sun.

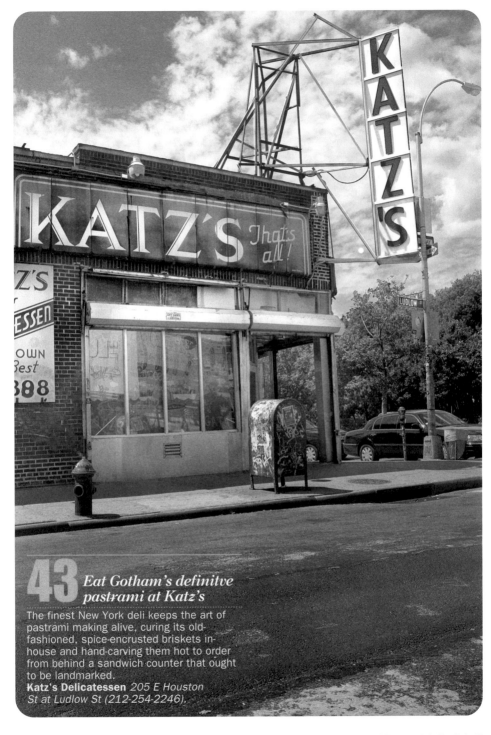

43 Eat Gotham's definitve pastrami at Katz's

The finest New York deli keeps the art of pastrami making alive, curing its old-fashioned, spice-encrusted briskets in-house and hand-carving them hot to order from behind a sandwich counter that ought to be landmarked.

Katz's Delicatessen *205 E Houston St at Ludlow St (212-254-2246).*

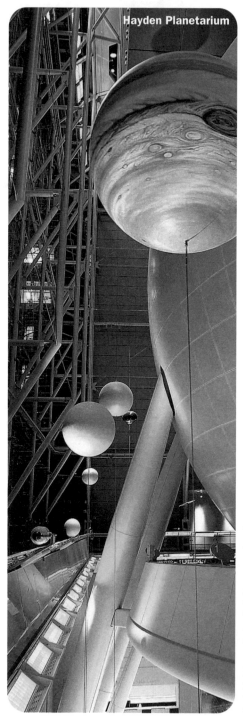

Hayden Planetarium

44-54

Put on some plus-fours and play a round of golf

Golf in this city isn't limited to launching balls off your tenement roof. There are plenty of great public courses nearby, most of which take about five hours to play 18 holes and cost a little over $50. Here are our favorites.

Clearview Golf Course
With epic, Saharan bunkers and great scenery, Clearview is popular—it's a good idea to secure tee times a few weeks in advance.
202-12 Willets Point Blvd, Queens (718-229-2570).

Douglaston Golf Course
Thanks to seven par 3s, this venue caters to those with Furyk-esque short-iron precision.
63-20 Marathon Pkwy, Douglaston (718-224-6566).

Dyker Beach
Tiger Woods' late father, Earl Woods, discovered golf at Dyker Beach while stationed at Fort Hamilton. And it's just a 15-minute walk from the subway.
Seventh Ave and 86th St, Brooklyn (718-836-9722).

Kissena Park Golf Course
The short (you should be able to play it in about three hours) and deceptively challenging layout offers a good view of Manhattan. It was designed by John Van Kleek, the same gentleman who shaped the course at Split Rock.
165 Booth Memorial Ave, Queens (718-939-4594).

La Tourette Golf Course
Probably the best public course in town. There's significant wait time, but quality has its price.
1001 Richmond Hill Rd, Staten Island (718-351-1889).

Marine Park
It's the longest course in NYC and conditions here have improved markedly in recent years.
2880 Flatbush Ave, Brooklyn (718-338-7113).

Mosholu Golf Course

Mosholu's a nine-hole course with double tees for a full round. There are lots of trees and very little water. Games are a speedy 2.5 hours.
3700 Jerome Ave, Bronx (718-655-9164).

Pelham Bay & Split Rock

Pelham Bay has rolling, open fairways and not much water. Hole #9 is notable for its myriad bunkers. Split Rock, on the other hand, is a series of challenging, Scottish-style holes that crescendo with a spirit-crushing back nine. Mind the mosquitos.
870 Shore Rd, Bronx (718-885-1258).

Silver Lake Golf Course

It's tighter than your gin-soaked uncle. You know—the one with the violent, explosive temper. Getting there involves a sea-crossing (it's Staten Island, dummy), but the connecting bus is pretty convenient.
915 Victory Blvd, Staten Island (718-447-5686).

South Shore Golf Club

To paraphrase Mike Tyson, its style is impetuous and its defense (by way of many greenside bunkers) is impregnable. And it's in excellent condition. You'll have a 40-minute bus ride from the ferry, though.
200 Huguenot Ave, Staten Island (718-984-0101).

Van Cortlandt Park

The oldest public US course, Van Cortlandt was conceived before women could vote in America. There are often crowds and long walks between holes, so allow 5.5 hours.
98 Van Cortlandt Ave East, Bronx (718-543-4595).

55 Watch a stellar show in the Hayden Planetarium

Gifted with a major facelift in 2000, the American Museum of Natural History's amphitheater dazzles audiences with changing productions like the Robert Redford-narrated "Cosmic Collisions," which explored the explosive encounters that created the Milky Way and altered the course of life on Earth.
Hayden Planetarium *American Museum of Natural History, Central Park West at 81st St (212-769-5100/amnh.org).*

A few of my favorite things

56-59

Jacques Torres, chocolatier

Most people forget that Manhattan is an island and that there are huge, wild, striped bass that swim in the East River and the bay in front of the Statue of Liberty. It's something unbelievable to sit in a boat next to New York City—where you have the background of all those downtown buildings and the beautiful Statue—and catch these huge fish. I've caught some that were 40 inches long. I charter boats with Captain John McMurray (718-791-2094, nycflyfishing.com) or Captain Ralf Burtis (516 887-2784, apralph@optonline.net).

The authenticity of foreign cuisine in New York is incredible. I love going to different restaurants for different types of food because it's as though I'm eating in any number of countries.

For Italian, I go to Roberto Passon (741 Ninth Ave, 212-582-5599, roberto passon.com). Roberto, the owner, is from Northern Italy and the food really has the flavor from the region. It has a good chef, low prices, amazing food and the best preparation of octopus in the city.

For Spanish food, La Nacional Tapas Bar (239 W 14th St, 212-243-9308, lanacionaltapas.com) has the absolute best paella in New York. A lot of my family is from Ibeza so I know what real Spanish food is. This is it.

For other cuisines, I love the smoked eel at Fuji (238 W 56th St, 212-245-8594), while Victor's Café (236 W 52nd St, 212-586-7714, victorscafe.com) is a fantastic Cuban restaurant where the oxtail is just unbelievable.

60

Learn to trapeze

For most people, watching a flying trapezist from a third-row circus seat is as close as they've ever gotten to experiencing the thrill. But thanks to España-Streb Trapeze Academy (51 N 1st St, Williamsburg, Brooklyn, 718-384-6491/espanastreb trapeze.org), those daring enough can soar to new heights. Got the guts?

61 Shoot pool for cheap

Though playing pool nowadays requires nearly a roll of quarters (you'd better pray you don't scratch on the eight ball right away), old-time bars, such as Williamsburg vet Turkey's Nest Tavern (94 Bedford Ave at North 12th St, Williamsburg, Brooklyn, 718-384-9774), still offer archaic prices. One game—likely waged against a salty local—costs 75¢, a bargain akin to the $3.50 32-ounce Styrofoam cups of Bud. Still too pricey? Swing by Upper East Side sports haunt Brady's Bar (1583 Second Ave at 82nd St, 212-861-6070) on Sundays. This nearly 47-year-old saloon offers complimentary pool all day long (it's $1.50 otherwise), as well as $4 bottles of Miller. If you can't wait that long for no-pay pool, ride the F train to Dumbo's bar-restaurant Superfine (126 Front St at Pearl St, Dumbo, Brooklyn, 718-243-9005) for free pool daily. Sign up for a game on the chalkboard (first come, first served). With the money you'll save, you can splurge on a grilled pizza ($12) and a warming apple-brandy sidecar ($11). Hey, you gotta have your priorities straight.

62 Tango!

A vertical expression of a horizontal desire, tango is the world's sexiest dance, demanding a partner who can intuit your rhythms as well as match your steps. Learn all the caidas (falls), boleos (leg flips), ganchos (leg hooks), molinetes (windmills) and corridas (runs) at Triangulo (135 West 20th St, between Sixth and Seventh Aves, 212-633-6445, tangonyc.com), which offers beginner classes and advanced milongas (or dance salons) in a very social setting.

63 Laugh yourself healthy

We know what you're thinking: Ha! But seriously, laughter has been found to have major benefits for the mind and body, including strengthening the immune system and, well, raising one's spirits, which is important:

"Laughter releases endorphins, which elevates the mood," says Mandan Kataria, M.D., who founded the first laughter club in Mumbai in 1995 (now, he says, there are more than 6,000 such clubs around the world). He swears by chortling as an antidepressant. "If your mood is good, you have positive thoughts," he adds, "which greatly enhances your quality of life."

Through yogic exercises and breathing techniques, you can induce belly laughs even if you're not amused by anything (the body can't tell the difference between real and forced laughter, so you can essentially fake it till you make it). These deep chuckles greatly increase oxygen flow—which is especially good for mental function, as the brain needs 25 percent more O_2 than other organs do to be at its best. "Children laugh 300 or 400 times a day, while adults laugh only 15 times daily," says Dr. Kataria. "We adults evaluate what's funny, but children's laughter comes from the body, not the mind. This is the technique we use in laughter club."

You know where best to get your jollies, but for a hearty 30-minute session of belly laughter (which Dr. Kataria says is far more beneficial than any superficial giggling you might do at the Comedy Cellar) try the free weekly hooting fest at Yogalaff (1430 Broadway, No.1107, at 40th St, yogalaff.com) on Wednesdays at 8pm.

64

Devour Jewish deli treats at Sammy's

Sammy's Roumanian Steak House (157 Chrystie St between Delancey and Rivington Sts, 212-673-0330) is a subterranean LES holdover that doesn't seem to have noticed that the rest of the 'hood has changed. Arrive on a crowded evening and you may think you've stumbled into a bar mitzvah—Yiddish singalongs and impromptu dancing are ignited by a live synthesizer and further fuelled by the frozen vodka. But you don't have to join the horah to have a blast. Instead, focus on true-and-tried Jewish dishes, from chicken livers and garlicky karnatzlack sausage patties to enormous Romanian tenderloins with potato pancakes. Same as they ever were.

65-69 *Get to know cask ales*

Warm, flat and flavorful, live-culture cask ales bring wine's class to the pint glass. Joshua M. Bernstein sips his way across town.

Not to be alarmist, but chances are, you're drinking dead beer. Nearly all bottled and draft brews, from lowly Bud to microbrew Dogfish Head, are filtered to remove live yeast cultures. But leave yeasts in and ordinary beer becomes extraordinary cask ale. The fragrant brew is richer and more flavorful than filtered beers, which seem watery and harshly effervescent by comparison. If a conventional beer should be chugged, a cask ale should be savored.

Stored in metal kegs called firkins, cask ales evolve like well-aged wines, and unlike carbon-dioxide-injected brews, develop gentle bubbles. Because casks aren't pressurized, manually powered "beer engines" dispense the naturally carbonated quaff, best enjoyed at 55 degrees—about 15 degrees warmer than typical icy brews, but the perfect complement to a balmy spring evening.

Increasingly, saloons citywide are serving cask ale, but don't go searching for esoteric brands. You'll find a rotating cast of microbrew favorites such as Sixpoint's Bengali Tiger IPA or Brooklyn Blast, which become more distinguished and nuanced as cask varieties. (If you're fond of the original, you'll likely adore its yeasty stepchild.)

Downstairs at Jimmy's No. 43 (43 E 7th St between Second and Third Aves, 212-982-3006), an antler-decorated rathskeller, at least one tap pumps out cask brew. West Village beer mecca Blind Tiger Ale House (281 Bleecker St at Jones St, 212-462-4682),

meanwhile, supplements 28 microbrew drafts with two cask selections.

Drop Off Service (211 Ave A at 13th St, 212-260-2914) offers one, while celeb-packed West Village gastropub The Spotted Pig (314 W 11th St at Greenwich St, 212-620-0393) has two cask varieties. The Brazen Head (228 Atlantic Ave between Court St and Boerum Pl, Cobble Hill, Brooklyn, 718-488-0430) runs cask-ale festivals (brazenhead brooklyn.com has updates) in the spring, fall and winter, featuring 25 or so American creations, served so perfectly warm and flat that bubbly suds will never seem quite right again.

70 *Blade with glory*

Bring your skates (helmets and wristguards are also required) to the **Wednesday Night Skate** (weskateny.org), which convenes at 7:45pm at the south side of Union Square Park each week from the beginning of April to the end of October. The two-hour skate is free, open to all levels and follows a different route each week.

71 Request a screening at the Donnell Media Center

Though two of the center's most requested movies are *The Wizard of Oz* and *Fish Market*, a 1955 documentary about the Fulton fishmongers, the center houses some 8,000 other 16mm films. If you have an NYPL card, you can see double features like *Fall of the House of Usher* and *The Blue Angel* for—gasp!—free.
Donnell Media Center 20 *W 53rd St between Fifth and Madison Aves (212-621-0609/nypl.org).*

72

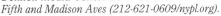

Visit the brand new MOCA

With New York's Chinese population nearly doubling since 1990, MOCA's measly 2,000-square-foot space on Mulberry Street—shuttered in February 2008—hadn't been cutting it for some time: "We would have to turn people away because it was too crowded," says public-affairs officer Amanda Heng. Designed by Vietnam Veterans Memorial architect Maya Lin, a new $15 million home on Centre Street—due to open to the public, at the time of writing, in fall 2008—incorporates organic elements like bronze walls, floors made of reclaimed wood, and a giant skylight that illuminates the museum's two-floor atrium.

This roomier 14,000-square-foot structure has allowed curators to develop several new gallery shows, including one on slinky, sleeveless qipao dresses and another, "Archeology of Change," that tracks gentrification in Chinatown by spotlighting five erstwhile landmarks (including the building the museum is housed in, the former Grand Machinery Exchange). In a nicely unostentatious touch, donor plaques have been eschewed in favor of a most tasteful "journey wall," where tiles reveal the paths contributors' families took to arrive in the US.
Museum of Chinese in America *211-215 Centre St between Grand and Howard Sts (212-619-4785/mocanyc.org).*

73 Costume up at Rubie's

If New York is a place where everybody comes to reinvent themselves, Rubie's Costume Company is the perfect place to begin your transformation. A supplier of costumes for everything from New Year's Eve balls to Saturday Night Live, this flagship store of what's become a ten-country enterprise has everything. Hillary Clinton masks, glow-in-the-dark beehive wigs, blood-sucking "leeches," prosthetic legs, reindeer antlers for your pooch… If you have no idea what to wear for Halloween, just pay Rubie's a visit.
Rubie's Costume Company *120-08 Jamaica Avenue at 120th St, Richmond Hill (718-846-1008).*

74 Drink and doodle

Though always a means for capturing digits, the cocktail napkin makes a convenient canvas for showing off Marcel Dzama-like artistic prowess, particularly at low-key bar Dusk Lounge's weekly Napkin Idol drawing contest, held every Tuesday from 6pm. Winners—announced at 9pm and 11:30pm—receive a free drink and an hour-long happy-hour extension (for everyone else it runs 5:30-9pm).
Dusk *147 W 24th St between Sixth and Seventh Aves (212-924-4490/dusklounge.com).*

75 Explore the collection at the Black Gay and Lesbian Archive

The pet project of Harlem writer and editor Steven G. Fullwood, the archive was started in 2000 to document LGBT life for people of color. Since 2004, the holdings—books, magazines, original flyers, and manuscripts—have been housed in the distinguished Schomburg Center for Research in Black Culture (515 Malcolm X Blvd [Lenox Ave] between 135th and 136th Sts, 212-491-2200, nypl.org), part of the NYPL system. Now anyone can explore this rarely told history.

PHOTO BY LEN PRINCE

"'Chicago' still **GLITTERS HYPNOTICALLY.**"

Ben Brantley, The New York Times

CHICAGO
THE MUSICAL

TELECHARGE.COM or 212-239-6200/800-432-7250
CHICAGOTHEMUSICAL.COM AMBASSADOR THEATRE · 219 WEST 49TH STREET
NEW YORK · LONDON
AMBASSADOR THEATRE, 49TH STREET AT BROADWAY · CAMBRIDGE THEATRE, SEVEN DIALS

76-84 *Prove you've got game at the city's best pickup basketball games*

Riverbank State Park

These four excellent, full courts, with well-marked lines, friendly rims and nylon nets, are frequented by uptown weekend sportsters and high-school kids. Games are relatively casual, with a slight edge, and anyone can play (those with a higher skill level might not want to). The wait in summer is around 20 minutes.
Riverside Dr and 145th St.

48th Ave at Vernon Blvd

The three full courts have well-maintained surfaces, and rims with a nice bounce. While this outpost attracts locals, Manhattanites often take the five-minute train ride from 42nd St to grab a spot too. It's easy to jump in and you can expect a solid game. Summertime waits can be around half an hour.
Hunters Point, Queens.

Rodney St at South 5th St

You'll find one full court and two half courts, all with clear lines, looked-after surfaces and soft rims. Like its neighboring courts two streets away, this stop gets a lot of locals. But the better court quality brings better players. Summertime waits can be around 60 minutes.
Williamsburg, Brooklyn.

Holcombe Rucker Park

A top-quality NBA regulation-size court with friendly rims, nylon nets, fresh lines and even a scoreboard makes this one of the premier pickup spots in the city. On sunny days, you'll find top-quality street ballers and players from the NBA. Locals insist it's not difficult to jump in a game, but make sure you're ready to step up to Allen Iverson or Shaq (who've been known to frequent Rucker) before calling "next game."
W 155th St at Frederick Douglass Blvd.

West 4th Street Court

The most famous of the city's high-level street courts, "the Cage" is accessible to regular joes—on weekdays. Come weekends, you're lucky if you can grab a spot of fence, let alone touch a ball. On any given summer weekend, you can see a smattering of Knicks players as well as the occasional sighting of L.A. Laker Smush Parker.
W 4th St at Sixth Ave.

Central Park's Great Lawn Courts

Double-rimmed hoops on both full courts makes for an unfriendly bounce, but the lines are visible and there are nets. The central location brings in quality ballers from all over. The competition is fierce, so no matter who's playing you'll get a good game. It's easy to jump in too, though in the summer the courts are crowded.
Midpark at 83rd St.

Riverside Park at 76th St

Frequented by local Upper West Siders, these courts aren't hosting a plethora of pre-professional players, but there is an occasional influx of athletic twenty-somethings with decent skill. Though the lines are faded and there are no nets, the rims are friendly, and the combination of seven rims and a casual neighborhood feel means finding a game is pretty simple; wait times, even on a summer Saturday, shouldn't exceed 20 minutes.
At Riverside Dr.

Clove Lakes Park

Exceptional surfaces on three full courts, very clean lines and springy rims make this a big local spot for some of the best ballers on Staten Island. Anyone with the skills should expect a solid game. It's very local, which means 'hoodies generally grab games first, but the vibe's friendly, so if you're patient you'll get in.
Victory Blvd at Clove Rd, Staten Island.

John Adams Park

There are no nets on the three hoops, but the lines are clear and the surface is good. Frequented by local residents, game quality is pretty high, and pretty much anyone can play.
Wales Ave at E 152nd St, Bronx.

85 Watch screenings among the sculptures

With a striking view of the midtown skyline as a backdrop, the Socrates Sculpture Park Outdoor Cinema (32-01 Vernon Blvd at Broadway, 718-956-1819, socratessculpture park.org) serves up an impressive array of free outdoor films most Wednesdays during July and August. Diversity is the word here, with movies (selected by curators from the Museum of the Moving Image) hailing from a different country each week—the screening is complemented by food from the movie's homeland, sold here by local eateries. Showings are at sunset, often preceded by musical entertainment. Bring a blanket.

86

Descend to the basement at the Cornelia Street Café

You could walk by Cornelia Street Café (29 Cornelia Street between Bleecker and W 4th Sts, 212-989-9319, corneliastreetcafe.com) and mistake it for one of the myriad touristy eateries in the West Village, but the restaurant hides a cabaret basement, home to readings and music. Running from adventurous jazz and classical music to folksy singer-songwriters, the music serves as a reminder that the neighborhood was once a haven for the downtown counterculture. The menu too (colorful and dated) is consistent with the venue's bohemian roots.

87 Dance to house at Sullivan Room

True to its reputation as one of the least pretentious clubs in Manhattan, Sullivan Room (218 Sullivan St between Bleecker and W 3rd Sts, 212-252-2151, sullivanroom.com) has established itself as a haven for straight-up, no-frills house music. And if you're not into house, the club features plenty of nights geared toward drum 'n' bass boffins and breakbeat fans.

88 Pay homage to John Lennon in Strawberry Fields

So you went to Paris and, despite your best intentions, went to see Jim Morrison's grave. Why not join the sad sack out-of-towners who flock each day to the John Lennon Imagine mosaic in Central Park? Same rules apply. Pretend you're going somewhere else and just happened to notice it. Pretend you're merely curious, that it's a sociological experiment. Then, when no one's looking, carefully place down that discreet little glittery white piano keyring you've been saving for the occasion. No one need know you were even there… tonight the park authorities will sweep the evidence away—candles, poems, flowers, paintings, your little white piano and all.

89

Climb aboard the Waterfront's barge

The rarity of a front view of the Statue of Liberty is reason enough for most to visit the 1914 barge that lodges at the Waterfront Museum and Showboat Barge (290 Conover St at Pier 44, Red Hook, Brooklyn, 718-624-4719, waterfrontmuseum.org). But the vessel, which has been docked in Red Hook since 1994, is also home to a circus in June, a bluesy sunset music series in July, and a year-round, child-focussed interactive exhibit on harbor history.

90 View the city's best Vermeer

Sure the Metropolitan Museum has more of them, but the single Vermeer in the Frick Collection, *Mistress and Maid* (1665-1670), is our stone-cold favorite. It shows the eponymous woman in a vivid-yellow dress trimmed in ermine—you may remember it from the biopic *Girl with a Pearl Earring*, in which the subject's philistine husband says, "You've glazed my wife in dried piss!"

The Frick Collection *1 E 70th St at Fifth Ave (212-288-0700/frick.org).*

91 *Walk*
Arthur Avenue

The Arthur Avenue district in the heart of working-class Belmont is small and utilitarian-looking—just six blocks, densely packed with a colorful collection of third- and fourth-generation restaurants, butchers, bakers, fishmongers and grocers. It remains the city's best source for everything Italian, from St Francis medals for pets (Catholic Goods Center, 630 E 187th Street) to Sicilian salt-packed capers and Francesconi canned tomatoes, sold by the case (Teitel Brothers, 2372 Arthur Ave). By day, the plenty spilling out onto the sidewalks includes homemade lemon, chocolate, and cremolata ices, and curbside raw bars manned by waiters in crisp white aprons. Meat vendors display skinned rabbits and baby lambs, dangling on hooks over bins piled high with tripe and trotters.

Drop by the Calabria Pork Store (2338 Arthur Ave, 718-367-5145), where soppressata, capocollo and prosciutto dangle from the ceiling in fantastic profusion, in a room thick with the funky, gamy smells of aging meat. Or tuck in at one of the pink vinyl banquettes at Mario's (342 Arthur Ave, 718-584-1188) for lump cheese ravioli, stuffed with milky-fresh ricotta and smothered in a fruity, bright-red marinara (beware the portion sizes). For picnic fare or a cold supper to carry home, few places can compete with the venerable Mike's Deli (2344 Arthur Ave, 718-295-5033), an overstocked butcher and café located in the city's most beloved food and kitchen-supplies market. The glossy menu may paralyze you with indecision; it lists more than 50 sandwiches, plus platters, pastas, soups, stromboli, salads, and sides. Pasta-lovers, meanwhile, should detour slightly from Arthur itself for Borgatti's Ravioli & Egg Noodles (632 E 187th St, 718-367-3799), where freshly made sheets are hand-fed through a vintage press right behind the counter and cut to order—just choose your width from a cardboard display. Is there a better example of Italian-American New York? Fuhgeddaboudit.

 ## Play in the arcade

Back in 1869, when Frederick Law Olmstead and Calvert Vaux, the men behind Central Park, completed Bethesda Terrace & Arcade—the highly ornate passageway that connects the plaza around the famed Bethesda Fountain to the elm-lined promenade to the south—it was deemed the architectural centrepiece of Manhattan's most treasured urban getaway, boasting a stunning tile ceiling designed by English-born Jacob Wrey Mould.

After decades of weathering—and a bursting city budget that had no room for extravagant repairs—the 16,000 intricately patterned Minton clay tiles (imported from Stoke-on-Trent, England) from the ceiling were put in crates and carted off to storage in the 1980s. Now, after three years and $7 million dollars spent, a painstaking (and long-overdue) restoration has returned this treasure to its former glory and made the arcade essential Central Park viewing once more.

Bethesda Terrace *Central Park 72nd Street entrance.*

Guest-bartend

If lingering at the bar isn't diversion enough, get behind it at uptown Irish tavern Trinity Pub (229 E 84th St between Second and Third Aves, 212-327-4450). Show up on Thursday nights, when booze-slinging aspirants of all stripes can take over the joint. Bring in 30 pals and the three-hour-long gig, along with free drinks and half of the tip jar, is yours for the taking. Downtowners with a good handle on the jigger can head to Stay (244 E Houston St between Aves A and B, 212-982-3532), where owner Rob Koda opens the place to guest barkeeps on Thursdays from 7pm to 10pm (sign up by e-mailing guestbartend@stay-nyc.com). You'll also need to rally your friends to make it happen. Stay, like Trinity, requires a minimum head count of 30 customers—but your modest buyback power just might just make it worth their while.

 ## Fill up for free

The best time to prowl for free food is at the weekend. First stop, Trader Joe's (142 E 14th St between Third Ave and Irving Pl, 212-529-4612; 90-30 Metropolitan Ave at Woodhaven Blvd, Rego Park, Queens, 718-275-1791), where vanilla yogurt with fresh blueberries is served to throngs who hover near the sample station. Both metropolitan TJs offer rotating samples daily, changing the breakfast-like morning offering at 2pm for something resembling an afternoon snack. Next, hit the Union Square Greenmarket, where a deft circumnavigator can almost satisfy the four food groups. On Saturdays, Breezy Hill Orchard maintains a steady supply of sliced apples. Ronnybrook Farm sets out flavored butters, yogurt cheese, and cups of rice and chocolate puddings. There's a protein fix from DiPaolo Turkey Farm, where turkey sausage pierced with toothpicks sizzles on an electric griddle. For dessert, stroll to Max Brenner (841 Broadway between 13th and 14th Sts, 212-388-0030; 141 Second Ave at 9th St, 212-388-0030), where a jar of praline-covered pecans sits on the counter with tongs for self-serving. Take one, then study the shelves of chocolates as if contemplating a purchase and, when nobody's looking, take another. Still hungry? At Chelsea Market (75 Ninth Ave at 15th St, chelseamarket.com), nosh peppered potato chips and cheddar cheese at Chelsea Market Baskets, hit Fat Witch Bakery for a brownie bite, then wash it down with red wine from nearby Chelsea Wine Vault.

Love the yellow condiment at Moutarde

Such is the artistry with which mustard is presented at Moutarde (239 Fifth Ave at Carroll St, Park Slope, Brooklyn, 718-623-3600) that it arrives on a ceramic painter's palette as a gratis appetizer. As well as the usual bread and butter, you get the palette with five different flavored mustards (including banana) to dip an assortment of raw veggies and toasted bread into.

100

Select from the free vinyl jukebox at Great Jones Café

It's one of the last left in the city. Spin a record while you still can. **Great Jones Café** *54 Great Jones St between Bowery and Lafayette St (212-674-9304/greatjones.com).*

Rib ticklers

Time Out New York*'s Eat Out editor* **Gabriella Gershenson** *feels the burn down in the pit on her quest for great barbecue.*

At Hill Country, a barbecue restaurant in Chelsea, three impressive pits bathe hundreds of pounds of meat in the smoke of smoldering Texas post oak. It's where dead pigs, cows and fowl come if they're lucky—a carnivore's heaven. So when the pit master asked me to work in the kitchen—a noon to 10pm shift—I jumped at the chance.

A pit is the most sanctified place for barbecuers, who are notoriously territorial when it comes to their craft. And with nearly a dozen NYC low-and-slow joints having opened in the last couple of years, I couldn't think of a better time to see exactly how they slice it.

Why are these folks so clannish? It's just meat, after all. Part of the reason is the distinct codification of the different styles of barbecuery. 'Cuers are apt to identify with their respective styles of food prep—Kansas City style, Texas, Memphis, North Carolina—as steadfastly as sports fans stick to their home teams.

Hill Country (30 W 26th St between Broadway and Sixth Ave, 212-255-4544), with its emphasis on beef and dry rubs and an aversion to sticky sauces, stays as true to its Texan roots as an NYC eatery can. A diner entering the cafeteria-style restaurant (orders are placed at a counter and brought tableside on a tray) would do best to order the spicy pork sausage links, made by Texan barbecue mecca Kreuz Market, and the superb moist brisket. Pit master Kenny Callaghan of Blue Smoke (116 E 27th St between Park and Lexington Aves, 212-447-7733) also does well with the Texan style, treating his chewy beef ribs to a salt-and-pepper rub and smoking them over hickory for close to seven hours. Brisket gets a non-Texan, though delicious, treatment at R.U.B. BBQ (208 W 23rd St between Seventh and Eighth Aves, 212-524-4300), where burnt ends—the 16-hour-smoked end pieces of brisket—taste better than candy.

Back at Hill Country, I'm outfitted with a white jacket with snaps, a white apron and an unlimited supply of vinyl gloves. In my front pocket went the pit worker's indispensable tools, among them a black Sharpie (for keeping

Hill Country

track of the meat that's been prepped) and a meat thermometer (it's as important to check the temperature of the raw meat as it is to see if cooked meat is done). I felt like Sam the Butcher.

At the pit, I checked the temperatures of glistening briskets (ideally, around 170 degrees), learned how to pull the hulking eight-pound pieces from the oven using just two sets of tongs, and layered them on a sheet pan when they were ready to be transferred to the warmers—carefully. Sold for some $18 per pound, dropping one would have been about a $144 loss for the restaurant. The pit crew deals with that kind of stress all day. Yet slicing meat is possibly the most revered—and nerve-racking—task you can have at any 'cue haven. In addition to learning how to cut the different types of meat, there's a specific Hill Country lingo to master. A "dolly" is the chicken's white meat (like Dolly Parton—get it?), a "tomahawk" is the thigh and leg, a "red" is a jalapeño cheddar sausage, a "white" is the nonspicy variety, and so on.

"I learned how to pull the hulking eight-pound briskets from the oven using just two sets of tongs, carefully—dropping one would have been about a $144 loss for the restaurant."

Though it's on most NYC barbecue menus, chicken is not the crown jewel of any barbecue joint—most revel in a devotion to beef, pork, or both, but never fowl. That doesn't mean that there isn't some first-rate poultry in Gotham's barbecue eateries. Southern Hospitality (1460 Second Ave between 76th and 77th Sts, 212-249-1001), co-owned by Justin Timberlake, does wonders with its fried chicken, a juicy on the inside, crunchy on the outside marvel, as does Georgia's Eastside BBQ (192 Orchard St between Houston and Stanton Sts, 212-253-6280) with its moist specimen coated in a well-seasoned crust that may leave you asking "what ribs?"

From the restaurant's standpoint, there is a bonus to shunning made-to-order dishes and focusing instead on meats that have been cooking for hours. That's the case at Hill Country, where the food is typically cooked overnight, then transferred to finishing pits. From these, carvers pull pork ribs, brisket, Cornish hens and other meats to slice up for patrons, who order them by the pound.

Although the pride and joy at Hill Country is the brisket, other barbecue restaurants have different strengths. The Smoke Joint (87 South Elliott Pl at Lafayette Ave, Fort Greene, Brooklyn, 718-797-1011), for instance, does a fine take on Carolina-style barbecue—which emphasizes pulled pork—with its smoked pork butt, chopped and served with one of three sauces, all made in-house (tangy "Hollapeno" is the best). And, of course, no barbecue experience would be complete without pork ribs. The dry-rubbed spareribs at Daisy May's (623 Eleventh Ave at 46th St, 212-977-1500) are a good bet, smoked for several hours, resulting in pink, smoke-ringed flesh and a deep woodsy flavor.

Though the main event—meat—is the true measure of barbecue superiority, there are other elements of the meal worth judging an eatery by. Sweet tea, aka brown-tinted sugar water, is a popular Southern accompaniment to a barbecue meal. Daisy May's arrives, tasty yet cloying, in a mason jar with several leaves of fresh mint for good measure. The Smoke Joint's version takes pity on Yankee palates, serving an unorthodox yet refreshingly semi-sweet version. Diners who prefer something harder (and hipper) with their meals should don their trucker caps and head to über-cool Williamsburg barbecue spot Fette Sau (354 Metropolitan Ave between Roebling and Havemeyer Sts, Williamsburg, Brooklyn, 718-

"At R.U.B. BBQ, burnt ends—the 16-hour-smoked end pieces of brisket—taste better than candy."

963-3404), which offers a mind-boggling array of bourbons with an otherwise pared-down menu.

Then there are the sides. Diners usually expect slaw, corn bread, baked beans, and mac and cheese—some of the basic barbecue accoutrements—to be on the menu, and the latest rash of NYC joints has brought along with it sides both daring and traditional. In the former group, at Harlem's Dinosaur Bar-B-Que (646 W 131st St at Twelfth Ave, 212-694-1777), a refreshing iceberg wedge salad seems better suited for a steakhouse, but does just as well cutting the fat in Dino's rich 'cue; in the latter category, fans of a acidic slaw should enjoy the piquant versions at Blue Smoke and Georgia's. And though most barbecue fanatics don't even acknowledge dessert, Hill Country's peanut butter and jelly cupcake, a juvenile guilty pleasure sprinkled with Reese Pieces, should make even the most stalwart purists reconsider.

When I finished my shift at Hill Country, I was sweaty, reeking of meat and had a sore finger that lasted through the weekend (many of the men sport injuries—one has what he calls "brisket elbow"). Knowing that I didn't have to repeat the intensely physical tasks the next day gave me a sense of relief. It also gave me a special appreciation for the guys here, and at all barbecue joints, and the techniques they've developed to streamline a job that's executed under the gun. Pit worker Donovan taught me how to hook my thumb under the wing of the raw Cornish hen just so, making it easier for me to season both sides with the rub. Victor instructed me to use the towel to get a good grip on the pesky membrane on the back of the rack of beef ribs. Some people are just cut out for this.

Additional reporting: Juanpablo Wright and Tom Berry.

110 Play Scrabble at Pete's Candy Store

It may be pocket-size, but Pete's Candy Store (709 Lorimer St between Frost and Richardson Sts, Williamsburg, 718-302-3770) is full of goodies. The train-car-shaped performance space and bingo Tuesdays at this former luncheonette and candy store have helped it become a Billyburg staple, but the highlight is Scrabble Saturdays (5pm-8pm), which lures in all the local wordsmiths. Come out and play—just be sure to bring a partner who knows their seven-letter words.

111 Go the theater for less than one dollar

For less than a buck (no joke—there's not even a service charge), you can get a Sunday ticket to any main-stage production at Soho Rep, thanks to a new program. "I'm always looking for how to take the ticket price out of the equation for young audiences," says artistic director Sarah Benson. In 2007, tickets for John Jesurun's *Philoktetes*, an adaptation of the classic Greek myth, sold out in three days. Check the website for upcoming productions.

Soho Rep 46 *Walker St between Broadway and Church St (212-941-8632/sohorep.org).*

112 Listen to a bit of everything at The Knitting Factory

Serving up an eclectic menu of experimental jazz, klezmer, indie rock—even hip-hop karaoke—The Knitting Factory has drawn in an unbroken stream of lounge lizards, industry sharks and uptown gawkers for over two decades, despite moving premises in 1994. The Main Space showcases big-name acts (Lou Reed, Jonathan Richman, Slick Rick), best viewed from the balcony, while the Tap Bar, a floor down, promises spoken-word performances and 18 draught beers. Venture even further below for the Old Office, which features a modest selection of wines.

The Knitting Factory *74 Leonard St between Broadway and Church St (212-219-3006).*

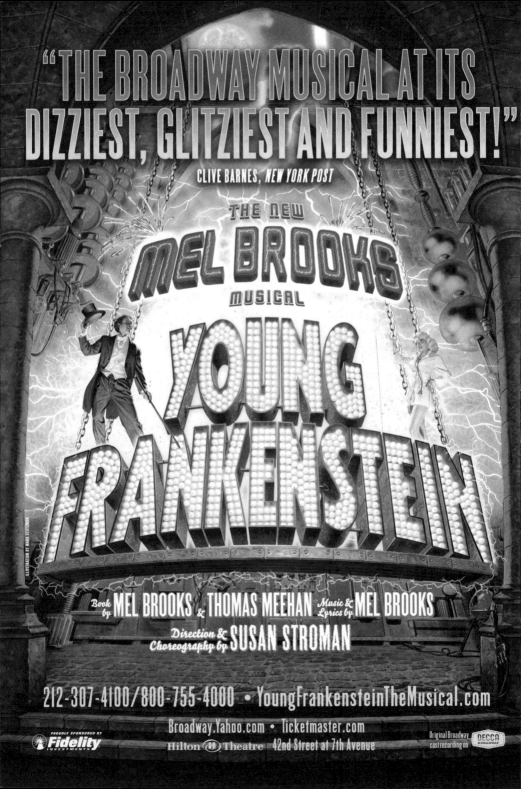

113

See Coney Island's sunken sub

Well, it's actually less sunken than… stuck. The *Quester I* was a deep-sea salvage vehicle designed and built in 1970 by a Brooklyn Navy Yard pipe fitter named Jerry Bianco. He hoped to use it to raise some of the treasure lost aboard the *Andrea Doria*, the Italian passenger liner that sank off Nantucket after colliding with another ship on the night of July 25, 1956. Unfortunately, the *Quester* didn't get very far. As it was lowered into the water, the vessel—painted a bright yellow like the craft in the Beatles song—listed severely and couldn't be launched. Already strapped for money after four years of construction work on the ship, Bianco left it tethered to the pier. It broke free from its moorings in 1981, drifting to its current position in Coney Island Creek, where it is visible at low tide.

114

Step into the Merchant's House

The sumptuous Federal-Greek Revival style Merchant's House Museum (29 E 4th St between Bowery and Lafayette St, 212-777-1089, merchantshouse.com) is the city's only preserved 19th-century family home. The house is laid out with the same furnishings and decorations that filled its rooms when hardware tycoon Seabury Treadwell and his family inhabited it from 1832 until 1933—note, in the double parlors, gas chandeliers that are believed to be the oldest in the country still in their original location. There are three floors to tramp around (tours are self-guided), but be sure to check out the exquisitely manicured garden. There's not another place like it in the East Village. Note that the Merchant's House Museum is closed every Tuesday and Wednesday.

115

Play (computer game) tennis at Wiimbledon

The closest most New Yorkers get to Wimbledon is the distance between the edge of their couch and the TV, but Clinton Hill's Lane Buschel and Steve Bryant have devised a way for fans to actually compete—sort of. In summer 2007, they hosted Wiimbledon, the world's first ever Wii tennis tournament (not actually affiliated with either Nintendo or the All England Lawn Tennis Club, we should point out). "It's sort of like leaving your living room and playing your Wii in public," explains Buschel, who works for a PR firm. Unlike Wimbledon's fortnight schedule, Wiimbledon ran for one day only; for details of the next event, visit wiimbledon.net.

116-118

Watch movies… in bars!

Catch a weekly flick at seasonal Brooklyn haunt Habana Outpost (755-757 Fulton St at S Portland Ave, Fort Greene, Brooklyn, 718-858-9500) every Sunday at 8pm. This Cuban-Mexican offshoot of the popular Nolita café—closed November through March—presents classic films (think *Godzilla* and *The Last Dragon*) in its bustling outdoor garden, preceded by a film short from a local auteur. Popcorn here makes for a fine accompaniment to an icy Corona, particularly as it's given away free. Low-key Soho spot Obivia (201 Lafayette St at Kenmare St, 212-226-4904), meanwhile, shows a free (though soundless) film every Sunday at 7pm on five plasma TVs. Astoria lounge Hell Gate Social (12-21 Astoria Blvd between 12th and 14th Sts, Astoria, Queens, 718-204-8313) projects B movies and cult classics on an outdoor screen during the summer and indoors in the chillier months. Showtime is Sunday at 9pm, but with house cocktails like the Chocolate Egg Cream—made with Bosco chocolate syrup, vanilla-infused Jim Beam bourbon, seltzer and cream—you might want to make it a double… feature, of course.

Flight to New York $1500.00

Two nights in
a luxury hotel $760.00

Champagne on
arrival $90.00

Not coming out of your room for 24 hours:
Priceless®

MasterCard

Accepted in over 26 million locations worldwide

119 Get into out films at Cinemarosa

Every third Sunday of the month, Cinemarosa (cinemarosa.org) presents queer-oriented and queer-themed films and videos free of charge at the Queens Museum of Art (New York City Building, Flushing Meadows Corona Park, Queens, 718-592-9700, queensmuseum.org). The museum's 110-seat auditorium provides an intimate setting, and Cinemarosa has become a meeting point and cultural mecca for the borough's highly diverse lesbian, gay, bisexual, and transgender community, many of whom submit their own works to the series.

120

Buy a decent bottle of wine for less than $20

Setting a two-sawbuck limit when you're an oenophile typically narrows the options to Carlo Rossi carafes, but there are a handful of half-off deals early in the week for your swishing pleasure. Take a Monday field trip to Brooklyn's intimate wine bar Donna da Vine (378 Atlantic Ave between Bond and Hoyt Sts, Boerum Hill, Brooklyn, 718-643-2250) for a choice of six half-price bottles. The barkeeps recommend New Mexico's fragrant sparkler Domaine St. Vincent ($17) or the peachy Big Tattoo white ($17.50). If boozing on Tuesday is more your speed, visit downtown gastropub Nolita House (47 E Houston St between Mott and Mulberry Sts, 212-625-1712), where all bottles are half off from 5pm to 11pm. Savor Australia's Yalumba Y Series shiraz or France's fruity Château Miraval rosé, each $18—just a smidge more than retail, and cheap enough to justify ordering the $9 cod tacos. Thirsting for more? All night Monday and Tuesday, bottles under $60 (except for sparkling varieties) are 50 percent off at the bordello-esque Bourgeois Pig (111 E 7th St between First Ave and Ave A, 212-475-2246). The best bang for your buck? Jacques-Yves sauvignon blanc or Domaine Laurent Miquel syrah, discounted to $13 and $14 respectively. Want another? Go on: being a wino has never been so affordable.

A few of my favorite things

121-125

Jacques d'Amboise, founder of the National Dance Institute

I'll go on the Staten Island Ferry at any time of day, but even jaded New Yorkers find that going at sunset is the best. On the way over, you get to see the Statue of Liberty bathed in the rays of the sun setting behind it. And on the return trip the lights of Manhattan welcome you back.

I love the rice wine at Sura (105 E 9th St, 212-982-6390, suranyc.com). It's one of a number of little Korean restaurants that have become regular dining spots for me. If I'm in the mood for Italian, I love eating at Bella Luna (584 Columbus Ave, 212-877-2267, bellalunanyc.com).

The Frick Collection (1 E 70th St, 212-288-0700, frick.org) is magical, and there's nothing better than sitting in the Cloisters (99 Margaret Corbin Dr, Fort Tryon Park, 212-923-3700, met museum.org) alone with a good book.

I often just find an artist whose work I love and go to the gallery that's showing their work. The ACA Galleries (529 W 20th St, 212-206-8080, acagalleries.com), for example. It's incredible to be surrounded by amazing artwork and then leave the gallery to find yourself in a narrow street in the west 20s.

My favorite place in the entire city is Roosevelt Avenue in Jackson Heights. Cultures piled on top of one another, a volcano of optimism. On one block it's as if you've stepped into New Delhi, then around the corner you're in Athens. Down the street it's Korea and then Mexico. I mean... god, what a city!

nationaldance.org

126

Wrestle gay

The city's preeminent gay freestyle wrestling club, Metro Wrestling (metrowrestling.org), offers a beginners' clinic on the first Sunday of every month, and you can practice grappling and takedowns every Saturday (5-7pm at 122 W 27th St, second floor) and Sunday (2-5pm at 208 W 13th St, room 412) in Manhattan. There are two annual Metro tournaments, and the better athletes are sometimes sent to tourneys like the International Gay Games.

127-130

Slurp oysters on the cheap

Jonathan Swift might have said, "He was a bold man that first ate an oyster," but we'd say it's bolder still to eat one on the cheap. Not at these fine fish joints, though—show up during oyster happy hours to take advantage of delicious, top-quality mollusks at knock-down prices.

Aquagrill (210 Spring St at Sixth Ave, 212-274-0505) has a lengthy and impressive list of oysters from all over the world. Weekdays, noon-7pm, six Blue Points go for $8 with a glass of house wine (PBRs cost $1.50 a can). The best spot in the house at Fish (280 Bleecker St at Jones St, 212-727-2879), meanwhile, is the bar, where you can watch your oysters being shucked and plated while you fill up on peanuts and throw the shells on the floor. Weekdays, noon-7pm, Blue Points go for a buck apiece and a pint of PBR costs $1.50.

Outdoor seating and stunning views of the Hudson—once a bountiful source of bivalves—make PJ Clarke's on the Hudson (4 World Financial Center at Vesey St, 212-285-1500) an ideal spot for shellfish. Their happy hour oysters (Pine Islands on our trip) go for $1-$1.50 from 4-7pm, Monday through Friday. Over in Brooklyn, cheap mollusks can be had Thursday through Sunday at Spike Hill (184 Bedford Ave at North 7th St, Williamsburg, Brooklyn, 718-218-9737), with littleneck clams going for $1 each and Blue Points for $1.50 each, 4-10pm. Get there early; the place fills up quickly.

131 Hear every Shaw

Project Shaw, a highbrow yet unpretentious monthly reading event, aims to present professional recitations of every single play penned by George Bernard Shaw. It takes place on Monday nights and draws packed houses to the genteel Players Club (16 Gramercy Park South between Park Ave South and Irving Pl, 212-475-6116, projectshaw.com). Performances in 2008 include *Jitta's Atonement* in November and *Saint Joan* in December.

132

Book the best seats at the Miller Theatre

Columbia University's boxy auditorium (2960 Broadway at 116th St, 212-854-7799, millertheatre.com) is the CBGB of contemporary classical music: an uninspiring facility (albeit one with nontoxic bathrooms) that has become iconic through its inspiring and consistently audacious musical offerings. According to theater director George Steel, the best seats in the house are in the middle orchestra, row F, right behind the railing. Not only are the sight lines great in this location, he says, but these seats are in front of the overhang of the balcony, which makes the acoustics ideal. Plus, there's plenty of legroom. Get booking!

133

Take in indie acts at the Seaport Music Fest

People think the warm season means SummerStage and Celebrate Brooklyn. But as those two live music behemoths wrestle with trying to be too many things to too many people, the Seaport Music Fest (South Street Seaport, Pier 17, Fulton St at South St, seaportmusicfestival.com) simply presents big names of the indie world, for free, on Friday nights, in one of the nicest settings to be had.

"Paul Simon attended the very first Seaport show, featuring Polyphonic Spree, in 2002," says producer Stephen Dima. "He and four other people made up the entire audience—there were more people onstage than on the pier. As we watched, we knew the venue was both surreal and special... we simply had to build awareness and a reputation. We achieved both this past summer. It's a beautiful thing seeing some 6,000 to 10,000-plus NYC music fans come out to support each band."

134 Order the warm roasted-duck salad at Sripraphai

It's made with red peppers, tomatoes, cucumbers, scallions and (of course) roasted mallard, then drenched in a lime and peanut sauce that is hot and sweet and savory all at once. Heaven.
Sripraphai *64-13 39th Ave between 64th and 65th Sts, Woodside, Queens (718-899-9599).*

135-137

Drink kalimotxo

Oenophiles, avert your eyes—*kalimotxo* (pronounced "calimocho") is an iconic Basque cocktail that mixes wine and cola, creating a none-too-sophisticated yet surprisingly refreshing concoction. Find it at Bar Carrera (175 Second Ave between 11th and 12th Sts, 212-375-1555). Owner Frederick Twomey blends Coke with Alquezar Moristel, a white wine with a strong taste of berrie. Xunta Tapas Bar (174 First Ave between 10th and 11th Sts, 212-614-0620) offers it as an off-the-menu refresher—ask and ye shall receive an unholy marriage of house red and cola. Kalimotxo's cousin, *uba lingorria* (wine mixed with lemon-lime soda) can be found at Pipa (ABC Carpet & Home, 38 E 19th St between Broadway and Park Ave South, 212-677-2233). This is an upscale version made with sauvignon blanc, Hendricks gin, pear puree, fresh lemon juice and Sprite.

Yelo

138 Have a snooze

LED lights operational? Check. Zero-gravity chair in optimal position? Check. Audio transmission engaged? Check. Not a trip to outer space but rather a visit to la-la land care of MetroNaps (Empire State Building, 350 Fifth Ave, Suite 2210, between 33rd and 34th Sts, 212-239-3344, metronaps.com). Wannabe sleepy-heads enter a pod chamber, basically a darkened room, filled with a half-dozen "EnergyPods"—futuristic chairs straight out of *2001: A Space Odyssey.* An oversized, bubble-shaped visor lowers over your head and soothing, sleep-inducing sounds lull you. "We get all kinds of people in here," says the attendant. "Mostly overworked business people and tourists seeking a little quiet time."

A few blocks away, the recently opened Yelo (315 W 57th St between Eighth and Ninth Aves, 212-245-8235, yelonyc.com) promises lowered stress levels, increased productivity and improved health via 20- to 40-minute power-nap sessions and concurrent reflexology massages. Inside your Yelocab, a futuristic 60-square-foot private cabin, you'll repose on a leather chair that reclines until feet are above the heart (which lowers the heart rate). A cashmere blanket adds a touch of cosiness. When our intrepid (OK, exhausted and sleep-deprived) reporter recently had a go on it, she was immediately won over. "Since I'm the sort of person who can nod off at the dentist's, I immediately felt drowsy, and as whales sang to me from speakers in the ceiling, I dipped into a light sleep," she said. After a standard 20-minute session the rooms at Yelo undergo a soothing sunrise—you can choose your hue, which brightens until you're awake. Still, you may suffer the same problem many have every morning at home: the miserable feeling of getting out of a warm, comfortable bed. To ease you into a lucid state, MetroNaps offers Wake Stations with reviving face misters, warm towelettes, mints and moisturiser. When our guinea pig finally rose from her brief slumber, the pre-pay approach and no-tipping policy at Yelo ensured that her calmer, more refreshed state wasn't befouled.

139

Browse the Jerome Robbins dance archives

These archives host the most comprehensive dance collection in the world. Yes, there are books and periodicals, but the biggest draw —for anyone who has an hour to kill—is the thousands of films and videotapes available for viewing. Selecting from them is like curating your own program, free of charge.

Jerome Robbins Dance Division of the New York Public Library for Performing Arts *40 Lincoln Center Plaza at Columbus Ave (212-870-1657/nypl.org).*

140

Sup a beer in a reformed factory

Like banks offering free toasters, bars nowadays tend to resort to free-pizza and Skee-Ball gimmicks to attract fickle tipplers. But such ploys are superfluous with a drinkery as meticulously conceived as Dumbo hideaway ReBar, carved out from an ex-factory's mezzanine. Past the handwrought gate and stained-glass windows, the tulip chandeliers' multi-colored glow illuminates 15 taps dispensing potent American microbrews (Penn Weizen, Captain Lawrence Smoked) and rich European beers (Delirium Tremens, Koeningshoeven Quadruple). The quality quaffs extend to by-the-glass organic wines, which paint-flecked artists swig as they munch on asparagus-and-smoked-salmon bocadillos and barbecued pulled pork by the fistful. Live jazz, blues and DJs provide the soundtrack after dark, when fuzzy-headed schemes lead to thoughts of purchasing a newly sprouted Dumbo apartment, making ReBar your permanent local.

ReBar *147 Front St between Jay and Pearl Sts, Dumbo, Brooklyn (718-797-2322/rearnyc.com).*

ReBar

141-143

Play beer pong

Beer pong, a drinking game that involves sinking a ping pong ball into beer-filled plastic cups, is the well-coordinated fratboy's lark of choice. Work on your skills any day of the week at Down the Hatch (179 W 4th St between Barrow and Jones Sts, 212-627-9747), where a sign-up chalkboard keeps the one highly coveted table in constant play. Show up on Thursday nights and bring your college ID (even if you graduated years ago) for half-price drinking all night long. There are further lowbrow high jinks at Jake's Dilemma (430 Amsterdam Ave between 80th and 81st Sts, 212-580-0556), where daily specials like $3 drafts on Mondays and $10 pitchers of shots on Thursdays should keep you occupied while you wait your turn on one of two tables. More serious pong enthusiasts can head to Biddy Early's (43 Murray St between West Broadway and Church St, 212-732-2873), where six regulation-size tables (that's eight by two feet for the layman) and $8 pitchers of domestic brew enhance your beer-pong experience.

DOWN THE HATCH

BEER PONG RULES

1. Each team must start with a full pitcher (No Exceptions)
2. 10 cups per side filled half-way
3. Each team member shoots once
4. If the ball goes into the cup - the opposing team must drink it and remove it from the table
5. If both teammates make their shot into different cups they get 1 ball back & continue to shoot, alternating turns until they miss
6. If both balls land in the same cup, it only co...
7. Any cup that is knocked over is c...
8. Cups are to be re-racked only un...
9. You may not shoot until you finish your b...
10. If you call your shot and make it - The opposing team drinks 2 cups
   • If you miss the called shot or it lands in a different cup - you drink one of your own
   • ...your cup only when you have finished your beer
   • ...the table or cup
   • ...on any disputes

Down the Hatch

BOURGEOIS OHR

HOLZER KRUGER
RAUSCHENBERG
PICASSO ARBUS
DUCHAMP
FREUD FRIEDLANDER
BUREN MATISSE
WARHOL
EAMES **WHITEREAD**
SHERMAN DALÍ
RUSCHA JUDD
BROODTHAERS
VAN GOGH MURRAY
RODIN MONDRIAN
WALKER
MIES VAN DER ROHE
KELLY **NEWMAN**
CHRISTO TWOMBLY
OLDENBURG RAY
MONET SMITH
HIRST BALDESSARI
WALL POLLOCK
SERR CALDER

MoMA

THE MUSEUM OF
MODERN ART
11 WEST 53 STREET
NEW YORK, NY
—
T (212) 708 9400
WWW.MOMA.ORG

144 Browse the shelves at Westsider Books till midnight

A former Mexican bar, Westsider (2246 Broadway between 80th and 81st Sts, 212-362-0706, westsiderbooks.com) is a Hollywood fave; the store has appeared in *You've Got Mail*, *Rescue Me* and 2008-released *Chapter 27*. A browser's dream, it's stuffed to its ceilings with bookwormy treasures, and the atmosphere is laid-back enough that you can take your time combing through the stacks. And thank our lucky Pynchon, it's open till midnight!

145

Watch films at MoMA

With nearly 22,000 titles, MoMA boasts one of the largest film collections in the world. Its state-of-the-art theaters (officially known as the Roy and Niuta Titus Theatres 1 and 2) aren't too shabby either—between the two of 'em, some 600 filmgoers can enjoy both classics and groundbreaking goodies. Titus 1 has all the history: Many filmic greats, including Martin Scorsese, Woody Allen and Mel Brooks, spent their formative years here. Greta Garbo preferred to watch her films alone in the greenroom adjacent to the projection booth; director Otto Preminger, meanwhile, staked out a favorite seat on the side balcony and spent half of the screenings talking back at the screen—to the annoyance of other patrons. **Museum of Modern Art** *11 W 53rd St between Fifth and Sixth Aves (212-708-9400/moma.org).*

146 See a dance work-in-progress—free!

With no cash on the line, both you and the performers can afford to be a little experimental with Movement Research (movementresearch.org), a dance lab that showcases works-in-progress every Monday at 8pm at Judson Church (55 Washington Sq South at Thompson St, 212-598-0551). Performances are free and no reservations or tickets are required; just arrive a half hour early to ensure a good seat.

147

Cheer on the Brooklyn Cyclones

Catch a rising star—or maybe just a stray foul ball—at a Brooklyn Cyclones game at Keyspan Park (1904 Surf Ave, Brooklyn, 718-449-8497, brooklyncyclones.com). The Mets' Class A minor league affiliate, the Cyclones are filling the void left by the Dodgers' 1957 flight from Brooklyn in an intimate seaside setting that is a world away (a D, F or Q train away, at least) from Shea or Yankee stadiums. Be sure to get seats along the right field line for a view of the Wonder Wheel and Cyclone rollercoaster all lit up in the background.

148

Enjoy the Greek cuisine of Michael Psilakis

Despite a recent string of bad luck and poor timing that cost him two restaurants, self-taught chef Michael Psilakis's Horatio Alger ascendancy (he was discovered by New York foodies while slinging pasta on Long Island) shows no signs of abating. A few years ago, he began—at Onera—the rather ambitious project of reinventing Greek food as we know it. Endowed with the culinary equivalent of perfect pitch, he transformed the flavors he grew up on into elevated creations that are catnip for critics—whether it was lobster poached in avgolemono (egg-lemon sauce) at the ill-fated Dona, deconstructed moussaka at the vanished Onera, or a gorgeous selection of classic spreads, like tsatsiki and taramasalata, at his casual spot, Kefi (222 W 79th St between Amsterdam Ave and Broadway, 212-873-0200). His 2007-opened venture, Anthos (36 W 52nd St between Fifth and Sixth Aves, 212-582-6900), yields a fresh slew of delights.

149-153

Buy a drink... eat for free!

Boss Tweed's Saloon

"Any bum off the street can come in and eat for free," remarks a gleeful bartender about the drippy, spicy wings at this LES barroom (115 Essex St at Rivington St, 212-475-9997). Freebies are served on Fridays from 5-7pm, but drinks are cheap enough (Bud pints $2, well drinks $3) that you'll be willing to fork over the cash for something to wash them down.

Brazen Head

This neighborhood beer haunt (228 Atlantic Ave between Boerum Pl and Court St, Cobble Hill, Brooklyn, 718-488-0430) serves up free Sunday breakfast from noon, in the form of all-you-can-eat bagels and cream cheese. Add a Bloody Mary or mimosa ($5) to make it a proper brunch.

Cha An Japanese Tea Room

The menu at Cha An (230 E 9th St between Second and Third Aves, 212-228-8030) changes every day, but from 5-7pm weekdays you're likely to come upon such appetizer-sized treats as spicy shrimp, pickled vegetables or "fish pieces". The cost: one drink. Beer prices start at $6, wine costs from $7.50 and sake from $10.

Sip

Snag a soda (from $3), wine or beer (from $4) and scarf free tapas every day at Sip (998 Amsterdam Ave between 109th and 110th Sts, 212-316-2747) from 5-7pm and 2-4am. Freebies include string-bean-topped crispy bread, sweet sausage and potatoes, and oil-and-vinegar-marinated beet salad.

The Watering Hole

Fill up on free fries and wings at happy hour (3-7pm) on Monday, Tuesday and Friday at this huge bar, formerly known as Tracy J's (106 E 19th St between Park Ave South and Irving Pl, 212-674-5783).

154 Go underground at 205

NYC's club scene may have been cleaned up and stripped of personality over the years, but if you can make it past 205's sometimes attitude-heavy door staff, head straight to the spot's basement—that's where you'll find some of the messiest parties around. Great music, often of the space-disco and electrohouse varieties, certainly doesn't hurt. Go to myspace.com/205club for more information.
205 *205 Chrystie St at Stanton St (212-477-6688).*

155 Do Nardicio

It could mean catching a Whore's Mascara and the Dazzle Dancers show or watching a screening of *Great Gay American Road Trip*. Either way, you haven't done gay nightlife in this town until you've done Daniel Nardicio. The party impresario is responsible for such legendarily sleazy soirees as Sundays at the Bijou with Daniel and Daniel Nardicio's Evening Service—a truly, um, religious experience. See dlist.com for upcoming events.

156 Find the Gubbio Studio at the Met

Not exactly hidden, but easy to pass by on the way to the Temple of Dendur, the tiny *studiolo* (study) from the Ducal Palace in Gubbio, Italy, is a marvel of trompe l'oeil woodworking. Dating to around 1480, the room, designed by Francesco di Giorgio Martini (1439-1502) and executed by Giuliano da Majano, uses a wood-inlay technique called intarsia to create the illusion of a cupboard-filled space containing books, musical instruments and other paraphernalia, using at least five different kinds of hardwood. Don't leave without looking behind the permanently open doors: There's an intricate trompe l'oeil of prison-like iron bars on the other side.
Gubbio Studio *Metropolitan Museum of Art, 1000 Fifth Ave at 82nd St (212-535-7710/ metmuseum.org).*

157

Bowl, Harlem-style

Sure, Harlem Lanes (2116 Adam Clayton Powell Jr. Blvd at 126th St, 212-678-2695, harlemlanes.com) boasts 24 well-maintained lanes, but this is more than a mere bowling alley. The complex, which opened right above the historic Alhambra Ballroom in the spring of 2006, also features two small sports bars with flat-screen TVs and a popular program of theme nights. Karaoke rages Mondays and Thursdays, while spoken word gets the open-mic treatment on Wednesdays. Happy-hour drink specials run throughout the week (5-8pm): Takes the sting off those gutterballs.

Just like the movies

Time Out film critic Ben Walters *investigates New York's impressive filmography and plots a course through the city's silver-screen sights.*

New York is the movies—or at least a certain aspect of them. There's something about it—that skyline, those stone-and-steel canyon avenues, the architectural resistance to a curve or an acute where a right angle will do… above all, the sheer scale of the place—that could do without humanity, if push came to shove, but will never let the camera down. What better subject for the quintessentially modern medium than the quintessentially modern space? And what better thing to do with such exquisite order than smash it up?

Apocalypse becomes Manhattan like nowhere else—from *Planet of the Apes* and *Escape from New York* to *Independence Day* and *Armageddon*, there are few spectacles to top a toppling skyscraper. For a brief, deceptive, post-9/11 moment it seemed that experience of the real thing might supplant the need for imaginative destruction, but then came *The Day after Tomorrow, War of the Worlds* and *I Am Legend* to put the city back in its ruined place.

Short of all-out annihilation, New York also makes a superb playground for gargantuan toddler-monsters—the sort of lumbering beasts who actually seem to be made to the same scale as the skyscrapers, unlike the puny people scurrying beneath their feet. King Kong remains the daddy of them all, larking about on the Empire State Building in his 1933 and 2005 incarnations, and the World Trade Center in 1978. Also worth a crick in the neck were *Q: The Winged Serpent* who took up residence in the Chrysler Building, the Stay Puft Marshallow Man from *Ghostbusters*, who ambled down Central Park West, and Godzilla, who dropped in on Madison Square Gardens in the 1998 film.

But lest we're giving too doomy an impression, let's not forget how achingly romantic a spot this city can be. No camera has made sweeter love to New York than Woody Allen's. *Manhattan* gave us that majestic shot of the Queensboro Bridge—a vista which, though somewhat obstructed, you can still recreate

from the Riverview Terrace at Sutton Square on East 58th St. But perhaps his single most sustained adoration of the place comes in *Hannah and Her Sisters*, in which Sam Waterson's architect gives Dianne Wiest and Carrie Fisher—and lucky us—a tour of his Manhattan highlights, including the Waldorf-Astoria (at Park Avenue and 50th St) and Abigail Adams' stone house (at First Avenue and York St). For an apologetically saccharine appreciation of the city, *Miracle on 34th Street* gives us sugar-coated Macy's department store, at 151 West, yes, 34th St.

There's no shortage of other landmark buildings that have taken celluloid bows. The scene in *The Fisher King* in which the main concourse of Grand Central Station at 42nd St is magically transformed into an elegant dance floor is impossibly dreamy. Columbia University, at Broadway and 116th St, has featured in *Ghostbusters*, *Malcolm X* and *Spider-Man*; the distinctive wedge of the Flatiron Building, at Fifth Avenue and 23rd St,

"New York...makes a superb playground for gargantuan toddler-monsters —the sort of lumbering beasts who actually seem to be made to the same scale as the skyscrapers."

was also in *Spider-Man* as the offices of the *Daily Bugle*. (The *Daily Planet*, from 1978's *Superman*, was played by the art deco News Building, former home of the *Daily News*, on 42nd St between Second and Third Avenues.)

The FAO Schwarz toystore (at Fifth Avenue and 58th St) was home to the famous outsized piano-playing sequence in *Big*, while, for those of a less cheery disposition, the Dakota (at Central Park West and 72nd St) was the birthplace of *Rosemary's Baby*. Everyone knows that Katz's Delicatessen (205 E Houston St at the corner with Ludlow Street) was the site of Meg Ryan's vocal fake orgasm in *When Harry Met Sally*, but it was also where Johnny Depp's Joe Pistone met his FBI superior in *Donnie Brasco*. And of course, if you fancy *Breakfast at Tiffany's*, the window-shopping is to be found at Fifth Avenue and 57th St.

Head a block northwest and you can take a walk on the other side of the tracks at the crossing—Sixth Avenue and 58th St—where Dustin Hoffman's Ratso Rizzo barked "I'm walkin' here!" in *Midnight Cowboy*. But many of the city's more conspicuously seedy celluloid

> "The distinctive wedge of the Flatiron Building was featured in Spider-Man *as the offices of the* Daily Bugle *(the* Daily Planet, *from 1978's* Superman, *was played by the News Building on 42nd)."*

Grand Central Station

appearances are no longer to be found. The downtown dangerous edge, for instance, was already giving way to gentrification when it was exploited by the likes of *Desperately Seeking Susan* and *After Hours*. The mean streets that so inflamed the troubled mind of Travis Bickle in *Taxi Driver* have largely been sanitised—Times Square today is more reminiscent of *Blade Runner* than *Saló*, and you'll struggle to find a porn theatre on 48th Street any more. Columbus Circle (at Eighth Avenue and 59th St) is still recognisable as the site of Bickle's botched assassination attempt, though, and the building at which the climactic massacre takes place is still at 226 13th St in the East Village (between Second and Third Avenues).

Such a list risks implying that New York and Manhattan are one and the same. Head over to Long Island and you can revisit some of the most iconic moments of the city's celluloid history. The spectacular car-versus-subway-train chase from *The French Connection* took place over more than two dozen blocks of the Bensonhurst Elevated Railway in Brooklyn, speeding from Bay 50th St down New Utrecht Avenue to 62nd St station—the end of the line for Frog Two. The route crosses 86th St, the hangout of Tony Manero (John Travolta) in *Saturday Night Fever*; the Phillips Dance Studio he frequented is still at 1301 West 7th St at Bay Parkway. Up at the northern end of Queens, meanwhile, you'll recognise the site of the 1964 World's Fair at Flushing Meadows from its use in *Men in Black*, which made spaceships of its Observatory Towers and used one of them to trash the globe-style Unisphere.

It all comes back to destruction. For all the brutalist poetry of its soaring towers and chichi cafés, it seems we never tire of seeing hubristic Manhattan laid low. The start of 2008, after all, saw *Cloverfield* make its own addition to the lumbering-behemoth menagerie —and casually eliminated the pleasure garden where Orson Welles took Rita Hayworth for a ride in *The Lady from Shanghai* and Dustin Hoffman pounded the tarmac in *Marathon Man*. Why try to deny the frisson that resulted from its trailer, which demarcated "the area formerly known as Central Park"?

184

Keep an eye on the chef at Degustation

There are 19 seats at Degustation, Jack and Grace Lamb's Spanish-themed small-plates restaurant, and every one of them is the culinary equivalent of a box seat. The chairs are arranged around three sides of the tiny open kitchen, putting diners within feet of the plancha—and face-to-face with up-and-coming chef Wesley Genovart. Rather than guess what went into this sauce or that broth, you can personally press him for details on his phenomenal dishes: crisp, smoky croquetas perched on pimenton aioli, say, or lamb loin with Laphroaig whisky. Design your own tasting menu or try his five-course version for $50—but whatever you do, show up hungry. As every groupie knows, the easiest way in with any chef is to order seconds.
Degustation *239 E 5th St at Second Ave (212-979-1012).*

185

Visit the Noguchi Museum

The former studio of eclectic Japanese-American sculptor Isamu Noguchi, who moved to Queens to be nearer the quarries that supplied the granite and marble for his inimitable works, the Noguchi Museum (9-01 33rd Rd at Vernon Blvd, 718-204-7088, noguchi.org; open 10am-5pm Wed-Fri; 11am-6pm Sat, Sun) is a shrine to the artist's exquisitely harmonious sensibility. Thirteen indoor galleries showcase his organic, undulating work in granite, marble, bronze, and wood, moving seamlessly into the adjoining gardens, which he himself laid out with fountains and small footpaths. Particularly intriguing is the all-white room devoted to his Akari works (light fixtures encased by inventive paper shades). To get there, take the N or W to Broadway and walk ten minutes towards the Manhattan skyline or call ahead for information about the weekend shuttle bus; the museum closed briefly in January 2008 for major refurbishment work.

186

Join in the West Indian-American Day Parade

On Labor Day, skip the staid traditional procession up Fifth Avenue and hop over to Brooklyn for the West Indian-American Day Parade. This is New York's carnival, a raucous flotilla of colorful, crowded floats and sound trucks booming (no, BOOMING) calypso music, all of them heading along Eastern Parkway. You can watch the festivities along the home stretch between the Brooklyn Museum and Grand Army Plaza, but it's much more fun to take the train to Franklin Avenue and dive right in. Both sides of the thoroughfare are lined with vendors selling johnnycakes, jerk chicken, curried roti, conch fritters, callaloo, macaroni pie, and coconut bread, so bring an appetite and end summer with a bang. The parade begins at 11am on Labor Day at Utica Avenue and Eastern Parkway, then follows Eastern Parkway to Grand Army Plaza.

187

Browse a non-pervy sex shop

Sex shops aren't exactly known for creating an inviting atmosphere, but Babeland (babeland.com) makes the search for titillating toys less daunting. Its two brightly lit Manhattan locations (94 Rivington St between Ludlow and Orchard Sts, 212-375-1701; 43 Mercer St between Broome and Grand Sts, 212-966-3674) seduce patrons with a huge selection of battery-equipped floor models to fondle, walls of gleaming strap-on harnesses, and informative descriptions for everything. The friendly staff are all trained sex educators, rather than the unsavory characters you might find at other joints. "We test and try everything in the store, and are continually trying to learn as much as possible about everything that we carry," says Babeland buyer Alicia Kay. Happily for those confounded by their purchases, the emporiums host enlightening workshops each month on fellatio, female ejaculation, and other lascivious subjects.

188

Pine for the brine

Founded almost a century ago by Russian-immigrant brothers Izzy and Benny Guss, Guss' Pickles (85-87 Orchard St between Broome and Delancey Sts, 212-334-3616) is the last of the Lower East Side's old-school pickle shops (the original store was on Hester Street). Guss purveys its briny wares—schlepped in daily by the barrel from its Brooklyn store—to legions of fans, who lap up the sour and half-sour pickles, not to mention a mouth- and eye-watering array of stuffed olives, pickled and sour tomatoes, marinated mushrooms and what is quite possibly the best sauerkraut in the city. Pickle fans in need of a fix should note that Guss' is closed on Saturday.

189 Get a birthday discount on beauty products

At designer markdown behemoth Loehmann's (101 Seventh Ave between 16th and 17th Sts, 212-352-0856, loehmanns.com), birthday-club membership is free, and saves you 15 percent, valid from four days before blowing out your candles to four days after. If you sign up for the birthday program at natural beauty label Aveda's retail outposts (visit aveda.com for locations), you can celebrate with gratis customized shower gels, soaps and body lotions. Skincare and makeup emporium Miomia (318 Bedford Ave between South 1st and 2nd Sts, Williamsburg, Brooklyn, 718-388-0149) offers 25 percent off on your special day, as long as you have a valid ID.

190

Hold your nose, swallow your pride… and take a pedicab

"I'll get you anywhere in midtown in under ten minutes, or I'll pay you," says Gregg Zukowski, driver and owner of pedicab company Revolution Rickshaws. "For example, Grand Central to Penn Station takes me seven minutes." What if there's gridlock? "Then it might take eight," he brags. Zukowski is trying to explain why any real New Yorker would want to ride in something that looks like it's made for newlywed out-of-towners. There are 500-odd pedicabs in the city (though if an impending law gets passed, the number will be limited to 325), found mostly around midtown near Fifth Avenue, Central Park, and the Theater District before and after showtime. The price, which you can negotiate before hopping in, normally hovers around $1 per block.

"It's 'transportainment,'" says New York Pedicab Association president Peter Meitzler. "It's cheaper than a limo but just as much personal attention. I like to think of it as a pedal-powered limo service."

Still, it's not exactly a bargain next to your unlimited MetroCard and you might have to brave bad weather. But if you've already paid for Broadway tix and are running late, go for it. Just don't breathe too deeply—think about all those fumes pedi passengers must inhale as they zip around idling cars. "I know, I know," sighs Zukowski. "It's a bitch. I'm trying to get those automobiles banned."

191 Chew Brooklyn Gum in Brooklyn

It's hard to imagine now, but Americans were once immensely popular in Europe, especially right after World War II, when GIs went around dispensing nylons, chocolates and chewing gum to the freshly liberated French and Italians. So it's no wonder that when two brothers from the Milan region—Ambrogio and Edgidio Perfetti—began to market their own brand of the bane of bridgework in 1946, they decided to name it Brooklyn Gum. For their logo, they chose Roebling's famous span, earning their product the nickname la gomma del ponte— "the gum of the bridge." Today, the company, Perfetti Van Melle, is the third-largest purveyor of confectioneries in the world. Brooklyn Gum, meanwhile, can be found in Italy just about anywhere there's a cash register, in ten flavors—including the mysterious-sounding Storming. And yes, you can buy it right here in Brooklyn, though only in four flavors, and at a slight markup: A pack that costs about 80¢ in Italy will set you back $1.50 in Park Slope.

192

Sail on the Bateaux New York

At certain times even the loveliest restaurant can't sublimate that craving you have to get out of town now—but still be back in time for work tomorrow. An evening aboard Bateaux New York's glass-enclosed Celestial (212-727-2789, bateauxnewyork.com) will see you leave Manhattan's shore, taking a gorgeously languid trip around its southern tip, and dine on a meal that's far better than the tourist fare you might expect. The vessel's patrons all seem to have the blissful demeanor of folks on vacation. Departures are from Pier 62, Chelsea Piers.

193

Be wowed by the meatless meat at Red Bamboo

Sprouts, shoots and leaves… we're all for healthy vegetarian eating. But sometimes the best way to judge a flesh-free joint is by how convincing its mock meat is. Red Bamboo Brooklyn, a vegan and vegetarian Caribbean home cookery, has mastered the art. Slip into the intimate, brick-walled space and start with the appetizer combo: A trio of soul chicken (in a light panko coating), barbecued chicken and collard-green rolls. The Willy Bobo sandwich, which layers soy ham, pickles and vegan mozzarella on grilled coco bread, is better known to carnivores as a classic Cubano —herbivores know it as a craveworthy alternative to duller veg fare.

Red Bamboo *Brooklyn 271 Adelphi St at DeKalb Ave, Fort Greene, Brooklyn (718-643-4352/ redbamboobrooklyn.com).*

194

Celebrate the season with the tree lighting ceremony

Global warming may be wreaking havoc on the seasons, but one thing hasn't changed: Whatever the weather, fall gives way to winter with the Rockefeller Center Christmas Tree Lighting Ceremony. Each year, on Thanksgiving weekend, a Norway Spruce at least 65 feet tall is installed behind the ice-skating rink at Rockefeller Center, topped with a star and lit by five miles of lights. The lighting, which is accompanied by musical guests, draws predictable throngs, but don't worry if you can't get close—the tree is illuminated every day from 5:30pm to 11:30pm until January 6 and on Christmas Day remains lit for 24 hours.

A few of my favorite things

195-199

Budd Mishkin, NY-1 on-air personality

One of my favorite places to spend a little downtime is on the rocks overlooking Riverside Park, with my guitar and a cup of coffee. It may not be as pleasant for the people around me, but it's a quiet oasis in the big city. **The top corned beef in the city is at the Carnegie Deli (854 Seventh Ave, at 55th St, 800-334-5606, carnegiedeli.com)—especially after midnight, when it tastes the best. I even spent my bachelor party there.**
It always thrills me to walk into Madison Square Garden (thegarden.com) and see the ice. I have such strong childhood memories of watching the Rangers (rangers.nhl.com) and hearing Marv Albert announcing that the "Rangers are flying!" Winning the Stanley Cup in '94 was pretty good too.
One place where I love to see shows is the National Dance Institute (594 Broadway, Room 805, 212-226-0083, nationaldance.org). It was founded by the great ballet dancer Jacques d'Amboise and it really is a symbol of the city's creativity, humor and wonder.
My wife and I had our first date at the best concert venue in the city—the Bottom Line. Years later, the owner let me take the stage on a quiet afternoon, play my guitar and ask her to marry me. We're still going strong, but the Bottom Line isn't. Like much of what made New York great, it no longer exists.

200

Kossar's Bialys still makes Gotham's finest version of the snack. They've certainly had practice, for Kossar's Bialystoker Kuchen Bakery, founded in 1934, is the oldest bakery in America dedicated to the onion-y, Bialystok version of the bagel, which has a depression instead of a hole and is not boiled before baking. The bakery (367 Grand St between Essex and Norfolk Sts, 212-473-4810, kossarsbialys.com), which is closed on Saturdays, also serves bulkas (long rolls topped with onions and poppy seeds), pletzels (small onion flatbreads) and, of course, bagels.

201 Cheer on the Puerto Rican Day Parade

Waved on by what has to be one of the largest concentrations of flags known to humanity, the National Puerto Rican Day Parade (nationalpuertoricandayparade.org) pulses its way up Fifth Avenue from 44th Street to 86th on the second Sunday in June each year. This exuberant display features floats, salsa bands, dancing, such celebrities as Jennifer Lopez, Marc Anthony and Ricky Martin, and countless politicos vying for the boricua vote. More than 2.5 million turn out for the festivities—extremely impressive considering the population of the island itself is less than four million.

202 Walk the line

In spring 2006, ground was broken for an inspired new public park along the inoperative elevated High Line freight-train tracks, built in the 1930s. Below and above it, shiny new residential buildings and hotels are rising in a breathtaking transformation of a neighborhood that was previously known solely for its auto body shops and its art galleries. The first section of the park, which will run from Gansevoort Street to W 20th Street, is scheduled (at the time of writing) to open in summer 2008 and, in a recent development, the Whitney Museum of American Art (945 Madison Ave at 75th St, 212-570-3676, whitney.org) has signed to build a satellite museum at the southern end of the High Line.

Time Out recently caught up with Joshua David, cofounder of Friends of the High Line, a not-for-profit group of community activists that spearheaded the campaign to turn the defunct elevated train track into a lush walkway. "The progress we are making is just amazing," says David. "Having the Whitney anchor one side of the park ensures its art-oriented identity. Both artists and local gallery owners were extremely supportive of the project from the beginning.

They really understood the aesthetic and creative vision, and got us off to a strong start within the local community, so we are thrilled to have such a strong cultural and artistic presence."

The last train to use the elevated High Line rattled along back in the early 1980s. Then, for more than two decades, this 22-block-long, three-story-high ribbon of rail on Manhattan's far west side, between Gansevoort Street in the Meatpacking District and 34th Street, was abandoned—an urban afterthought made lush by nature.

"What attracted us to saving the High Line was exactly that strangeness—this steel structure with wild flowers growing on top of it, in the middle of the city," says Robert Hammond, who in 1999 founded the Friends of the High Line with David. The two Chelsea residents started pitching a simple concept to anyone who would listen: Save the High Line and turn it into an elevated, urban oasis. In May 2007 it started to become a reality, with David Bowie curating the first ever High Line Festival (highlinefestival.com), an art fest celebrating High Line.

203 Forage in Central Park

Free food in Central Park? You'd better believe it—the trick is knowing where to look and what you're looking for. Along the Bridle Path, you'll find the common spicebush, whose leaves make a great tea (the Native Americans used it to treat fever). Then there's the very decent rhubarb substitute beside the Lake: You can put Japanese knotweed on salads and it will supply you with resveratrol, the same thing found in red wine that protects against aging. Kentucky coffee trees grow in the Ramble, which means that all around them on the ground are seeds that can be roasted into delicious, caffeine-free coffee. And, finally, you'll find cattails growing beside the water at Turtle Pond. If you pull up the stem and peel the shoot, it tastes just like cucumber or zucchini. But you have to do it before the plant's distinctive brown sausage-shaped flower appears—the shoot then becomes as hard as wood.

204-213 *Visit New York's ten prettiest residential blocks*

South Portland Avenue *between DeKalb and Lafayette Avenues, Fort Greene, Brooklyn*

The king of all New York blocks (*pictured*) seems straight out of Sesame Street, not only for the unbroken rows of brownstones and brick townhouses, but also because it's still home to the diverse crowd for which Fort Greene has become known: The old guard of the black middle class lives with transplants from far and near; kids and senior citizens roost on stoops. Slate sidewalks and a canopy of London Plane trees make this block a standout.

Gramercy Park South *between Park Avenue South and Irving Place, Gramercy Park*

Gramercy Park has been considered an elite urban oasis for more than 150 years, and its southern stretch offers a rare mix of early-19th-century townhouses, including one of the city's largest Victorian mansions, the National Arts Club. Yet it's the gated private park, occupying a densely green plot between East 20th and 21st Streets, that defines the enclave. The leafy expanse is accessible only to residents in the surrounding buildings, granted coveted keys.

West 20th Street *between Ninth and Tenth Avenues, Chelsea*

Few streets offer such respite from Manhattan's frenetic pace as this part of 20th Street (and its neighbors immediately to the north and south). The southern side is flanked by a pristine collection of Greek Revival row houses, while the north side is home to the General Theological Seminary, occupying an entire city block. The seminary's 19th-century architecture comes with all the trimmings, including ornate wrought-iron fencing, lush overhanging trees and a colossal bell tower that transforms the one-block strip into a provincial European village.

45th Avenue *between 21st and 23rd Streets, Long Island City, Queens*

Ten Italianate townhouses, high-stooped and made from Westchester stone, are the stars of the block-long Hunters Point Historic District. The houses on this stretch of 45th Avenue, mostly built during the 1880s, also include well-preserved examples of the French Empire, Queen Anne and neo-Grec styles popular at that time.

Convent Avenue *between 143rd and 144th Streets, Sugar Hill*
As Manhattan's affordable middle-class neighborhoods rapidly become extinct, this block—with architecture that echoes the City College of New York's Gothic Revival style—shines as a movie-perfect example of quiet excellence. Sunday afternoons find residents holding forth on stoops or playing touch football on a side street.

Montgomery Place *between Prospect Park West and Eighth Avenue, Park Slope, Brooklyn*
Stunning brownstones, old-world apartment buildings and a terracotta-colored minimansion fill this tranquil block-long street. A mix of late-19th- and early-20th-century limestone and brick buildings flaunts grand detailing; arched doorways and curved staircases suggest you're in a European fairy tale.

Beck Street *between Longwood Avenue and East 156th Street, Longwood, Bronx*
Turning onto Beck Street from Longwood Avenue is like entering a New York City of yesteryear. It's lined with stunning Renaissance Revival brownstones, which in turn are often lined with neighbors who hang out while kids play soccer or basketball in the street.

Coffey Street *between Conover and Ferris Streets, Red Hook, Brooklyn*
Red Hook isn't everybody's thing, and that's a huge part of what draws residents here. The quaint townhouses are nestled amid peace and quiet (and birdsong!), and the warehouse on the block helps create an industrial vibe without making the place feel grotty.

Charlton Street *between Sixth Avenue and Varick Street, Soho*
Tucked into a pocket between commercial Varick Street's daily hustle and bustle and the splashy all-night swagger of Soho, the trees that line this wide, sunlit block are healthier than most New Yorkers, and the string of primarily owner-occupied brownstones has staggeringly clean sidewalks.

West 78th Street *between Columbus and Amsterdam Avenues, Upper West Side*
Sandwiched between the Museum of Natural History and Amsterdam Avenue, this block is lined with gorgeous brownstones, each boasting wide staircases that ascend to large glass-plated doors. Along the curb on either side stands an abundance of tall, thick trees whose branches reach out and meet in the middle, creating a green cathedral effect when the leaves are full.

214-218

Do the alternative art fairs

Everyone knows New York is at the center of global contemporary art, but trawling the galleries can be a bit of a bore. But at the end of February each year, you can take advantage of a cluster of brilliant—and in some cases thoroughly eccentric—art fairs. Artgoers who secretly prefer the MoMA to Chelsea will love the Art Show of the ADAA (artdealers.org). Celebrating its 20th year in 2008, the Art Dealers Association of America show is a classy event featuring mostly museum-quality pieces. Organizers go for a sleek design and lots of contemporary art, but you attend for the gravitas: yes, that is a Diego Rivera landscape having its US debut.

Wii lovers and webheads are likely to be happier at DiVA New York (divafair.com/ny_07), a small fair dedicated exclusively to digital and video art. A handful of galleries take rooms on a floor of a hotel, while another group are represented in bare shipping containers parked up and down the streets of Chelsea.

For an indie alternative to the Armory Show, head to the site of the original Armory, where Marcel Duchamp rocked the art world with *Nude Descending a Staircase* in 1917. Indie kids who hate labels—and their hippie dads—will find quality painters like Karen Arm of the New York-based P.P.O.W gallery at PULSE (The 69th Regiment Armory, 68 Lexington Ave at 26th St, pulseart.com/ny). Or you can forget conventional framing techniques (and dodging the guard to get up close to the artworks) at relative newcomer Red Dot (reddotfair.com), where you'll find work lying on mattresses, leaning up against the wall or hanging out in the loo. "People should realise that art's a tangible commodity," said one exhibitor in 2007. "It doesn't have to seem so precious."

But 2007's most sprawling affair was Scope New York (scope-art.com), perfect for fans of performance art, drag queens and *Jackass*. Participants showed off works as weird as a hairstyling service; a floor installation of moving cloth inspired by the Red Sea; and a performance by Gabriel Martinez, who appeared in a skintight suit, sporting a 12-foot Vegas-style headdress.

219
Find stiff drinks and stuffed squirrels at Home Sweet Home

Taxidermy-themed bar Home Sweet Home (131 Chrystie St between Broome and Delancey Sts, 212-226-5708) is homey, we suppose—assuming you keep stuffed animals in your living room. Descend the chandelier-lit stairwell of this Lower East Side bar to a concrete-floored, signless subterranean den bedecked with stuffed critters: there's a raccoon, an eagle, even a jackalope. Sassy bartenders dispense drafts and bottled beers from a bar inlaid with display cases containing icky knickknacks (we like the dental molds).

220
Visit the lavender library

It began humbly, 30 years ago, as a stack of writings stored in the Upper West Side pantry of Joan Nestle and Deborah Edel. But today the Lesbian Herstory Archives (484 14th St between Eighth Ave and Prospect Park West, 718-768-3953), which has been housed in a Brooklyn brownstone since 1990, is the world's largest (and oldest) collection of sapphic materials, including books (notably the personal photo albums of dancer Mabel Hampton, which date back to the 1940s), memorabilia from the first DC Dyke March in 1992, audio- and videotapes, photos, clothing and much more. Tour its holdings at one of the biannual open house events—in December and on the day of the Dyke March (a lesbian-led march held the week before the Gay Pride March) in June.

221
Dunk your cookies at Ronnybrook Milk Bar

The walls are made from milk crates at the Chelsea outpost of upstate milk farm, Ronnybrook. Sidle up to the counter for two freshly baked cookies and a tumbler of whole, skim or flavored milk for $3.50.
Ronnybrook Milk Bar *Chelsea Market, 75 Ninth Ave between 15th and 16th Sts (212-741-6455/ronnybrookmilkbar.com).*

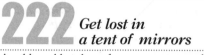 **Get lost in a tent of mirrors**

An old-world-style performance venue parked on the former site of the Fulton Fish Market, Speigeltent (spiegelworld.com)—the word means "tent of mirrors" in Flemish—follows a tradition that became popular throughout Europe during the early 20th century, when mobile dance halls traveled from town to town, luring the locals with their opulent ambience and eclectic rosters of entertainment. Erected at Pier 17 at the South Street Seaport from late July to September, the tent can accommodate 400 people standing, 320 seated and 300 with full cabaret tables. Among the performers to have graced the tent are various burlesque and drag acts, not to mention musical outfits ranging from the Spanish Harlem Jazz to Nashville Pussy. The Spiegeltent (which, despite being retro, is air-conditioned) is adjacent to a beer garden that offers refreshments—as well as free outdoor performances and East River views.

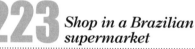 **Shop in a Brazilian supermarket**

Situated in a capacious, high-ceilinged garage, Rio Bonito Supermercado—a 2002-minted replica of a São Paulo, Brazil supermarket—stocks everything Brazilian expats need to remind them of home, including fresh oxtails from the butcher in the back. It also carries frozen pão de queijo (baked bite-size cheese rolls, an excellent party snack; $3.99), unique sweets including bananinhas (miniature bananas baked in sugar—buy one for 75¢ at the register), a peanutty halvah-like confection called pacoquinha (also available in coconut and cashew—try the mixed pack for $4.99); and one of the best coffee deals in town ($3.99/pound for the excellent Café Pilao). Check out the lunchtime buffet ($4.99/pound) and barbecue ($7.99/pound) in the back and don't even think of passing up the homemade empadinhas de frango, hot, flaky muffins stuffed with minced chicken and green olives ($1.50 each).
Rio Bonito Supermercado *32-86 47th St at 34th Ave, Astoria, Queens (718-728-4300).*

Track down the Treats Truck

This silver delivery truck, which runs on compressed natural gas, tours Gotham all year round, distributing treats such as Mexican chocolate brownies, caramel-cream sandwiches, and the Oatmeal Jammy (an oatmeal cookie with a jam center), all baked in Red Hook. The brainchild of Kim Ima, a theater professional with no previous food experience, the 15-foot truck might be coming to a street near you—check the Truck website (treatstruck.com) or call a recorded information line (212-691-5226) for route details.

 **Visit the South Street Seaport Museum**

The history of the Port of New York has been the subject and soul of quaint South Street Seaport Museum (212-748-8600, southstseaport.org) for nearly 40 years. But recently, next-door galleries and a minifleet of privately held exhibition spaces have moved in. The 2006-refurbished Schermerhorn Row Galleries (12 Fulton St between Front and South Sts, 212-748-8725) serve as the museum's home base, repository of an intriguing collection of nautical artifacts. Equally fascinating are the vestiges of the early 19th-century mercantile-exchange buildings the museum now occupies—look out for the 1800s graffiti.

The museum operates two galleries on Water Street: The Walter Lord Gallery (209 Water St between Beekman and Fulton Sts) is home to a permanent exhibition of enormous ocean-liner models; the Melville Gallery (213 Water St between Beekman and Fulton Sts) hosts rotating exhibits and literary readings. Admission to the museum ($8) includes tours of the lightship *Ambrose* and 1911 bark *Peking*, both docked at Pier 16.

226 *Shop for old-fashioned glasses at Fabulous Fanny's*

The city's premier source of period eyeglasses for roughly two decades, Fabulous Fanny's (335 E 9th St between First and Second Aves, 212-533-0637) is a former 26th St flea market booth that now boasts more than 30,000 pairs of spectacles dating as far back as the 1700s.

Whether your look is Jules Verne gold-fill round-wire rims, a pair of aviators from the disco era or 1970s rhinestone-encrusted Versace shades, this jam-packed boutique's got it—hundreds of aged frames are arranged by size, shape, color or period.

Keys to the city

Amateur crooner Adam Feldman ***hits Gotham's piano bars on a singalong tour.***

At 11pm on Friday night, I pass through a heavy scarlet door and descend into a low-ceilinged dive. In the middle of the room, 15 people are gathered around a piano. They are adults of all ages, harmonizing loudly and often off-key, like drunken Christmas carolers. But they're not singing noëls: They are singing, from memory, a medley from *Annie*—a clutch of daddies, belting out songs that were written for prepubescent girls. Here at Marie's Crisis (59 Grove St between Seventh Ave South and Bleecker St, 212-243-9323), in the heart of the old gay Village, I'm beginning a survey of the city's most popular piano bars—a vital corner of New York's musical nightlife whose virtues often go unsung. During the week, these places tend to have a quiet, neighborhood feel, but on weekends, especially late at night, they're stuffed wall-to-wall. There are songs in more people's hearts than you might think.

One of the city's rare refuges for communal singing, Marie's Crisis is a second home to New York's most fervent musical-theater devotees. It's a parallel-universe Cheers, where everybody knows not only your name but also the complete score to Stephen Sondheim's *Pacific Overtures*. The bespectacled weekend pianist, Dexter Watson, pauses between songs to chat with the regulars—like show-tune fan Catherine Skidmore, a nurse from New Jersey. Skidmore is hard-core: On her left forearm she has a tattoo of the Georges Seurat painting from Sondheim's *Sunday in the Park with George*. The swarming room also includes some less-savvy visitors, and at one point a table of women shouts a request to hear something from *West Side Story* or from *The Sound of Music*. In tacit response, Watson chooses a tune from Sondheim's *Company*: "You Could Drive a Person Crazy."

I hop in a cab uptown, and it is past midnight when I arrive at the fancy entrance of my next destination: the Townhouse (236 E 58th St between Second and Third Aves, 212-754-4649),

Marie's Crisis

a tastefully stuffy gentlemen's club that seems like a time capsule from a bygone era of gay gentility. The crowded room is dotted with floral arrangements and architectural prints, and middle-aged men in blazers and cardigans mill about the full-size piano in the corner. There, Rick Unterberg is tickling the ivories pink. A frail man in his 70s steps up for a solo; grasping the microphone tightly with both hands, he sings a heartfelt, atonal rendition of "Send in the Clowns." His listeners applaud supportively.

From there it is on to Brandy's (235 E 84th St between Second and Third Aves, 212-650-1944), where the atmosphere is entirely different. The walls are decorated with posters from recent Broadway shows and ancient French cafés, and pianist David Budway is playing pop songs from yesteryear—"The Gambler," "Country Roads," "Let It Be"—to a joint packed with young, straight women and men. The audience joins in loudly at the choruses, like happy summer campers. Customers are allowed to do solo numbers—for a price. "If you tip me, you can sing," says Budway, not quite jokingly, and gestures to the clear plastic fishbowl full of

dollars bills that sits atop his small upright instrument. Nearly an hour later, just before closing time, I make it to the mic and belt out an old Paul McCartney tune. By now it is 3:30am: Time to head home and rest the vocal cords for more piano-barhopping.

A week later, properly recovered, I begin a second round of musical tourism at Midtown's cozy Broadway Baby Bistro (318 W 53rd St between Eighth and Ninth Aves, 212-757-5808). It is spanking new, which is notable: Piano bars have been disappearing gradually from the city for years, and few new joints have taken their place. Outside of Broadway Baby, flamboyant pianist Ricky Ritzel is sharing a smoke with fellow pro Terri White, who has appeared in multiple Broadway shows and makes her living as a singing waiter between gigs. "I've had a rough year," he says, and names three venues that have closed in the last year alone. "You and me both," White replies. One of the city's most popular piano bars, Rose's Turn, closed its doors for good six months ago; White had worked there, on and off, for four decades. Such is the piano-bar performer's lot: Life may be a cabaret, but cabaret isn't much of a life.

"It's a parallel-universe Cheers, *where everybody knows not only your name but also the complete score to* Stephen Sondheim's Pacific Overtures.*"*

A smallish audience—not that many people yet know about the neonatal Broadway Baby—listens appreciatively as Ritzel and White begin a song. The energy level is higher a few blocks away, where a sizable group is huddled in front of a velvet rope outside Don't Tell Mama (343 W 46th St between Eighth and Ninth Aves, 212-757-0788), and the doorman says it'll be a half-hour wait just to get in. The place is packed with out-of-towners looking for entertainment in Times Square; the comically disheveled George Saunders waits tables wearing nothing but spandex underwear and an apron. ("The tourists love it," he tells me. "We want to make sure it's called Don't Tell Mama for a reason.") Patrons are welcome to sing pop or musical-theater songs alone at the microphone, and for many people, this is the main appeal of piano bars today: a kind of cabaret karaoke.

Continuing my southward path, I head off to the Laurie Beechman Theatre—downstairs at the West Bank Café (407 W 42nd St between Ninth and Tenth Aves, 212-695-6909)—for the After Party: a weekly open-mic show-tune night popular with young musical-theater talents. Host Brandon Cutrell lubricates the proceedings with outrageously ribald patter, and keeps a list of those who want to perform with the proficient piano man Ray Fellman. Cutrell tends to stack the beginning of the show with ringers from Broadway musicals; but it is now past 1am, and the amateurs are getting their time. Among them is a young woman completely obsessed with the cult musical *Grey Gardens*; nearly every week

she gets up to perform the same song from that show, complete with makeshift props and costumes—tonight is no exception. When my turn at the mic arrives, I sing Edith Piaf's "La Vie en Rose." (A week later, I discover that an older Romanian couple at the front table has videotaped the performance and posted it on YouTube.) Although it's getting quite late, I grab another cab and head down to the Village to visit another open-mic night: Mostly Sondheim, at the Duplex (61 Christopher St, second floor, at Seventh Ave South, 212-255-5438). To my surprise, it is still raucously busy, with drunkenly enthusiastic audience members clamoring for a turn on stage.

By now it's three in the morning and time to go home, but I find myself drawn back to where I started: the dark womb of Marie's Crisis. Other bars may be hipper, livelier, younger, classier, but Marie's feels special. I recall what Marie's alternate pianist Jim Allen—off duty, but still hanging around—told me the week before. "I play here on Christmas and New Year's and all the holidays, with people who don't have family," he said. "This is my living room: the Fellini version of *The Waltons*."

234

Be a hero on Guitar Hero

On Tuesday nights (10pm-4am), wanna-be Claptons compete onstage for the hottest virtual riff via Guitar Hero II at LES venue Pianos (158 Ludlow St at Stanton St, 212-505-3733). The guitar-shredding PlayStation game's cult-like following might be intimidating, but watching other people is entertainingly anxiety-free, particularly when regular joes attempt to rock "Sweet Child o' Mine."

235 *Hunt unicorns in the park*

In the lovely Frederick Law Olmsted-designed Fort Tryon Park, which overlooks the Hudson River, a path winds through peaceful grounds to a castle at the northern edge that seems to have survived from the Middle Ages. It was actually built in 1938, using pieces of five medieval French cloisters shipped from Europe by the Rockefeller clan. This holds part of the Met's collection of medieval art and architecture, including the 12th-century Fuentidueña Chapel, the Annunciation Triptych by Robert Campin and—best of all—the famous Unicorn Tapestries.

The Cloisters *Fort Tryon Park, 99 Mary Colvin Drive (212-923-3700/metmuseum.org).*

236

Splash out on caviar at Caviar Russe

They take their fish roe seriously at Caviar Russe (538 Madison Ave between 54th and 55th Sts, 212-980-5908), whether the stuff is offered by the mother-of-pearl spoonful (sevruga $26; golden osetra $35; triple zero $59) or in portions of 25 to 250 grams (priced from $130 to a mighty $2985), served with traditional blini, toast or potatoes. At the seven-seat caviar bar that faces the open kitchen, every detail has been designed for an experience that's refined without collapsing over into fussiness. Ask the bartender for a pairing recommendation, then order a "taste"—two chilled oysters with beluga and chilled sake, or a lobster-and-caviar profiterole accompanied by chilled vodka, champagne or a glass of white wine from the well-considered list.

237 Get five shots of anything for ten bucks at the Continental

No longer the gritty music venue that saw Iggy and the Ramones grease the stage, the Continental Bar (25 Third Ave at St. Marks Pl, 212-529-6924) still offers the cheapest—and most lethal—drink special in Manhattan. Indeed, the $10 for five shots of anything deal is such a part of the spot that the old sign offering it is now out front, as if masquerading as the bar's name. Happy hour (4-8pm) sees at least a dollar off every drink, and a lot of happy regulars who get the Continental drift.

238 Pay your respects on 9/11 at the Floating Lanterns Ceremony

Every September, the New York Buddhist Church uses the Japanese tradition of floating paper lanterns to honor those lost at Ground Zero. Members of the public are invited to write the name of a loved one (or a message of peace) on a note to be carried down the Hudson. See newyorkbuddhistchurch.org for details of this year's ceremony.

Buck up, commitmentphobes. Museum memberships may be the best way to get into your favorite institutions on the cheap. Here's the breakdown: A single MoMA (212-708-9400, moma.org) membership goes for $75 (or $120 for a dual membership—and you can sign up with a friend, not just a life partner). This means you'll have to visit four times in a year to make the deal worthwhile. Perks include up to five $5 guest passes per visit (some ticket sellers have been known to give 'em to you free) and a 10 percent discount at the MoMA store.

Meanwhile, the $75 membership at the Guggenheim (212-423-3500, guggenheim.org), which breaks even at five visits, will gain you free admission to all of the Gugg museums worldwide (hello, Bilbao!). A full membership at The Met (212-535-7710, metmuseum.org) costs $95, which is worth it if you tend to pay what they wish ($20) at least five times a year. But we'd go for the more simple $60 "Met Net" membership, which gets you into the Trustees Dining Room once (worth it for the view of Central Park), as well as an admission card—

and passes to the Cloisters. At the Whitney (212-570-3676, whitney.org), $75 gets you annual membership (worth five single visits; a dual membership is $100), private morning viewings with breakfast and tickets for an opening cocktail reception.

Even if art isn't your bag, there are some enticing membership privileges to be had. At the American Museum of Natural History (212-769-5606, amnh.org), annual membership costs four suggested donations ($70; $115 for families) and gets you invites to private tours, lectures and workshops, as well as deep discounts on planetarium shows, IMAX films and freeze-dried ice cream at the gift shop. The annual Garden Party is a big draw for Cooper-Hewitt National Design Museum (212-849-8349, cooperhewitt.org) members, but the $75 a year membership means you'll get special treatment outside the walls of the Carnegie Mansion as well: Previous events have included a daylong jaunt to Long Island City for an exclusive tour of the Noguchi Museum and of Getty Museum architect Richard Meier's warehouse gallery. Individual dues at the New York Botanical

American Museum of Natural History

Garden (718-817-8724, nybg.org) sprouted from $60 to $75 at the end of 2007, but you still get early entrance to special exhibits, access to the grounds before the gates open and complimentary admission to green spaces around the country. Members are also invited on behind-the-scenes tours with garden botanists and inspired day trips, like an outing to the Philadelphia Museum of Art's Renoir landscape show. Best of all (this goes for all the memberships), this is a way to avoid that I-need-to-see-the-whole-shooting-match-in-one-afternoon feeling.

Still not sold? How about joining the Young Lions program at New York Public Library (212-930-0885, nypl.org)? At $350 it sure ain't cheap, but then the under-40 crowd is hipper than your typical blue bloods: The Frick doesn't get Ethan Hawke and Terrence Howard at their benefits. Tax-deductible membership grants access to exclusive parties (perhaps *Us Weekly*'s Janice Min and painter Delia Brown debating voyeurism) and film previews (*Into the Wild*, hosted by Sean Penn, in September 2007). Money burning a hole in your pocket? Bump your membership up to $750 Conservator status and you'll get into Reading Circle talks (from the likes of *Then We Came to the End* author Joshua Ferris) and advance tickets to the always-sold-out Library Lions gala.

247-250

Ignore the plastic Irish bars— have a real Gaelic night out

If it's authentic craic you're after, you'll find plenty in Woodside, Queens. At The Cuckoo's Nest (61-04 Woodside Ave at 61st St, 718-426-5684), the banter crackles around the bar, and the traditional music on Sunday evenings will have you sighing into your Guinness. The blarney is more boisterous at Sean Og's Tavern (60-02 Woodside Ave at 60th St, 718-899-3499), popular with new immigrants from the Emerald Isle who come to dance to the video jukebox—it feels like a Dublin disco.

In the Bronx, in County Woodlawn, The Rambling House (4292 Katonah Ave at 236th St, 718-798-4510) pulls a good-natured transplant crowd for its live weekend music and Irish bangers and mash—and from here it's just a short crawl to the always-packed Rory Dolan's (890 McLean Ave between Central and Kimball Aves, 914-776-2946), just over the checkpoint-free border in Yonkers.

251

Shop in a bike shop that's, like, friendly

The Bicycle Station (560 Vanderbilt Ave between Bergen and Dean Sts, Prospect Heights, Brooklyn, 718-638-0300) is an absolute godsend for cyclists on their way to or from Prospect Park—and the many others who make a detour just to get their steed serviced by owner Mike Rodriguez and his crew. In a refreshing change from the usual attitude-laden bike store, the Stationmasters want to find exactly the right cycle for you, they don't up-sell, and they don't look down on newbies who can't tell derailleurs from crank arms. "Quick, efficient and friendly" seems to be the shop's unofficial motto. "I think customer service means being nice," says Rodriguez. Amazingly, this freakish philosophy hasn't hurt the shop, which has been around for approaching ten years.

252-261

Get snapped in the city's best photo booths

Who doesn't love photo booths? Here are New York's finest.

Bubby's

Famous for their pies, both locations also offer a slew of other comfort foods like macaroni and cheese and gravy-smothered meat loaf—best ingested after you've posed.

120 Hudson St at North Moore St (212-219-0666); 1 Main St between Plymouth and Water Sts, Dumbo, Brooklyn (718-222-0666).

Bushwick Country Club

The jukebox plays the best of the 1980s, action figures and lunch boxes decorate the walls, and you can play mini-golf right outside the bar. Four black-and-whites will set you back a mere three bucks.

618 Grand St at Leonard St, Williamsburg, Brooklyn (718-388-2114).

Coney Island

Though there's an array of sticker photo booths here, the authentic original is just by the Wonder Wheel.
Surf Ave at Atlantic Ave (no phone).

Dave & Buster's

A "photomorph" booth—when you and your fellow "victim" have your photos snapped, your images will be morphed together to create the image of what your child might look like. Whoa. Prints come out on a postcard.
234 W 42nd St between Seventh and Eighth Aves (646-495-2015).

Kmart

If the shot isn't flattering, you can retake photos before printing.
770 Broadway at Astor Pl (212-673-1540).

Lakeside Lounge

They just might immortalize you by putting your shots on lakesidelounge.com, plus the kitschy 1950s rock 'n' roll vibe is a nice escape from everyday New York.
162 Ave B at 10th St (212-529-8463/ lakesidelounge.com).

Niagara

This bar is so big that you can escape from the freako hitting on you by hiding out in another party room on another floor. The basement level is generally less crowded and features more-intimate rooms lined with benches.
112 Ave A at 7th St (212-420-9517).

Otto's Shrunken Head

The Kills used the booth at this tiki bar to shoot images for their album covers.
538 E 14th St between Aves A and B (212-228-2240/ottosshrunkenhead.com).

Ricky's

Here you can add "extras": a border, a background or even a new hairstyle.
112 W 72nd St between Columbus Ave and Broadway (212-769-3678).

Union Pool

An outside patio provides the perfect place to enjoy late-summer weather.
484 Union Ave at Meeker Ave, Williamsburg, Brooklyn (718-609-0484).

A few of my favorite things

262-267

The Naked Cowboy, naked cowboy

I hang out in Times Square all of the time, so I really love sitting in the Starbucks (1585 Broadway between 47th & 48th Sts) and watching people. I'm always in my underwear, so it's fun to see people's reactions to me. There are so many different people who come to the area, this is the best place to people-watch.

One place I love to go in Times Square itself is Spotlight Live Karaoke Lounge (1604 Broadway at 49th St, 212-262-1111, spotlightlive.com). It's one of the city's best places for karaoke because when you go up to sing, they have a live feed of you singing on the enormous billboard outside. It lets you become part of the whole Times Square thing.

I always get a turkey sandwich at Times Square Hot Bagels (200 W 44th St, 212-997-7300). It's close by and the minute I walk in, the deli guy immediately starts making my sandwich for me. I don't even have to order it.

I really enjoy going to the various TV studios for their morning shows. Fox (1211 Sixth Ave, 212-301-3000, foxnews.com), CBS (524 W 57th St, 212-975-3247, cbs.com), NBC (30 Rockefeller Plaza, W 49th St, 212-664-3700, nbc.com)—they all have crowds outside the studio who presenters talk to during the show. I used to hang out outside and when the camera turned near me, I'd jump out in my underwear and start singing just to get attention. Now I get invited to the studio and everyone acts like my best friend.

268

Jazz things up at Minton's

Few clubs in the city can boast as rich a history as Minton's Playhouse (208 W 118th St between St. Nicholas Ave and Adam Clayton Powell Jr. Blvd, 212-864-8346, uptownat mintons.com), which Miles Davis dubbed "the black jazz capital of the world." During the 1940s, when Thelonious Monk was resident pianist, late-night jams brought in such luminaries as Dizzy Gillespie and Charlie Parker, giving birth to bebop. Today, the long wooden bar offers a good vantage point for the nightly shows, or you can grab a table closer to the action. Minton's presents five house-bands from Sunday through Thursday, and guest acts on weekends,

www.treesforcities.org

Trees for Cities
Charity registration number 1032154

Travelling creates so
many lasting memories.

Make your trip mean
something for years to
come - not just for you
but for the environment
and for people living in
deprived urban areas.

Anyone can offset their
flights, but when your
plant trees with Trees for
Cities, you'll help create
a green space for an
urban community that
really needs it.

Leave Your Mark
Create a green future for cities.

269-271

Order the best sangria in town

The fruity wine-based refreshment, typically associated with the Spanish, has been adopted as one of Gothamites' unofficial summer quaffs. Havana Central at the West End (2911 Broadway between 113th and 114th Sts, 212-662-8830) serves a selection of tasty vino-and-fresh-fruit concoctions, all garnished with an appropriately festive plastic hula girl. In addition to classic red and white varieties, guzzlers can choose from champagne, rosé, shiraz or port-infused versions. During happy hour (Mon-Fri 4-7pm) glasses are $5 a pop. In Inwood, meanwhile, 809 Sangria Bar & Grill (112 Dyckman St between Nagle and Post Aves, 212-304-3800) features six inspired selections ($15-$35 per pitcher) like the 809 Passion, a blend of Alizé cognac, merlot, brandy and passion-fruit nectar. Or visit the bar at Suba (109 Ludlow St between Delancey and Rivington Sts, 212-982-5714) where two types of sangria—we like the "ginger-amontillado" with Reed's ginger beer—can be yours for $11 a glass. *Salud!*

272-273

Chill in two secret gardens

Behind an iron gate at St. Luke's church (487 Hudson St at Barrow St) is a hidden sanctuary that bursts with pink rhododendrons, yellow daffodils, and magnificent perennials. The garden was founded in 1842 with the planting of a tiny slip taken from England's famous Glastonbury Thorn (which survived until 1990, when it tragically succumbed to a freak windstorm). Sit on a wooden bench under the knobby cherry tree in the center and you can't help but think beautiful thoughts.

Almost as lovely is Battery Park's Oval Lawn, which is hidden in a small maze of tulip-fringed hedges in the southeast corner of North Cove. Lie on a dreamy expanse of grass, encircled by trees, and gaze up through the blossoms while the setting sun casts a rosy glow across the river.

274-277

Take a dip

You know what it's like: You hit the middle of July and it's hotter than Satan's grundle out there. Doesn't matter how many iced teas you throw down, you need a swim. Lucky for you there's no shortage of brilliant public pools in the city. If you don't want to leave Manhattan, the medium-sized indoor pool at Chelsea Piers Sports Center (Pier 60, 23rd St and Eleventh Ave, 212-336-6000; $50 all-access day pass) is a prince. Just beware of drowning: The facility's glitzy magnificence is so distracting, you might forget to paddle.

Brooklyn has a couple of exemplary pools—even better, both of them are free. Olympic-sized Red Hook (Bay and Henry Sts, 718-722-3211) was opened by Mayor Bloomberg in 2006, while the smaller Floating Pool Lady (Furman and Joralemon Sts) is even newer: It became the city's hottest cooling spot in 2007, its first summer season. Opened in Brooklyn Bridge Park, you'll find this oxymoronic, outdoor "floating pool" anchored between Piers 4 and 5 (though it may relocate to the Bronx in the future).

There are two other essential sites for New York's swimmers. The largest pool in the city is the outdoor Astoria Park Pool (19th St and 23rd Dr, 718-626-8620). Relatively clean and well maintained, it is also free—which means it can get kind of crowded. If you want more space, stump up the $75 annual membership for access to St. Mary's Pool (450 St. Ann's Ave, Bronx, 718-402-5155)—it's an excellent, medium-sized, indoor pool.

278 See Monday Night Magic

It's simple but brilliant sleight-of-hand illusions that make MNM so charming. Impresario Michael Chaut maintains a topflight roster of prestidigitators, illusionists, mind readers, and other crafty tricksters in this long-running magic show at Theatre at St. Clement's (423 W 46th St between Ninth and Tenth Aves, 212-615-6432, mondaynightmagic.com).

279 Order lemonade at Kitchenette

All too often, what gets passed off as lemonade is a sorry disappointment. A glass of sour water with wayward floating seeds. A sugary drink lacking that requisite citrusy tang. Where do you head for a proper glass? Try Kitchenette (156 Chambers St between Greenwich St and West Broadway, 212-267-6740; 1272 Amsterdam Ave, between 122nd & 123 Sts, 212-531-7600), where the pitcher-perfect pink lemonade recipe is a family recipe from co-owner Ann Nickinson's grandmother. The refreshing quaff, which gets its fun tint from berry juice, is served in mason jars—a fitting match with the restaurant's country-kitsch decor. A 16-ounce glass costs $2.75.

280 Check out the used bookmarks at Unnameable Books

Some say that Brooklyn is the city's most literary borough. And where do all of those well-read people take their excellent used books? To Unnameable, of course. With a cluttered, top-shelf inventory that could keep you reading great tomes for the next decade, this is a definite boon to Brooklyn's literati. There's more: The Unnameable staff collect and post items they find tucked inside traded books. Quirky discoveries include a 19th-century advertisement for Perry & Co.'s Patent Aromatic Elastic Bands, an Echo & the Bunnymen concert ticket from 1988, and an index card scrawled with the words "It's a mental image of something you've already perceived." Not long ago, owner Adam Tobin found a stranger's high-school portrait inside a book. He's now using it as a bookmark.

Unnameable Books *456 Bergen St between Fifth and Flatbush Aves, Park Slope, Brooklyn (718-789-1534/unnameablebooks.net).*

281 Swing down to the new Sports Museum of America

In a nation as obsessed with sports as ours, it seems rather odd that there's never been a museum dedicated to America's various athletic pastimes. That should all have changed by the time you read this, with the Sports Museum of America due (at time of writing) to open at 26 Broadway in May 2008. More than 28,000 square feet of exhibit space will be available in the three-storey building, room for some 600-plus bats, balls, skates, uniforms and other pieces of memorabilia, as well as more than 1,000 iconic photos. This is also to be the new site of the Heisman Trophy ceremony and the Women's Sports Hall of Fame.

Among museum cofounder Phillip Schwalb's favourite planned displays are Jesse Owens' diary from the 1936 Berlin Olympics; "Goalie's Nightmare," a virtual simulator that sends a 120mph slap shot racing toward your face; and "Dreaming Big," which glimpses today's sports stars when they were young.

Sports Museum of America *sportsmuseum.com*

282 Listen to new plays for nothing

Script readings around the city offer free theater for the ear.
Amanda Cooper *listens up.*

Once a year, Ben & Jerry's celebrates Free Cone Day—for the Chunky Monkey junkie, it's Christmas, New Year and Thanksgiving rolled into one. Theater has its own such holiday, only it's a weekly occurrence. The budget-conscious playgoer can find free readings throughout the city, by companies large and small. Many are open to the public, some involve genuine professionals. They come in two main flavors: readings of classics (such as the starry renditions you'll hear at Project Shaw) and sneak previews of new works, the latter type constituting its own unusual drama subculture.

A play reading is just that. Dialogue and stage directions are heard; set, costumes and blocking must be visualized. Although some works will be unfinished, they can still make for moving moments of theater sans production polish. If you've never heard of this world, it's no real surprise: Marketing and publicity budgets for reading series are minuscule to nonexistent. Since there's no box-office revenue or need to fill a big house, getting the word out is done on the cheap. Common promotional tactics involve e-mail blasts to troupe Listservs, Web postings and the occasional flyer or postcard distributed to like-minded venues.

Actors and directors who participate in readings get little if any compensation, but both established and emerging artists are happy to join in. "It's a chance to get involved at an early stage with a play that could very likely go on to have a longer life and, hopefully, be produced," says Kim Rosenstock, who programs Out Loud, Ars Nova's biweekly reading series (arsnova nyc.com). Past participants have included Michelle Williams and *Saturday Night Live*'s Rachel Dratch. Even celebrities find inspiration from fresh theater voices. As a by-product of having star-studded casting, Rosenstock says that Out Loud does see its share of "people who just want to come stare at Paul Rudd for free on a Monday night."

Though the readers may be far more established than the writers, the focus of successful play readings is the text. At New Dramatists (newdramatists.org), the revered nonprofit dedicated to developing playwrights, artistic director Todd London says the author oversees every aspect of the event, including casting and who can attend. "If the reading is engaged as a true experimental process at the right time and in the right environment," London says, "it can be important in the process of the writer discovering the play."

London, who himself sees from five to ten readings a month, tends to avoid them at producing theaters. "More often than not, they're a substitute for a production," he says. "I respect theaters that truly use play readings to cultivate audience appreciation of the new and different. Too often, though, companies present readings to convince funders (and themselves) they're nourishing the future of the art."

It's a dirty little secret of the nonprofit world that most plays get a reading or a workshop but no full production, leading playwrights to use the term "development limbo." However, readings are still the best way to move a play forward. The Vineyard Theatre often culls main-stage productions from the 15 or so readings that it conducts each year (though free, these affairs tend to be members-only).

Checking websites and joining e-mail lists can keep you in the know: Recent reading series have been run by 29th Street Rep's Brutal Readings (29thstreet rep.com), York Theatre Company's musical series (yorktheatre.org), Partial Comfort Productions' Welcome Mat Reading Series (partialcomfort.org) and Red Bull Theater's Revelation Readings (redbulltheater.com). Other companies to find out about include the Public Theater, Manhattan Theatre Club, Naked Angels, Irish Repertory Theatre and Soho Rep.

They'll never replace full productions as a theatergoer's favorite, but free readings come in just as many flavors as Free Cone Day—and they give your imagination a bit of a workout too.

283 Check out the map room at the NYPL

The world is truly at your fingertips in the Lionel Pincus & Princess Firyal Map Division of the New York Public Library (Fifth Ave and 42nd St, first floor, 212-930-0830, nypl.org). Restored in 2005 to its original 1911 Beaux Arts splendor, the map room's gold ceiling and elegantly carved wooden chairs and tables make an inspirational setting for poring over its collection of more than 400,000 maps, as well as 20,000 atlases, books, and periodicals dating back to the 16th century. From medieval conjectures about the earth's four corners to surveys of the city's five boroughs, you'll find it here.

284 Snag a window seat at Angel's Share

More clandestine than clannish, Angel's Share (8 Stuyvesant St between Third Ave and E 9th St, second floor, 212-777-5415) is an Asian-inflected cocktail den secreted behind an unmarked side door toward the front of second-floor Japanese restaurant Yokocho. It's a classy two-room spot, with suave, tuxedo-wearing bartenders, expertly chilled cocktail glasses, and some rules: Standing and parties of more than four are forbidden. If you can score a window table with a view over bustling Stuyvesant Square, savor one of many sakes or set the meticulous bartenders to work on a cocktail of your choice. You won't be disturbed.

New York Public Library

Time Out
Travel Guides

USA

285-289

Come to the zoo and say "Awww!"

Bronx Zoo

With more than 4,000 animals and 465 species, the Wildlife Conservation Society's NYC flagship zoo is the absolute must-see. The zoo's $49.7 million annual budget provides such wonders as 20 great apes in the lush, realistic habitat of Congo Gorilla Forest (open in summer); awesome Siberian striped tigers in the snow of Tiger Mountain; and, in Astor Court, a monkey den and sea lion pool. There are less salubrious pleasures in the World of Darkness, where your eyes will slowly adjust to meet bats, caimans and spooky, cave-dwelling eyeless fish, and in the Mouse House, where the three-feet-long cloud rat should be enough to give you nightmares. A $5 monorail helps to get you round the 265 acre site. It's all a bit like walking onto National Geographic Channel live. *Bronx River Pkwy at Fordham Rd, Bronx (718-220-5100).*

Central Park Zoo

You want gay penguins? Silo and Roy are so famous their breakup made local gossip pages. You want an ursine psych crisis? Gus, the polar bear, has been in therapy and likes to swim laps to work out his angst. With more than 1,400 animals (of 130 species) in only 6.5 acres, some of these creatures live in Manhattan-apartment-sized quarters, which might leave you feeling bad. But hey, look—tamarinds, those creepy primates that look as though human heads (complete with Tina Turner hair) have been stuck onto itty-bitty monkey bodies. You can tour the zoo on your lunch break and smile as city kids see a sea lion for the very first time. *Southeast corner of Central Park, enter at Fifth Ave at 64th St (212-439-6500).*

Queens Zoo

Never dragged to a National Park as a tyke? This 11-acre, America-themed zoo will give you the idea. It is home to only 400 animals of 70 species, but having more space for fewer critters seems like a worthy trade-off. Our country's misunderstood predators (pumas and bald eagles) are present, well defended and easy to see—still, it makes you shudder when the coyotes come right up and look you in the eye. (One coyote, Otis, was settled here after being found wandering in Central Park in 1999.) You can also see big-headed bisons and Spangles, the Andean spectacled bear. *53-51 111th St at 54th Ave, Flushing Meadows, Queens (718-271-1500).*

Prospect Park Zoo

This tiny zoo is aimed expressly at kids: They can observe and draw the animals and even get to touch them in the barnyard. Watch the meerkats fight at close range, see cute rust-colored furballs (red pandas to naturalists) and technicolor rubber toys (poison dart frogs), but watch out for Esther the kangaroo—she occasionally surprises visitors by sneaking up and plucking out their leg hairs. Since 54 of the 106 species are reptiles and amphibians, you'll get through this tiny zoo pretty quickly if you're not a fan of the squirmy stuff. And avoid the temptation of entering the prairie dog tunnels—they, too, are designed for little ones and you might get stuck. *450 Flatbush Ave at Empire Blvd, Prospect Park, Brooklyn (718-399-7339).*

Staten Island Zoo

There are no glossy maps or WCS funding for this zoo, but this eight-acre site has some spunk the others don't. Aside from the 858 creatures of 220 species, it's got a mascot, the famous *Groundhog Day* star Staten Island Chuck. The sleek, clever river otters and adorably pudgy black-tailed prairie dogs are also well worth the $7 entry fee. On weekends, zookeepers wriggle dead mice to tempt the reptiles. Too gross? Check out the fossa from Madagascar. It looks part bear, part mongoose, and it springs around its enclosure. With its dilapidated grounds and strains of (we shit you not) "The Hokey Pokey," this zoo is perfect for a date who is up for a laugh and a long-ass hike for a critter fix. *614 Broadway between Harvest Ave and Colonial Court, Staten Island (718-442-3100).*

290 See Bollywood in a deco cinema

While Bollywood movies are starting to make inroads across the multiplex videoscape, the best place to have a peep at one is surely the Eagle Movie Theater (73-07 37th Rd, 718-205-2800, eaglemovietheater.com), a focal point of the Jackson Heights Indian community. Formerly a notorious porn theater called the Earle—the new owners simply changed the "r" to a "g"—this tattered art deco gem is the first stop in the city for the subcontinent's boisterous, musically driven dramas, comedies, and action films, perhaps the latest Aishwarya Rai vehicle. Subtitles are in English.

291 Chew on a BB cheese steak

Purists may scoff at the absence of Cheez Whiz, but the cheese steak devised by BB Sandwich Bar seems destined to be New York's answer to the Philly classic. The only item on the menu, this cheese steak comes layered with thin slices of medium ribeye steak, sautéed herb-marinated onions, a topping of ketchup-vinegar cornichon relish and a slice of white American cheese on each side of a poppy-seed kaiser roll. The wax paper-wrapped sandwiches come with a moist towelette and two mints. Use them.
BB Sandwich Bar *120 W 3rd St between MacDougal St and Sixth Ave (212-473-7500).*

292 Browse at ADAA's annual art show

Having reached its 20th year in 2008, the Art Dealers Association of America (ADAA) February show is still classy, featuring mostly museum-quality pieces. Sounds boring, huh? They know, they know. So, back in 2007, the organizers premiered a sleeker design and lots of contemporary art. Nonetheless, you come here for the gravitas: Yes, that is a Diego Rivera landscape having its US debut.
Seventh Regiment Armory, Park Ave at 67th St (212-766-9200 ext 248/artdealers.org).

293 Do the midnight run

Those Gothamites who are looking for a jumpstart on their fitness resolutions should join the New Year's Eve Midnight Run. Fun starts at 10pm at the Central Park Bandshell with DJ-fuelled dancing, giving way to a costume parade with judges on hand at 11pm. Fireworks ring in the New Year, and then the run begins: a five-kilometer jaunt around the park beginning at 68th St and doing a counterclockwise circuit that ends up back at the Bandshell. And if you can keep your resolutions, your time by the next December 31 should have improved. Register to run at nyrr.org.

294

Take time to reflect on the Holocaust and Jewish culture

Opened in 1997 and expanded in 2003, New York City's Holocaust remembrance archive, the Museum of Jewish Heritage (Robert F Wagner Jr Park, 36 Battery Pl at First Pl, 646-437-4200, mjhnyc.org, admission free-$10), provides one of the most moving cultural experiences in the city. Exploring Jewish life and detailing the horrific attacks on it over the past century, the collection consists of 24 documentary films, 2,000 photographs and 800 cultural artefacts, many donated by Holocaust survivors and their families. The Memorial Garden features English artist Andy Goldsworthy's permanent installation Garden of Stones, 18 fire-hollowed boulders, each planted with a dwarf oak sapling.

The Jewish Museum (1109 Fifth Ave at 92nd St, 212-423-3200, thejewishmuseum.org, admission free-$12), which is located in the 1908 Warburg Mansion, takes a broader look at Jewish culture. The museum contains a fascinating collection of over 28,000 works of art, artefacts and media installations. The two-floor permanent exhibit called "Culture and Continuity: The Jewish Journey," an account of the survival of Judaism, may offer some form of consolation.

295

Pull up a stool for coffee at D'Amico Foods

There's a convivial authenticity that comes from family-run D'Amico Foods' almost 60 years in the neighborhood—a feeling that neither the offer of free Wi-Fi nor mustachioed hipsters hunkered on grungy couches can compete with. From one of the ratty stools pulled up to the granite-topped counter in the back, you might see the guy who pulls your espresso (8 o'clock shadow, big basketball shorts) parrying flirty insults from a gaggle of tweens sipping self-serve (but irreproachable) coffee. When the skirmish gets out of hand, the group of weathered Italian men (derby hats, glasses thick as osso buco) headquartered at the rickety tables nearby gently scolds them all. Starbucks, eat your heart out.

D'Amico Foods *309 Court St between DeGraw and Sackett Sts, Cobble Hill, Brooklyn (718-875-5403).*

Block booking

Drew Toal **grabs a stack of books and hits the streets.**

New Yorkers, in their particular "we don't care what everyone else is doing because we do what we want anyway" way, don't seem to be suffering from the shameful decline in quality reading that plagues the rest of the country. In all five boroughs, the city's diverse, enlightened denizens devote all of their rare and precious spare moments of leisure to books. And not just pop tripe like Harry Potter or Dan Brown; in a place where your tastes can't help but be made public, it is not uncommon to see a mother with a stroller in one hand and Baudelaire in the other, or a self-important hipster doofus with a copy of Georges Perec prominently on display for everyone to admire.

It wasn't always like this. New York today is almost unrecognizable from the city of a century ago—the one Edith Wharton so deftly described in her classic novel, *The House of Mirth*. In this tragic tale of love and money,

socialite Lily Bart becomes entangled in a web of lies that ultimately results in her suicide by sleeping draught overdose; maybe not the best way to go, but perhaps better than Madame Bovary's rat poison-flavored snack. All that is left of those stuffy Victorian days of Gotham is the UES historic district, still home to snooty venues that you can't get into, like the Knickerbocker or Metropolitan clubs. You can, however, enjoy a highbrow lunch nearby at davidburke & donatella (133 E 61st St between Lexington and Park Aves, 212-813-2121, dbdrestaurant.com); their three-course (and unpoisoned) prix fixe lunch special is an innocent $24. Alternatively, you could salute Ms Bovary over some fancy French fare at Orsay (1057 Lexington Ave at 75th St, 212-517-6400, orsayrestaurant.com). For a greater sense of New York history, definitely stop by the Museum of the City of New York (1220 Fifth Ave at 103rd St, 212-534-1672, mcny.org) for a

look at the ephemera that characterized Wharton's Gotham in days gone past.

Wharton's dear and balding friend, Henry James, also a product of old New York, wrote what many consider his most "American" novel about where he was born: *Washington Square*. Read a copy on a bench near the Arc de Triomphe-lite at the center of eponymous Washington Square Park. Then stop by Jane (100 W Houston St between Thompson St and W Broadway, 212-254-7000), a restaurant that isn't named for, but does recall public-space activist Jane Jacobs and her struggle to stop megalomaniacal urban planner Robert Moses from extending Fifth Ave through the park.

If writers like Wharton and James represented the pinnacle of the traditional American novel, Paul Auster represents a whole new phase of New York lit, one that eschews the hifalutin problems of old money for the pomo mindfucks of Alain Robbe-Grillet and the gritty ambience of a detective novel. His *New York Trilogy* (*City of Glass*, *Ghosts*, *The Locked Room*) will leave

"It isn't uncommon to see a mother with a stroller in one hand and Baudelaire in the other, or a self-important hipster doofus with Georges Perec prominently on display for everyone to admire."

you scratching your head and wondering what is what, much like the book-bound grandeur of the Strand (828 Broadway at 12th St, 212-473-1452, strandbooks.com), the iconic New York bookstore with "18 miles of books," where a browser could lose themselves for days rooting through four floors of discounted print.

Nearby in the East Village, setting of Adam Rapp's semi-autobiographical tale of a Midwesterner's migration to early 1990s New York, there are plenty of places that still have a greasy, grunge-era sheen. In *The Year of Endless Sorrows*, Rapp's unnamed hero often supplements his pathetic, ramen-flavored eating habits with trips to nearby cafés, like the Café Orlin (41 St. Marks Pl at First Ave, 212-777-1447), where he often saw another sad-sack regular and "assumed we had a silent brotherhood, a kind of East Village private café camaraderie, something small and wordless and telepathically respectful." After a bracing coffee, head over to the 11th Street Bar (510 E 11th St between Aves A and B, 212-982-3929, 11thstbar.com) for a subdued atmosphere, perfect for proper drinking and a bit of reading or even one of the occasional poetry recitals.

The scarred communal psyche of New Yorkers in the years since the 9/11 attacks has provided a bleak backdrop for many contemporary purveyors of American lit. Both Ken Kalfus and Don DeLillo's most recent novels have used the fallen towers as metaphors for all kinds of things. Kalfus's *A Disorder Peculiar to the Country* is a black comedy that charts a family's disintegration in the wake of the attacks. After escaping the fallen towers, Marshall Harriman attends a multifaith memorial service at the Cathedral of St. Patrick (Fifth Ave between 50th and 51st Sts, 212-753-2261, saintpatrickscathedral.org), a church that was mentioned in Jack Finney's answer to the Wellsian monopoly on time-travel fiction, *Time and Again*, which mainly takes place in 19th-century New York. (It is worth noting that this particular place of worship also happens to be ground zero for the doomsday weapon in *Beneath the Planet of the Apes*.)

DeLillo's book, *Falling Man*, relates the tortured recovery of another survivor, named Keith. In an effort to move on, Keith often distracts himself with pickup hockey games on the Sky Rink at Chelsea Piers (23rd St and the Hudson River, 212-336-6666), the huge, upscale sports and rec center by the water. Jump on the subway there with a copy of Colum McCann's *This Side of Brightness*, a fantastic novel about the myriad dark and abandoned corners that lie beneath the surface of the city. It will give you a whole new appreciation of public transport, the workers who made the city what it is today, and the tribulations of the light-fearing morlock caste that exists below.

As you ride under the East River, consider one of Brooklyn novelist Jonathan Lethem's best-known books, *Motherless Brooklyn*, which takes place in New York's most populous borough. It's a comedic noir centered on the dim, Tourette's-addled protagonist Lionel Essrog, who is on a quest to solve the murder of friend and small-time Italian gangster, Frank Minna. Joe's of Avenue U (287 Ave U between Lake St and McDonald Ave, Brooklyn, 718-449-9285), in Gravesend, is a Sicilian-style restaurant with a menu that Essrog and the other "Minna Men" would certainly appreciate. Essrog's condition wouldn't even be a problem at Union Pool (484 Union Ave at Meeker Ave, Brooklyn, 718-609-0484), a popular and very loud bar for cool kids, where his weirdness would fit right in with the contemporary Brooklyn aesthetic.

"Jump on the subway with a copy of This Side of Brightness, a fantastic novel about the myriad dark and abandoned corners under the city. It gives a whole new appreciation of the light-fearing morlocks below."

Coney Island

Tim McLoughlin's anthology *Brooklyn Noir* chronicles this stark transformation of Brooklyn over the years. From this collection, Pearl Abraham's depiction of old Williamsburg bears no resemblance to the one of today, where—in addition to Union Pool—bars like Royal Oak (594 Union Ave at Richardson St, Brooklyn, 718-388-3884) and Daddy's (435 Graham Ave at Frost St, Brooklyn, 718-609-6388) bring in the artsy types that now predominate the area. In another story, Pete Hamill's writer protagonist, Carmody, discusses his leaving for the West Coast in 1957, the same year as the Dodgers, and laments, "When they left, I left too, because that was the end of Brooklyn as I knew it." The new Brooklyn is, on the other hand, perhaps best exemplified by McSweeney's, the self-consciously hip and irreverent publishing company whose titles include work by David Eggers, Chris Adrian, and David Byrne. The Brooklyn Superhero Supply Store (372 Fifth Ave between 5th and 6th Sts, Brooklyn, 718-499-9884) is McSweeney's weird base on the East Coast and has all manner of appropriately bizarre bric-a-brac for sale.

Speaking of superheroes (albeit of the non-Brooklyn variety), Michael Chabon's *The Amazing Adventures of Kavalier and Clay*, arguably the author's finest novel to date, begins at a fictional office building on 25th Street at Madison Square Park during the World War II years, where Joe Kavalier and Sam Clay launch their comic book careers. Today, their stuff would be sold at Forbidden Planet (840 Broadway at 13th St, 212-473-1576, forbiddenplanet.com), a two-level comic emporium near Union Square.

Those wishing to take the N, Q, D, or F trains down to Coney Island will want to take some books along for the longish trip. Kevin Baker's *Dreamland* is a poetic novel about dwarves, Mexican royalty, and old Coney Island. Although the Elephant Hotel that hides Kid Twist is no longer there, there are still a few historic Coney landmarks, notably Astroland (1000 Surf Ave at W 10th St, Brooklyn, 718-372-0275), home of the Cyclone, and Nathan's Famous (1310 Surf Ave between Stillwell Ave and W 15th St, Brooklyn, 718-946-2202), site of hot dog eating champion Kobayashi's greatest gastronomic victories.

321 Eat Czech at Zlata Praha

Or Golden Prague, to translate it into English. One of New York's only Czech restaurants, Zlata Praha (28-48 31st St between Newtown and 30th Aves, Astoria, Queens, 718-721-6422) is decked with folk costumes, ornamental plates, old currency and pictures of Prague. The Czech platter for two is one of the best deals going: smoked pork, flavorful pork loin and half a crisp roasted duck. Three types of cabbage and doughy "bread dumplings"—steamed sourdough slices—guarantee a satisfied stomach, as does the stuffed cabbage. Wash them down with a liter of Staropramen.

322 Disappear in Prada's high-tech changing rooms

Don't be put out if the lavish leathers, sumptuous shoes, and Miuccia outfits at Prada Soho (575 Broadway at Prince St, 212-334-8888) are beyond your means. Money is no object if you're making a visit to the fabled changing rooms, whose sliding doors are made from a glass that fogs up at the touch of a button. The effect is like that of a two-way mirror: you can watch the outside customers, who can't see you changing inside. No really, they can't.

323 Play shuffleboard at Nancy

A gritty, blue-collar dive in sleek, upscale Tribeca, Nancy Whiskey Pub (1 Lispenard St at W Broadway, 212-226-9943) is a neighborhood in the wrong neighborhood. It maintains its identity with $8 Bud pitchers, a jukebox that tends towards Lynyrd Skynyrd and the Allman Brothers, and the only bank shuffleboard in the city. For $1, you can push, bank and cajole the red pucks down a 12-foot-long table. Beginners are welcome—or at least not discouraged—and the pub holds tournaments on most Saturday and Sunday evenings. You may never go back to pool.

324–327

Put the alcohol into arts and crafts

Back in 2002, Corinna Mantlo established an informal knitting class at Luca Lounge (220 Avenue B between 13th and 14th Sts, 212-674-9400, boozeandyarn.com) to attract guys and girls from different walks of life. "A lot of formal classes charge obscene amounts of money, and some were actually banning guys from enrolling," she says. "I wanted to keep the community-minded part of knitting alive." Mantlo, who has also held "booze and yarn" sessions in New Orleans, says alcohol helps relax newcomers to the weekly Wednesday gathering and facilitates flirting, but that "some people are so focused on getting the stitch right, they order a drink but don't take a sip all night." Knitters can bring their own tools or buy a starter kit from Mantlo for just $20.

Want to relive the glory days of elementary school but this time with a tequila chaser? On the first Tuesday of every month, participants in Freddy's (485 Dean St at Sixth Avenue, Prospect Heights, 718-622-7035, freddys backroom.com) "diorama night" dive into their craft kits for foil, Popsicle sticks and other random bits to help nail the evening's theme, with the best display chosen by consensus.

You won't find boring bowls of fruit at Molly Crabapple's biweekly drawing class at the Lucky Cat (245 Grand St between Driggs Ave and Roebling St, Williamsburg, 718-782-0437, drsketchy.com); instead you'll see comely burlesque queens pose for amateur Da Vincis. Patrons compete for honours such as the "Best Left-Handed Drawing," with winners treated to a suitable drink (a shot of Chartreuse, say, for a green-haired model).

Like the kitschy club it's held in, PAINTStain is a rather casual affair. The idea for this weekly crafts night came to Krista Madsen when she first opened Stain Bar (766 Grand St at Humboldt St, Williamsburg, 718-387-7840, stainbar.com). "My friends were coming in to help decorate anyway, so I decided to make it a regular thing." Each Monday, Madsen offers free paints, fabrics and other gems from her box of goodies, or patrons bring their own projects.

Dr Sketchy at Lucky Cat

328-332 *Approach foie gras afresh*

While other cities ban foie gras, in New York the chefs are using fatty liver in ever more creative ways.

Experimental

One of the more adventurous dishes on the menu at the newly opened Dennis Foy restaurant (313 Church St between Lispenard and Walker Sts, 212-625-1007) is the torchon of foie gras with "Eis and Snow." In this creation the pate is served with an ice-wine gelée (ice wine is a sweet white made from frozen grapes) and "snow" (powdered foie gras).

For brunch

Meatpacking District steakhouse STK (26 Little W 12th St between Ninth Ave and Washington St, 646-624-2444) riffs on traditional morning fare with its "foie gras French toast." The dish consists of liver, French toast brioche and green apples, sauced with a sherry gastrique (a syrupy reduction) and dusted with powdered sugar.

Child's play

Foie gras is the star in one predictably eccentric appetizer that appears on the winter menu at davidburke & donatella (133 E 61st St between Park and Lexington Aves, 212-813-2121). Eric Hara, new chef de cuisine at the restaurant, takes no prisoners with his foie gras peanut-butter-and-jelly sandwich using grilled brioche toast, foie gras, vanilla-strawberry jam and macadamia nut butter.

Slavic style

Pelmeni were on the menu at the old Russian Tea Room. At the recently relaunched restaurant (150 W 57th St between Sixth and Seventh Aves, 212-581-7100), chef Marc Taxiera fills these little dumplings with foie gras and rabbit and floats them in an oxtail broth with root vegetables.

Fancy French

Terrance Brennan offers an unusual adaptation of foie gras at the refurbished Picholine (35 W 64th St between Central Park West and Broadway, 212-724-8585). Order his new Chicken "Kiev" and you'll get to watch your server lance the meat at the table so that the liquid foie gras in the center can ooze out.

333 Drink on the roof at the Met

Ogle the Greco-Roman statuary, admire the Impressionists, gawk at the Temple of Dendur—but make sure you then zip up the elevator to The Roof Garden at the Metropolitan Museum of Art (1000 Fifth Ave at 82nd St, 212-277-8888, metmuseum.org) for a drink. No matter that the bar menu is limited, it's the chance to suck in the unmatched view—accompanied by overpriced daiquiris and sandwiches—that makes the sculpture-cluttered terrace special. To the south, you get a terrific shot of the midtown skyline, while Central Park unfurls majestically to the west, Cleopatra's Needle and all.

334 Find Improv Everywhere

Although Improv Everywhere creates some of the flat-out funniest scenes in New York, you won't see them in any theater. And unless you join the group's e-mail list, you won't know when the performances happen, either. Founder Charlie Todd eschews mean-spirited pranks and says his goal—and that of his cadre of agents—is simply "to make scenes happen." This could involve putting a bathroom attendant in a McDonald's or staging an Olympic-trial synchronized-swimming practice in Washington Square Park fountain. Watch footage of past stunts on its website (improveverywhere.com), and then join in the next one.

335 Browse the celebrity bookshelves at the Housing Works

We love the local reading series at this excellent bookstore. The writers who pass through are a high-minded mix of the already established and up-and-comers: Lydia Davis, Jonathan Lethem, Samantha Hunt and Dave Eggers, to name just a few of them. For recognisable names of a different sort, simply browse the bookstore's shelves: Many celebs have donated their books to this shop. Interesting volumes from Salman Rushdie, Woody Allen, Paul Giamatti, Gwyneth Paltrow (who inscribed her name on the sides) and Cindy Sherman have all graced the shelves, and you can figure out what Peter Sarsgaard has been up to by seeing what he brings in: war titles when he was filming *Jarhead* and natural-pregnancy books donated after the birth of his daughter, Ramona.

Housing Works Used Book Café *126 Crosby St between E Houston and Prince Sts (212-334-3324/ housingworksbookstore.com).*

336 Appreciate the sound at Cielo

This club has one of the richest, warmest sound systems in NYC, and hosts some of the city's—and the world's—best DJs. And despite the bottle-service tables and somewhat exaggerated reputation for a snotty door policy, Cielo is actually a relatively chill spot to dance to those top-notch spinners. Why is the joint's sound so good? The folks behind the audio equipment, Sound Investment, have a top-secret sound processor that's "customized to the size, shape and acoustical characteristics of the room," according to tech dude Daniel Ange. "When you're on the dance floor you can actually start to hear notes, and sounds take on a third dimension. A cocktail or two doesn't hurt as well…."

Cielo *18 Little W 12th St between Ninth Ave and Washington St (212-645-5700/cieloclub.com).*

It's fun and strangely karmic to gaze at images of the Buddha in the Rubin Museum of Himalayan Art (150 W 17th St, 212-620-5000, rmanyc.org). On Friday nights, the museum runs a "Naked Soul" all-acoustic music series drawing on themes inspired by art in the museum: spirituality, peace, wisdom, tolerance and compassion. The performances take place in a marvelous wood-lined theater. As [singer-songwriter] Susan Werner said, it's like holding a concert inside a guitar. I also love the museum's lighting at night: a combination of blue jewel, sunset in Santa Fe and illuminated aquarium.

I love walking across the Brooklyn Bridge from the Manhattan side—gazing out at New York Harbor, taking in all that water and amazing light—and lunching at the River Café (1 Water St, 718-522-5200, rivercafe.com). Afterwards I take the New York Water Taxi (nywatertaxi.com) home to Chelsea from Fulton Ferry Landing. Also for lunch I love the cozy and literary Half King (505 W 23rd St, 212-462-4300, thehalfking.com) in Chelsea. There's a Monday night reading series and changing photography exhibits. I like to sit on the black leather couch under the eaves, having the portobello and goat's cheese sandwich, and reading over my day's work. **I love to go owling in Central Park. In 2004, a rare boreal owl visited, roosting in near Tavern on the Green (Central Park West at 67th St, 212-873-3200, tavern onthegreen.com). This year, three long-eared owls spent the winter in the Ross Pinetum (Central Park West at 85th St), a pine arboretum within the park.** The most romantic spot in the city is the park's Boathouse Café (E 72nd St & Park Drive N, 212-517-2233, thecentralpark boathouse.com). In the winter there's a fire in the fireplace, in summer there's a breeze off the lake.

342

Far more exotic and entertaining than pigeons pecking at discarded pretzels in Central Park, watch sea lions at the Bronx Zoo (Bronx River Parkway at Fordham Rd, Bronx, 718-367-1010, bronxzoo.com) gorge on fish twice a day. The ocean mammals satiate themselves with 35 pounds of herring every day. The first feeding is at 11am (10:30am in winter and fall), the second at 3pm.

343

Enjoy classical music on the river

This former coffee-bean barge presents four chamber concerts a week (plus one jazz program), set against a panoramic view of Lower Manhattan. It's a magical experience, but wrap up in winter. When the weather warms, you can enjoy a drink on the upper deck during the concert's intermission. Admission is $25-$40.
Bargemusic *Fulton Ferry Landing between Old Fulton and Water Sts, Brooklyn (718-624-2083/bargemusic.org).*

344

Visit the National Museum of the American Indian

At the bottom of Broadway (which, many moons ago, began as an Indian trail), this branch of the Smithsonian Institution displays its collection around the grand rotunda of the 1907 Custom House. The life and culture of Native Americans are presented in rotating exhibitions—from intricately woven, fibre Pomo baskets to beaded buckskin shirts—along with contemporary artwork. On show until September 23 2008 is "Beauty Surrounds Us," a collection of musical instruments, games and ceremonial clothing that celebrates the importance of decorative art in native cultures. The Diker Pavilion for Native Arts & Culture, opened in 2006, has already made its mark on the cultural life of the city by offering the only dedicated showcase for Native American visual and performing arts. The Diker's 6,000 square feet contain ten exhibition cases set into niches between a series of sloping walls, all paneled in a wonderfully rich cherry wood.
National Museum of the American Indian *George Gustav Heye Center, Alexander Hamilton Custom House, 1 Bowling Green between State and Whitehall Sts (212-514-3700/nmai.si.edu).*

345

 Take a heli-tour

There's no daredevil swooping and diving on a flight with Liberty Helicopter Tours (212-967-6464, libertyhelicopters.com), but the views of Gotham are excitement enough. Even a five-minute ride (durations vary, $69-$186) is long enough to get a thrilling look at the city from above. Catch a 'copter from Downtown Manhattan Heliport (Pier 6, East River, between Broad Street and Old Slip) or VIP Heliport (Twelfth Ave at 30th St).

346

Watch the Westminster Kennel Club Dog Show

America's most prestigious dog show prances into Madison Square Garden each February. One of the oldest "sporting" events in the country, it's your chance to see some of the most beautiful and best trained pooches on the planet compete for the coveted Best in Show trophy—and a few tasty dog treats. Visit westminsterkennelclub.org for details of next year's event.

347

Sample the simplest of pizzas

The pizza bianca ($1.75/slice) doesn't look or smell or taste like a pie. But one bite of the rectangular flatbread reveals waves of flavor brought on by the simplest of ingredients: salt, olive oil and rosemary.
Sullivan Street Bakery *533 W 47th St between Tenth and Eleventh Aves (212-265-5580).*

348

Get a corset custom-made

In addition to Selima Salaun's slinky lingerie and loungewear, including antique camisoles and vintage silk kimonos, this boudoir-like boutique will custom-make Victorian- and Edwardian-inspired corsets for a perfect fit.
Le Corset by Selima *80 Thompson St between Broome and Spring Sts (212-334-4936).*

349 *Go for Grom*

Try finding fault with the soft-but-not-melted texture of Grom's silky gelato. The pristine store (the Italian company's first stateside post, to be joined at the time of writing by a new joint on Bleecker in summer 2008) is delightfully inviting, with a wide-open front counter where passers-by can pop in for a $5 cone, as well as a spacious restaurant area if you're inclined to sit down. The standout flavor is crema di Grom—velvety vanilla gelato with crunchy Italian sugar cookies and chunks of Valrhona chocolate. Flawless.

Grom *2165 Broadway at 76th St (646-290-7233/grom.it).*

350
Join the Gay & Lesbian Pride March

Downtown Manhattan becomes a sea of rainbow flags every June as gays and lesbians from the city and beyond parade down Fifth Avenue in commemoration of the 1969 Stonewall Riots. After the march, there's a massive street fair and a dance on the West Side piers. See hopinc.org for more details.

351 *Wait for news of a Giant Step party*

Giant Step parties have been among the best of the nu-soul scene since the early 1990s—back before there was a nu-soul scene. Sadly, the gang doesn't throw as many fetes as it once did, now preferring to concentrate on live shows and record promotions. But on the rare occasion that Giant Step does decide to pack a dancefloor, you'd be a fool to miss it: The music is always great, and the multicultural crowd gorgeous beyond belief. Keep an eye on giantstep.net.

Gay & Lesbian Pride March

Time Out
Travel Guides

Worldwide

All our guides are written by a team of **local experts** with a unique and stylish insider perspective. We offer essential tips, trusted advice and honest reviews for everything you need to know in the city.

Over 50 destinations available at all good bookshops and at timeout.com/shop

Time Out Guides

352 Ignore the floor piano at FAO Schwarz

That damn piano that Tom Hanks danced on 20 years ago in the movie *Big* is still a major draw at FAO Schwarz's Fifth Avenue flagship store. But it's not the only thing luring visitors through the front doors of this 145-year-old company. The play palace has gradually shifted its focus from superpricey products (the dance-on piano costs $250,000) to high-quality toys that don't require shoppers to take out a second mortgage. "We want to inspire children to be happy through unstructured play, and for us, that means five things: quality, design integrity, originality, environmental friendliness and safety," says the company's CEO, Ed Schmults.

Over the past few years, FAO has added more than 20 specialty boutiques, including several customizing workshops (take that, Build-A-Bear). In the Styled by Me Barbie area, kids design their own dolls, choosing everything from skin tone and hair color to designer clothes and accessories—breasts are still regulation Barbie size. Over at the Hot Wheels Factory, speed demons create a personalized car in mere minutes.

Intrepid explorers of the huge space will find more than toys to distract them. In the Harry Potter section, fans of the books and movies can ogle the largest selection of Hogwarts memorabilia in the country. And the upscale Zutano boutique on the lower level is filled with baby and toddler gear.

Like other retailers, FAO has been feeling pressure from the green camp, and the store is heeding the call. Its colorful new wooden toys are made with nontoxic, water-based paints, and in June 2008 it introduced "All-Natural and Organic for Infants," a line of plush animals made from organic cotton. (The line includes a newborn-size version of the popular Patrick the Pup toy.) The country of origin of most items in the store is now displayed, to reassure parents made wary by the recent spate of recalls. Sure, FAO is still larger than life, but in the end, reminds Schmults, "it's all about providing good, safe toys."

FAO Schwarz *767 Fifth Ave at 58th St (212-644-9499, fao.com).*

353 Get "le cassoulet" at La Luncheonette

The way they've been doing it in Toulouse, France, for centuries works equally well in Chelsea. This cassoulet (£21.50) puts chunks of tender braised lamb, a leg of duck confit and garlic pork sausage in a cassole (an earthenware crockery pot) of slow-cooked white beans. Just as it should be.

La Luncheonette *130 Tenth Ave at 19th St (212-675-0342).*

354 Feel the Feinstein

Cabaret's crown prince, Michael Feinstein, draws A-list talent to this swank room in the Regency. It's pricey (cover is $60-$75 and there's a $40 food and drink minimum) but you usually get what you pay for. Recent performers have included top names such as Chita Rivera, Diahann Carroll and Ben Vereen. Shows are from Tuesday to Saturday at 8:30pm, with extra 11pm performances on Friday and Saturday.

Feinstein's at the Loews Regency *Loews Regency Hotel, 540 Park Ave at 61st St (212-339-4095/feinsteinsattheregency.com).*

355 See the sharks and sea jellies at the New York Aquarium

See a living recreation of the Pacific coastline (what, Coney Island's shore isn't good enough?), and catch a glimpse of the species that somehow survive in the East River. There's also a lively sea lion show plus some truly awesome sharks, sea jellies and a young walrus. If you're longing to get away but can't quite swing a Caribbean vacation, be sure to check out Glover's Reef, a 150,000-gallon tank stocked with some 35 species of marine life brought here from the coast of Belize.

New York Aquarium *Surf Ave at W 8th St, Coney Island, Brooklyn (718-265-3474/nyaquarium.com).*

356

Get into hardcore cornography at Café Habana

The fashionable set milling around Nolita at all hours may not look as if they eat, but they do— at Café Habana (17 Prince St at Elizabeth St, 212-625-2001). They storm this Cuban-Mexican chrome corner spot for the sexy scene and the addictive grilled corn ($2): golden ears doused in fresh mayo, char-grilled and generously sprinkled with chili powder, lime and grated cotija cheese. Locals also love the takeout annex next door, where you can get that corn-on-a-stick to go.

Agent Provocateur

Trick yourself out like a retro pinup at this cheeky English firm's pink-and-black flagship. Cofounded by Joe Corre, the son of designer Vivienne Westwood and Sex Pistols manager Malcolm McLaren, AP is known for its slightly frisky designs such as beribboned garter belts ($90–$300) and "playsuits," pasties and matching strappy bondage-esque thongs ($40–$200). Those with tamer tastes can indulge in pure silk stockings ($55), ruffled satin panties ($70) and culty beauty products (starting at $40).
133 Mercer St between Prince and Spring Sts (212-965-0229)

A.W. Kaufman

Call it witchcraft or just decades of experience, but the employees at the family-run storefront can pluck the best piece for a client's silhouette just by eyeing her. A.W. Kaufman's decor is nondescript and verges on ramshackle, as men's and women's briefs, boxers and bras are stowed in plastic bins, and you can't try things on. But the high-quality, oft-discounted European offerings and the old-school service are what make this place legendary.
73 Orchard St between Broome and Grand Sts (212-226-1629).

Brooklyn Fox

Alexis Schoenberg's 400-square-foot nook opened last winter in what was formerly home to wine emporium Uva, but its handful of unsung high-end labels can be just as intoxicating. Alluring slips (starting at $88), bras ($35 and up) and thongs (from $62) from Spanish label Andres Sarda are arranged by hue along racks that hang from the cream and antique-papered walls. Aesthetic snobs won't want to miss Brit designer Shiri Zinn's vibrators ($84–$150) that look like portable art.
132 North 5th St between Bedford Ave and Berry St, Williamsburg (718-599-1555).

E Lingerie by Enelra

Originally located in the East Village, this venerable depot once outfitted Madonna for '80s flick *Desperately Seeking Susan*. But you don't have to be a material girl to appreciate its

Agent Provocateur

mainly French and Italian unmentionables, including culty Cosabella thongs ($16–$33) and adorable Eberjey triangle bras ($27). In a nod to its baby-laden nabe, E Lingerie also offers maternity bras ($39 and up).

140 Fifth Ave between Butler and Degraw Sts, Park Slope (718-399-3252).

Kiki de Montparnasse

Man Ray's lover serves as the muse for this sleek, high-end emporium, which is part sex shop, part lingerie boutique. The art-filled joint features spacious changing rooms with dimmer switches so you can see how your corset ($345 and up) will look in candlelight. Scads of vibrators ($75–$1,500 for 18-karat goldplated styles), whips ($150–$1,500) and, yes, crotchless panties ($125) are all up for grabs alongside slinky sleepwear ($295–$695) that might be mistaken for Jil Sander when worn outside the bedroom.

79 Greene St between Broome and Spring Sts (212-965-8070).

Myla

Naughty London outfit Myla has garnered a reputation for its seriously sexy designs. Its first stateside boutique dishes up side-tie knickers costing $100 and up, and diamanté nipple tassels starting at around $135; slightly less expensive pick-me-ups include feather ticklers ($80). And for nothing at all, you can try to guess the uses for its sculptural sex toys ($115–$470).

20 E 69th St at Madison Ave (212-327-2676).

La Petite Coquette

For more than 25 years, proprietor Rebecca Apsan has been girding New Yorkers' loins, thanks to her immensely popular emporium and expert staff. Its moniker is French for "the little flirt," and Apsan's come-hither goodies don't disappoint: She was the first in NYC to carry the Bracli pearl thong ($69). Her boudoirish depot also features scads of gamine to ultrasexy wares imported from Europe, along with its own collection of silk-and-lace G-strings ($70) and kimono cover-ups ($220). Ladies with a foot fetish can walk out in Jacques Levine's marabou high-heeled slippers.

51 University Pl between 9th and 10th Sts (212-473-2478).

See Brooklyn's "Little Liberty"

Although no one would confuse the parking lot behind the Brooklyn Museum (200 Eastern Pkwy at Washington Ave, Prospect Heights, Brooklyn, 718-638-5000, brooklynmuseum.org) for New York Harbor, it does contain a Statue of Liberty: a 40-foot-tall sheet-metal replica, actually, that once stood atop the Liberty Warehouse on 64th Street and Broadway. The recipient of a Memorial Day makeover in 2007—including cleaning and a new galvanized-steel pedestal—"Little Liberty" is just the latest addition to the Steinberg Family Sculpture Garden, a leafy sanctuary for architectural ornaments rescued from New York buildings long since demolished or remodeled. The impetus for the garden was the runaway development that plagued the city in the 1960s. "All this wonderful architecture was coming down with no thought to preservation," says curator Kevin Stayton. "The demolition of the first Penn Station was devastating. But it brought people to their senses." Night, a Beaux Arts relief of a winged female figure salvaged from that wreckage, was one of the first items brought to this island of lost souls, which also includes a massive zinc lion that once guarded Coney Island's Steeplechase Park. "They're a reflection of a time when craftsmanship was treasured," says head conservationist Lisa Bruno. "These pieces were handmade by immigrants who were literally helping to build this country."

365

Picnic among the foliage in Sara D. Roosevelt Park

Leave behind the crowds of Central, Prospect and Battery parks, and nosh in a lesser-known oasis. Bring your basket to the Lower East Side's Sara D. Roosevelt Park (Chrystie St between Canal and Houston Sts), where you'll find tables amid vegetation so lush you might feel as though you've stepped into a rain forest.

Finger food

Forks, spoons, knives—who needs them? Lee Magill takes her kids to five ethnic eateries where everything is finger food (towelettes not included).

There's a reason just about every toddler on earth loves Cheerios. Kids are crazy about eating with their hands—and crave finger foods even once they're old enough to distinguish a soup spoon from a regular one. Rather than discourage the habit, I decided to use it as a way of introducing my kids—Gabriel, six, and Madeleine, almost four—to some of the world cuisines they might otherwise have felt were just too adult.

Our first stop was the fanciful Hell's Kitchen shop Empanada Mama (763 Ninth Ave between 51st and 52nd Sts, 212-698-9008). With a pop soundtrack playing in a bright lime-and-red-painted room and a menu listing delectable half moon–shaped pockets, the place instantly intrigued my kids—and put them at ease. Here deep-fried but surprisingly ungreasy empanadas in corn- and wheatflour varieties come piping hot in paper bags, whether you're staying put or not. Each costs $2-$3 (you need

between two and four to fill up; the children will do fine with one or two). We loved the cornflour kind with delectably gooey mozzarella; the wheatflour spinach-and-cheese version; and, for dessert, the decadent if dubious-sounding caramel-and-cheese pockets.

Next we headed to tiny Awash (338 E 6th St between First and Second Aves, 212-982-9589, awashnyc.com), which stands out among its Curry Row neighbors for offering authentic Ethiopian fare in a no-frills but welcoming environment. Ethiopians eat primarily with their fingers, aided in the task by spongy, sour injera, a wholly unique counterpart to India's nan that accompanies or is part of nearly every meal. Order a tasting assortment of five dishes (all-veggie, all-meat or a combo of both), which artfully comes atop an enormous swath of injera. Among my family's favorites were the buttery, garlicky string-beans-and-carrots entrée and the sambusas: Danish pastry-like

pockets filled with a choice of mixed vegetables (collard greens, potatoes, cabbage, onions), chicken or beef. Typical kid fare? No. But Gabriel and Madeleine didn't seem to care.

While sushi is an obvious, if decidedly upscale, finger food, colorful comfort zone Sushi Samba 7 (87 Seventh Ave South at Barrow St, 212-691-7885, sushisamba.com) goes out of its way to offer a smörgåsbord of other items that you can eat utensil-free. Peruvian anticuchos (grilled skewers) beckon alongside an array of tempura options; for grown-ups who prefer a traditional raw bar to the rice-topped stuff, there's also one of those, featuring shrimp, king crab legs and oysters galore. Being avid sushi fans, Gabriel and I had no need for the menu. Both of us opted for our tried-and-true faves, which didn't disappoint: avocado and eel-and-avocado rolls for him, à la carte sushi and rolls for me (sashimi eaten with one's hands was a bit too weird). Madeleine, who came mostly for the company and for whom chocolate trumps all, struck pay dirt when we finished: Chocolate Fondue for Two, with Rice Krispie balls, marshmallows, apple slices and strawberries for dipping.

Less exotic fare awaited us at Moustache (90 Bedford St between Barrow and Grove Sts, 212-229-2220), a small, moody, European café kind of spot with communal tables. I learned long ago that pita and hummus are one of the best ways to introduce a PB&J-obsessed tot to "foods of the world," and no place does mashed chickpeas better than Moustache. And that's just for starters: Mediterranean specialties like

> *"Ethiopians eat primarily with their fingers, aided in the task by spongy, sour injera, a wholly unique counterpart to India's nan that accompanies or is part of nearly every meal."*

falafel, spanakopita and chicken kebabs make choosing difficult, sharing advisable and utensils unnecessary. Should you hit no homers with these, Moustache also serves the city's most inventive and delicious pizzas—try the Moustache Pitza, topped with roasted peppers, tomatoes, fresh mozzarella, onions and parsley, or the Lahambajin Pitza, with ground lamb, onion, tomato and parsley.

For our last stop, we hit the mod, *Jetsons*-esque Thai spot Spice (60 University Pl at 10th St, 212-982-3758) and went entirely the small-plates route, choosing five of the 12 appetizer options, all of which were perfectly finger-friendly. Since only the sauce accompanying the Spice Crispy Calamari was piquant and not the calamari itself, the dish scored points with my heat-averse kids. Two other winners were the Emerald vegetable dumplings—soft, round and plump—dipped in a luscious black plum sauce, and Martini Crispy Shrimp, a martini glass filled halfway with a sweet-and-sour mixture and stuffed with five or six tall rice-paper-wrapped fried shrimp. Less successful was a salad served with Asian ginger shrimp and bathed in a spicy dressing Gabriel and Madeleine couldn't abide. If you bring your kids here, I advise ordering the dressing on the side. As for how to go about convincing the kids that they can't eat every meal with their hands from now on, you're on your own.

371 Catch the Brazilian Girls at Nublu

Nublu's prominence on the local globalist club scene has been inversely proportional to its size—not to mention its seemingly out-of-the-way location. A pressure cooker of creativity, Nublu gave rise to the Brazilian Girls, who started jamming at one late-night session and haven't stopped yet, as well as starting NYC's romance with the northern Brazilian style forró. Even on weeknights, events usually start no earlier than 10pm and can run into the small hours—but if you show up early (and find the unmarked door), the bar is well stocked with wine selections, among other beverages, and the staff as warm as the music.

Nublu *62 Ave C between 4th and 5th Sts (no phone/nublu.net).*

372-375 Get the picture at Gotham's best photography galleries

Bonni Benrubi

You'll find a wealth of 20th-century American photography (like Lewis Hine and Walker Evans) and contemporary photography from emerging artists (such as Abe Morell and Matthew Pillsbury) at this gallery, which turned 21 in 2008.
41 E 57th St, 13th floor, at Madison Ave (212-888-6007/bonnibenrubi.com).

Edwynn Houk Gallery

A respected specialist in vintage and contemporary photography. Among the artists exhibited are Brassaï, Lynn Davis, Dorothea Lange, Annie Leibovitz, Man Ray and Alfred Stieglitz, each commanding (as you'd expect for talent of this caliber) absolute top-dollar prices.
745 Fifth Ave, fourth floor, between 57th and 58th Sts (212-750-7070/houkgallery.com).

Howard Greenberg Gallery

Named Photofind at its inception in 1981, the Howard Greenberg Gallery was one of the first spaces to exhibit photojournalism and street photography. The gallery's collection includes countless images snapped by Berenice Abbot, Edward Steichen and Henri Cartier-Bresson.
41 E 57th St at Madison Ave (212-334-0010/howardgreenberg.com).

Pace/MacGill

Pace/MacGill shows work by such well-known names as Walker Evans, Robert Frank and Irving Penn, in addition to groundbreaking contemporaries Chuck Close and Kiki Smith.
32 E 57th St, ninth floor, between Madison and Park Aves (212-759-7999/pacemacgill.com).

376 Admire the George Delacorte Music Clock in Central Park

How many times have you strolled through Central Park without stopping to admire this local icon, located between the Wildlife Center and the Children's Zoo? Commissioned by namesake publisher and philanthropist Delacorte in 1965, the whimsically designed timekeeper features a parade of eight beautifully sculpted bronze animals—including a bear with a tambourine, a horn-playing kangaroo and a drumming penguin—that dance around the clock on the hour and half hour. Listen out for the clock's renditions of nursery-rhyme tunes such as "Three Blind Mice" and "Row, Row, Row Your Boat."

377 Go German at the Goethe-Institut

The Goethe-Institut New York is a branch of the international German cultural organization, founded in 1951. Housed in a landmark Fifth Avenue mansion across from the Met, the institute mounts shows featuring German-born contemporary artists and presents concerts, lectures and film screenings. German-language books, videos and periodicals are available in the library. *Fantastisch!*

Goethe-Institut New York/German Cultural Center *1014 Fifth Ave at 82nd St (212-439-8700/goethe.de/ins/us/ney).*

378

Flick your BIC at Nat Sherman's smoking room

Just across the street from the New York Public Library, Nat Sherman (12 E 42nd St at Fifth Ave, 212-764-5000, natsherman.com) offers its own brand of slow-burning cigarettes, as well as imported cigars and cigarillos, company memorabilia and various smoking-related accoutrements. Marvel at the city's largest humidor and then repair to the downstairs smoking room for a puff.

379 View Asian art at the Asia Society...

The Asia Society sponsors study missions and conferences, as well as promoting public programs in the US and abroad. The headquarters' striking galleries host major exhibitions of art culled from dozens of countries and time periods—from ancient India and medieval Persia to contemporary Japan—and assembled from public and private collections, including the permanent Mr and Mrs John D Rockefeller III collection of Asian art. The spacious, atrium-like café, with a pan-Asian menu, and the beautifully stocked gift shop, make the society a one-stop destination for anyone who has even a passing interest in Asian art and culture.
Asia Society & Museum *725 Park Ave at 70th St (212-288-6400/society.org).*

380 ...and the China Institute

Consisting of just two small galleries, the China Institute is somewhat overshadowed by the nearby Asia Society. But its rotating exhibitions, including works by female Chinese artists and selections from the Beijing Palace Museum, are compelling. The institute offers lectures and courses on myriad subjects such as calligraphy, Confucius and cooking.
China Institute *125 E 65th St between Park and Lexington Aves (212-744-8181/chinainstitute.org).*

381 Ride the Jazz Trail trolley in Queens

Jazz diehards will love the three-hour Queens Jazz Trail trolley tour, which starts at 10am on the first Saturday of the month. It stops by Addisleigh Park and showcases haunts of jazz greats like Louis Armstrong, Ella Fitzgerald, Billie Holiday and Dizzy Gillespie. The $35 entrance fee also gets you a cool illustrated guide. Meet at Flushing Town Hall (137-135 Northern Blvd at Linden Pl, 718-463-7700, flushingtownhall.org); reservations recommended.

382 Tuck into wiener schnitzel at Wallsé

Native Austrian Kurt Gutenbrunner wrings maximum flavor from first-rate ingredients in his elegantly stark West Village restaurant, turning Viennese specialties—like thin, crumb-coated veal schnitzel—into contemporary masterpieces. Other exemplary dishes include a vivid spring pea soup, poached lobster with fennel and figs, and lamb loin slices in a classic zweigelt (a peppery red wine) sauce that takes two days to make. The staff ably suggests fine flavor marriages from the selection of Austrian wines. Finish with the renowned apple strudel. Art from the personal collection of painter-epicure—and Wallsé regular—Julian Schnabel hangs on the white walls.
Wallsé *344 W 11th St at Washington St (212-352-2300/wallserestaurant.com).*

383 Shop for mystery books at the Mysterious Bookshop

If you're a devotee of the mystery, crime, suspense, spy or detective genres, you're probably familiar with owner Otto Penzler, both as an editor and from his book tips on Amazon.com. The ground floor of his brownstone shop displays a wealth of paperbacks; climb the spiral staircase for hardcovers (including many autographed first editions).
Mysterious Bookshop *58 Warren St between Church and West Broadway Sts (212-587-1011/mysteriousbookshop.com).*

384 Get Gothic at Poe Cottage

Edgar Allan Poe Cottage is the very house in which he wrote literary gems including "Annabel Lee" and "The Bells." A presentation film and guided tour are available. Admission costs $3.
Edgar Allan Poe Cottage *2640 Grand Concourse at Kingsbridge Rd (718-881-8900/bronxhistorical society.org).*

385-391

Play tennis on New York's finest public courts...

A $100 permit ($20 for seniors, $10 for juniors) grants access to all the City Parks Department's public courts from April 1 to November 30, usually from 7am to 7pm daily. Single-play tickets are $7, plus an additional $7 ticket before you can secure an advance reservation. The 26 fast-dry and five asphalt Central Park Courts (midpark at West Dr and 96th St, 212-280-0205) are the Parks Department's best-kept outdoor courts. Access is easy, with wait times rarely exceeding an hour; you can also book up to a month ahead. Another favorite is Prospect Park Tennis Center (Parade Ground at Parkside Ave, Windsor Terrace, Brooklyn, 718-436-2500) is open year-round (a bubble is installed mid-November), but costs $32 per hour after 7pm, even for permit holders. Book one of nine Har-Tru or two hard courts in advance for prime times (before noon and after 6pm) and at weekends. There are also private and group classes, youth instruction, night tennis, center rentals for parties and a gourmet café. Meanwhile, it's first-come, first-serve at the ten hard courts of Riverside Park (Riverside Dr at 96th St, 212-978-0277). Surrounded by trees, flower beds and a view of the Hudson, these outdoor courts are as lovely as those at any private facility. Permits and passes for all the City Parks courts can be purchased at Paragon Sporting Goods (867 Broadway at 18th St, 212-255-8036), as well as other locations (check nyc.gov/parks for a list).

Of course, the Parks Department doesn't run all the public courts in New York. The excellent indoor and outdoor courts (33 hard outdoor, 9 hard indoor) at Flushing Meadows' USTA Billie Jean King National Tennis Center (Flushing Meadows Park, Queens, 718-760-6200) is, of course, the best. It's not only the home of the U.S. Open, but also the largest public tennis center in the world—and, except during the Open, it's accessible all year. Book up to two days in advance and expect to pay $16-$56 for a central court (a further 11 courts just outside the gates are NYC Parks owned and hence free for permit holders). Also open

all year are Midtown Tennis Club (341 Eighth Ave between 26th and 27th Sts, 212-989-8572), where you'll pay $45-$100 per hour, and Yorkville Tennis Club (1725 York Ave at 89th St, 212-987-0301), costing $60-$160 per hour. Midtown's eight indoor Har-Tru courts (supplemented by rooftop courts during the summer) are popular, so you'll need to book up to two weeks in advance—there's no chance of a game here unless you have a reservation. At Yorkville, there are just two indoor hard courts, so book at least a week ahead. The quality is excellent: Located on an Upper East Side garage roof, the Yorkville center houses high-ceilinged competition courts with state-of-the-art lighting. From late September to late April each year, the eight indoor, red clay courts of Sutton East Tennis (488 E 60th St at York Ave, 212-751-3452) cost $80-$160 per hour and should be booked a week in advance. Housed in a big white bubble under the 59th St Bridge, this facility boasts NYC's largest staff of pros—you can get lessons at satellite courts all summer.

392-394

...or splash out on membership to play somewhere more exclusive

Cityview Racquet Club

This $10 million, 80,000-square-foot facility opened its doors in late 2007, providing luxury tennis, squash and spa facilities, as well as fine views of the Manhattan skyline. The hardest part is scoring a membership (enrollment is limited), but once you're in, claiming one of the seven indoor Har-Tru courts is no sweat. Membership costs $1,200 initiation fee plus the annual dues: $4,000 for full access; $2,200 off-peak access. Then to play costs $24-$30 per hour.

43-26 32nd Pl between Queens Blvd and 43rd Ave, Long Island City, Queens (718-698-3664/ cityviewracquet.com).

Manhattan Plaza Racquet Club

Built on a rooftop overlooking the Manhattan skyline, this members-only club offers group lessons, as well as singles and doubles leagues.

There are five outdoor hard courts, which become indoor courts when they erect a bubble after Labor Day. Membership starts at $1,350, with each game costing $42-$70 per hour. *450 W 53rd St between Ninth and Tenth Aves (212-594-0554).*

Roosevelt Island Racquet Club

Located on a remote island, this club is appointed with a dozen heated indoor Lee green clay courts, nonglare lighting, and two lounges with food and drink. You'll need to claim a game at least 24 hours in advance, or 48 hours for weekdays after 6pm and weekends before 3pm. The hourly rate is $42-$64 for members ($66-$100 nonmembers), with annual membership costing from $950, plus $100 initiation fee. *281 Main St (212-935-0250/rirctennis.com).*

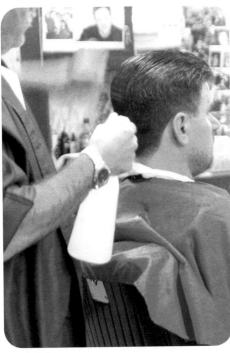

395

Get an uncomplicated cut at Astor Place

Here an army of barbers does everything from neat trims to more complicated and creative shaved designs. You can't make an appointment; just take a number and wait outside with the crowd. Sunday mornings are usually quieter. Cuts start at $12.
Astor Place Hair Stylists *2 Astor Pl at Broadway (212-475-9854).*

396

Buy the best cheese grits in all of Gotham

The folks at Williamsburg breakfast spot Egg (135A North 5th St at Bedford St, Williamsburg, Brooklyn, 718-302-5151) blend four ingredients to create porridge to end all porridges: deliciously corny organic Anson Mills grits, Ronnybrook cream, a dash of salt and aged Grafton Village Cheddar so sharp it'd make even the Cream of Wheat guy cry.

Time Warner Center

Fernando Botero's lobby sculptures of a naked woman and man are such a big hit with shoppers that the man's penis has been worn to a different color from people touching it.
59th St at Columbus Circle.

Grand Central Terminal

Look for the 50-foot pediment, which features a naked Mercury, god of commerce and trade, posing atop a clock with his pals Hercules and Minerva.
42nd St at Park Ave.

The Plaza

The Pulitzer Fountain, in front of the Plaza Hotel, has a naked statue of the great Audrey Munson, a famous nude model and muse throughout the modern period. There are also nude sculptures of her at the Manhattan Bridge and the Frick Collection. She was so hot that a man murdered his wife in hopes of marrying her; he later hanged himself while awaiting death by electric chair.
Fifth Ave at 59th St.

United Nations

Let Us Beat Swords into Plowshares, a bronze sculpture by Evgeniy Vuchetich, depicts a naked man with a sword in one hand and a hammer in the other. It represents man's desire to end war—nakedly.
Rose Garden, 1 United Nations Plaza.

The Lever House

Kooky artist Damien Hirst's *Virgin Mother*, a 35-foot sculpture of a grossly anatomic pregnant woman, stands guard outside the steel-and-glass Lever House.
390 Park Ave between 53rd and 54th Sts.

New York Health & Racquet Club

Get worked up while you work out. A set of bronze nude statues flank the entrance of the Chelsea location of this leisure chain.
60 W 23rd St between Fifth and Sixth Aves.

Queens Boulevard

"*The Civic Virtue* is one of the ugliest nude sculptures in New York history," says Bret Watson, president and founder of the Watson Adventures scavenger hunts, of this statue. It features a naked male standing over a woman. "It was given to the city to be placed in City Hall in 1922, but it was so ugly the city banished it to Queens."
Queens Blvd at Union Tpke.

404 Cook your own at Swish

Getting New Yorkers to cook for themselves isn't easy, but Swish is giving it a shot. The main offering is shabu-shabu (named for the swishing sound of meat being stirred in boiling broth); mini hot pots are provided for beginners, along with all the fixins—beef or fish, cabbage, mushrooms, noodles, and your choice of seafood, sake, or spicy broth—plus a list of confusing instructions. More advanced cooks can order ingredients à la carte or share whimsically named meals for two, such as Dive into the Sea: shrimp, crab, squid, scallops, sliced fish, and fish balls. Tapioca bubble-tea and fruit smoothies are free with each entrée.

Swish *88 W 3rd St between Sullivan and Thompson Sts (212-777-8808).*

405 Bag a bag at Edith Machinist

Check out one of the city's best collections of (mostly) fine leather bags, not to mention an army of shoes, here at this slightly below-street-level shop. There's no trash—just the cream of the vintage crop. The front rack displays Edith & Daha's own line of designer clothing.

Edith Machinist *104 Rivington St between Essex and Ludlow Sts (212-979-9992).*

406

Relive the Crash at the Museum of American Finance

In September 2007, the museum packed up its loot and moved into the former headquarters of the Bank of New York. The newly renovated Banking Hall makes an excellent place to view the museum's permanent collection, which traces the history of Wall Street and America's financial markets. On display are the ticker tape from the morning of the big crash of October 29 1929, an 1867 stock ticker and a $10,000 bill.

Museum of American Finance *48 Wall St at William St (212-908-4110/financialhistory.org).*

A few of my favorite things

407-412

Elettra Rossellini Wiedemann, Model

One of the best places to have tea is Caravan of Dreams (405 E 6th St, 212-254-1613, caravanofdreams.net). There is an amazing tea called "Good for Everything Tea," a combination of ginger, lemon, cayenne pepper and goji berries—great for flu season. **Diablo Royale (189 W 10th St between W 4th and Bleecker Sts, 212-620-0223, diabloroyale.com) in Greenwich Village has a vibe that feels like *Cheers*, except for the Mexican food and frozen margaritas —which are totally worth the calories. Maybe it's the tequila, but people are quick to pick up conversations with their neighbors at the bar, and staff treat you like you've been a regular for years.** My New Year's resolution was to ease myself into veganism, and places like Candle Cafe (1307 Third Ave at 75th St, 212-472-0970, candlecafe.com) make that really easy. The food is delicious and after a full meal (even dessert!) I feel nourished without feeling like I have to loosen my belt. **Taking the A train to the Far Rockaway neighborhood in Queens is fun. I wouldn't necessarily take a dip in the ocean there —it's no Thailand—but it feels great to get out of the city using public transport and to realize there are seagulls, sand and waves not too far from Manhattan.** I love to work out with my trainer at this small baseball field near Sheep's Meadow in Central Park. It's a really fun place to hang anyway because there are always these super-cool roller-skating dancers, and a lot of people playing beach volleyball or ultimate frisbee and sunbathing. **Sometimes I rent a bike in the park (212-541-8759, centralparkbiketour.com/ bikerentals.htm) and then ride through Manhattan all the way into Brooklyn via the Williamsburg or the Manhattan Bridge. The views are awesome.**

413

Watch poets battle at Nuyorican
Poetry is a contact sport
at Loisaida landmark the
Nuyorican Poets Café (236
East 3rd St, 212-505-8183,
nuyorican.org). Especially
on Friday's slam night, when
lyricists from the boroughs and
beyond square off. The winner
is decided by an animated, jam-packed house—arrive early to get
one of the few tables. This is the house that Miguel Algarín built
(with help from Allen Ginsberg and William Burroughs) in 1975,
spawning the New York spoken-word scene.

414 See Milne's inspiration for Winnie the Pooh

Visit the Central Children's Room at Donnell Library (20 W 53rd St between Fifth and Sixth Aves, 212-621-0636, nypl.org) to see a permanent display of the original Winnie the Pooh toys, on which A.A. Milne based his classic books. The stuffed bear was purchased at Harrods in 1921 by Milne as a gift for his son, Christopher; he bought the other playthings (among them Eeyore and Piglet) steadily over the next several years.

415 Cheer on the Harrison Street Regatta—or race yourself

Held every year in August, this race (from Pier 96 to the 72nd Street dock) is open to any human-powered craft and is considered the highlight of the paddling season. The event is topped off by a rollicking barbecue open to all, where you'll pay nothing for the food and soft drinks. The Downtown Boathouse's fleet of public kayaks is available for use in the race, or participants can bring their own vessel. If you're not the river-faring type, you can still show up to watch and cheer on the sailors. For information, call 646-613-0375 or go to downtownboathouse.org.

416 Join the National Chorale Messiah Sing-In

Hallelujah! Chase those Christmas blues away by joining with the National Chorale and hundreds of your fellow audience members in a rehearsal and performance of Handel's *Messiah*. No previous singing experience is necessary to take part, and you can buy the score on site, though picking one up early for advance perusal would certainly help novices. The Sing-In takes place every December at Avery Fisher Hall in the Lincoln Center (Columbus Ave at 65th St, 212-333-5333, lincolncenter.org). Visit nationalchorale.org for more information.

417 Drink down the spirit of Dylan Thomas—literally

It is said that in 1953, on the night before he died, Dylan Thomas pounded 18 straight whiskeys here. Now the old-school bar and its adjacent outdoor patio play host to a yuppie crowd and clutches of tourists, drawn by the outdoor seating, a fine selection of beers (seven on tap include $6 Anchor Steam, and 14 are available by the bottle). But pay your tribute to the master poet with a scotch.
White Horse Tavern *567 Hudson St at 11th St (212-989-3956).*

418 Encourage an addiction at Grand Sichuan International

A General Tso's for the thinking man, Grand Sichuan's strangely addictive Guizhou spicy chicken ($9.95) delivers a more sophisticated brand of fire—derived from dry-fried hot chilies and tongue-tingling Szechuan peppercorns—without a drop of gloopy sauce.
Grand Sichuan International *745 Ninth Ave at 50th St (212-582-2288).*

419 Discover the African Burial Ground

A major archeological discovery, the African Burial Ground is a small remnant of a five-and-a-half-acre cemetery where between 10,000 and 20,000 African men, women and children were buried. The cemetery, which closed in 1794, was unearthed during the construction of a federal office building in 1991 and designated a National Monument. In October 2007, a ceremony of dedication was held for the newly erected stone memorial designed by architect Rodney Leon, a 37-year-old African-American New Yorker. The two-story-tall curved monument draws heavily on African architecture and contains a spiral path that leads up to an ancestral chamber. There is a visitor center located inside 290 Broadway.
African Burial Ground *Duane St between Broadway and Centre Sts, behind 290 Broadway (212-637-2019/nps.gov/afbg).*

420-423

Load up with precious cargo from the city's hottest jewelry shops

Though Fifth Avenue's illustrious diamond houses such as Cartier and Tiffany retain their posh allure, NYC also offers a bevy of highly intimate boutiques for one-of-a-kind adornments, particularly in the West Village. This area of town is quickly becoming the new Gold Coast, thanks to Ginette_NY Jewelry Bar (172 W 4th St between Sixth and Seventh Aves, 212-627-3763), the first boutique dedicated to Provençal native Frédérique Dessemond's chic line. Her signature 14-karat gold flat disks—which can be personalized with custom monograms, words or numbers—are actually based on the traditional adornments worn by women in her Marseille hometown. Just a short walk away is perhaps the city's smallest bauble boutique, Phoenix Roze (183 W 10th St between Seventh Ave South and W 4th St, 212-255-2362, phoenixroze.com), a nook (formerly an alley) lined with second-generation jewelry maker and owner Guy Rozenstrich's handmade creations, along with Pamela Norris's chunky quartz bracelets. You'll find goods for both sexes, including superfemme moonstone-drop earrings and handsome silver shark's tooth pendants. Rozenstrich will also whip up custom pieces.

For accessories with worldly flair, visit Jane Eadie (248 Elizabeth St between E Houston and Prince Sts, 212-334-7975), the eponymous boutique of a former assistant to the Prince of Wales and the president of Polo Ralph Lauren. Her tiny, shabby-chic spot brings together Italian designer Daniela de Marchi's cocktail rings and, from Brazil, JMR Fontan's cuffs, among other hard-to-find pieces from designers all around the world.

If you're tired of cliché charms, pluck ungirly creations from Bittersweets New York (37 Broadway between Kent and Wythe Aves, Williamsburg, Brooklyn, 718-218-8595, bittersweetsny.com). Here artist and co-owner Robin Adams's quirky embellishments, such as 18-karat gold-plate cuffs modeled after earthworms, walk the line between creepy and beautiful in a former gallery bedecked with vintage wallpaper and antique cabinets.

Trip to where Teddy Roosevelt was born

The actual birthplace of the 26th Prez was demolished in 1916, but it has since been fully reconstructed, complete with a vast amount of authentic period furniture (some of it collected and restored from the original house) and a trophy room. Roosevelt lived here from his birth in 1858 until he was 14 years old. Check it out for a mere $3.

Theodore Roosevelt Birthplace *28 E 20th St between Broadway and Park Ave South (212-260-1616/nps.gov/thrb).*

Make like a mermaid on Coney Island

Decked-out mermaids and mermen of all shapes, sizes and ages share the parade route with elaborate, kitschy floats, come rain or shine. It's the wackiest summer solstice event you'll likely ever witness, and draws an appropriately diverse crowd. Check the website for route details, since the parade location changes each year.

Mermaid Parade *Coney Island, Brooklyn (718-372-5159/coneyisland.com).*

Give olive oil ice cream a try

We love the GelOtto cart that orbits Washington Square Park in the summer, serving up frozen (if, at $7.50 per cup, pricey) treats from the beloved Mario Batali restaurant. At first, olive oil gelato—a favorite on the Chowhound message boards—sounded like a head-scratcher, but we found it surprisingly sweet, with enough cinnamon to give it a nice kick and a drizzle of said oil right on the top.

427 *Catch an auction at Christie's…*

Dating from 1766, Christie's is known throughout the world for its high-profile sales of seriously upmarket items. The company's building in NYC is worth a visit purely for the architecture, in particular the cavernous three-floor lobby, which features a specially commissioned mural by Sol LeWitt. Otherwise, come by to watch a sale (most are open to the public) or nose around the items that are to be put under the hammer (viewing hours are scheduled in the days leading up to sales). Hours vary with each sale; call or visit the website for information.

Christie's *20 Rockefeller Plaza, 49th St between Fifth and Sixth Aves (212-636-2000/christies.com).*

428 *…or at Sotheby's*

Sotheby's, which has offices everywhere from London to Singapore, is the world's most famous auction house. The New York branch regularly holds public sales of antique furniture and jewelry in one lot, and pop-culture memorabilia in another. Spring and fall see the big sales of modern and contemporary art. Public viewings are held prior to each auction; call or visit Sotheby's website for details.

Sotheby's *1334 York Ave at 72nd St (212-606-7000/sothebys.com).*

429 *Browse historic snaps at the International Center of Photography*

The library at the International Center of Photography—a major photographic resource—houses back issues of photography magazines, and thousands of biographical and photographic files. Founded in the 1960s as the International Fund for Concerned Photography, ICP has work by photojournalists Werner Bischof, Robert Capa and Dan Weiner, all of whom were killed on assignment. Photojournalism remains an important part of the center's program, which also includes contemporary photos and video. In 2003, the first-ever ICP Photo Triennial further solidified ICP's presence on the contemporary photography scene. The two floors of exhibition space often showcase retrospectives devoted to single artists; recent shows have focused on the work of Sebastião Salgado, Weegee and Garry Winogrand.

International Center of Photography *1133 Sixth Ave at 43rd St (212-857-9700/icp.org).*

430 *Tour a studio and spot the next big thing*

It ain't cheap ($18.50 for adults) and you'll have to put up with camera-wielding tourists, but guided tours of the NBC Studios (30 Rockefeller Plaza, 49th St between Fifth and Sixth Aves, 212-664-3700, nbc.com) are led by pages, many of whom will go on to bigger and better things in showbiz—just as Ted Koppel, Kate Jackson, Michael Eisner and Marcy Carsey have already done. So when you meet them in the future you'll always be justified in shouting, "I knew you when you were nothing!"

431 *Tap your toes while getting your fingers greasy at the Lenox Lounge*

The lure of this Harlem spot is its rich history: James Baldwin and Langston Hughes used to hang out here. In the Zebra Room, tucked in back and decorated with the requisite animal-print wallpaper, listen to jazz and blues while tucking into crab cakes or shrimp. Or lean at the main bar—a 65-year-old wooden Art Deco masterpiece—where regulars sip high lifes. On weekend nights, take a pass; tourists come out in droves.

Lenox Lounge *288 Malcolm X Blvd (Lenox Ave) between 124th and 125th Sts (212-427-0253/ lenoxlounge.com).*

432

*Argue (or agree) with
the conspiracy theorists
in Union Square*

Home to candlelight vigils in the aftermath
of 9/11, Union Square has since become
something of an impromptu soapbox for
conspiracy theorists for whom that tragedy—
as well as numerous other historical events—
offers irrefutable interpretations. Should you
wish to refute them, drop by when there's
a political demonstration and you're
sure to find a suitable wall to bang
your head against. Pearl Harbor,
the JFK assassination, the 2000
election, the smoking ban—
all are quality debate fodder
with those who believe
two plus two equals the
Trilateral Commission.

433

Devour a bowl of English chips at the Atlantic ChipShop...

Set in a 100-year-old building with tin ceilings, this offshoot of the Park Slope ChipShop serves the same fish 'n' chips, bangers 'n' mash, mushy peas and other U.K. staples made popular at the original. This is more of a pub, and boozers will be happy to find 16 draught beers, bitters and ales, as well as a variety of single-malt Scotches, small-batch bourbons and specialty Irish whiskeys.
Atlantic ChipShop *129 Atlantic Ave between Henry and Clinton Sts (718-855-7775/chipshopnyc.com).*

434-439

...then get a further taste of England in America

The cheeky campaign to name a block of Greenwich Avenue (between 12th and 13th Streets) "Little Britain" may have come to naught, but the homesick expat and incurable Anglophile can find solace—and even sausage rolls—at a number of city establishments. Richard Koss explores Albion's finest outposts in her former colony.

Myers of Keswick

Ground zero for anything that combines the attributes of Britishness and edibility, Myers boasts the only authentic Cumberland sausages in America, minced and twisted into shape on the premises. The store also makes its own pies, scones and cheeses, the produce on its shelves looking like it would be more at home in a Sainsbury's than your local Gristedes. This is the place to stock up on Weetabix, Walkers crisps, McVitie's digestive biscuits, Wilkin & Sons jams, Heinz sponge puddings, bottles of Ribena or Robinson's barley water, and Rowntree's fruit pastilles.
634 Hudson St between Horatio and Jane Sts (212-691-4194/myersofkeswick.com).

Tea and Sympathy

Invariably crowded, this small eatery has been on a mission since opening its doors in 1990 to serve up British staples like bangers 'n' mash, shepherd's pie, Cornish pasties and sticky toffee pudding (positively dripping with hot custard). The sumptuous Sunday dinner ($23) of roast beef and Yorkshire pudding is popular, but the real highlight is a classic, very traditional afternoon tea, a $20 spread that includes a fresh pot of the brown stuff, finger sandwiches, cakes and scones with clotted cream and jam.
108-110 Greenwich Ave between 12th and 13th Sts (212-989-9735/teaandsympathynewyork.com).

A Salt & Battery

So dedicated to authentic fish 'n' chips that it wraps its vinegar-drenched portions in day-old copies of Brit-newspaper *The Independent*, this small storefront with limited seating is owned by Tea and Sympathy next door. Cod, haddock, sole or whiting are available, the staff is mainly Cockney and the satellite radio emanates from London. Cap your meal off with a deep-fried Mars bar ($3.25)—if you think your heart is strong enough for it.
112 Greenwich Ave between 12th and 13th Sts (212-691-2713/asaltandbattery.com).

The Park Slope ChipShop

Brooklyn's answer to A Salt & Battery offers a more extensive menu (including three sorts of shepherd's pie, as well as an $8.50 ploughman's lunch featuring stilton or cheddar) in a cozy spot decked out in British memorabilia. Mars, Twix, Bounty, Reese's Peanut Butter, Snickers and Twinkies all get the deep-fried treatment here, while the Hangover Special is a full English breakfast kicked up a notch with buck's fizz (a mimosa) and coffee.
383 Fifth Ave at 6th St (718-832-7701/ chipshopnyc.com).

St Andrew's Pub

St Andrew's claims to be New York's only Scottish pub—it's certainly the only one with bartenders in kilts and haggis on the menu (made with lamb and oats, rather than ground offal boiled in a sheep's stomach, and served over neeps and tatties), not to mention cock-a-leekie soup. The pub carries an impressive array of 200 single-malt whiskies, and offers Tennent's and Belhaven brews on draught.
120 W 44th St between Sixth Ave and Broadway (212-840-8413/standrewsnyc.com).

Mind the Gap Theatre

So far off-off-Broadway that it's really more off-West End, the Mind the Gap Theatre has been showcasing new British drama in New York since 1998 in a variety of small theaters (check the current program on the website). With Dame Judi Dench and Dame Helen Mirren both on the advisory board, the company must be on the right track.
535 W 23rd St (212-252-3137/ mindthegaptheatre.com).

440 Get to know gold at the Federal Reserve Bank

Here's your chance to descend 80 feet below street level and commune with the planet's most precious metal. Roughly a quarter of the world's gold (more than 100 billion dollars) is stored here in a gigantic vault that rests on the bedrock of Manhattan. Tours take place every morning, once an hour on the half-hour (phone for reservations). Keep your fingers to yourself.

Federal Reserve Bank *33 Liberty Street between Nassau and William Sts (212-720-6130/newyorkfed.org).*

441 Take a temporary fast at the Irish Hunger Memorial

Among Battery Park City's restaurants, cafés, shops and marina, between the esplanade with its sweeping views of the Hudson River and the city's financial district, you'll find the Irish Hunger Memorial (Vesey Street, at North End Avenue). Skip lunch and put the money instead toward your favorite charity, then stroll quietly around the landscaped plot in tribute to those who suffered so greatly in the face of others' greed during the Irish Famine. Sometimes it's good to take stock.

Irish Hunger Memorial

442 Take your favorite doll to the doctor

"There isn't a doll that we can't repair…
we fix them even if they were made before
the birth of Christ," claims Irving Chais, owner
of New York Doll Hospital. His family started
the business in 1900, and the second-floor
shop is cluttered with mounds of doll limbs
and bodiless heads. Chais explains that many
customers come to him because he can often
repair a beloved Barbie or teddy the same
day (unlike many other repair shops, which
can require several weeks to do similar work).
But some "operations" can't be rushed: He
once pieced together a porcelain head that
had shattered into 40 tiny shards. "It took
me six months," Chais says, "but it looked
like new again."
New York Doll Hospital *787 Lexington Ave
at 61st St (212-838-7527).*

443

Embrace the zaniness of Zenkichi

Noirish lighting, narrow passageways lined by
trompe l'oeil mirrors that turn a small bamboo
garden into a forest, seemingly endless twists
and turns—you're right to wonder just where
you're headed when the host at Zenkichi leads
you to your table. Fortunately, the quixotic
journey, which begins at a concealed entrance,
has a happy ending. Your destination is a
private booth—complete with tatami—that
becomes your intimate dining alcove. When
you're ready to choose from the menus of sake
and small-plate izakaya (that's Japanese pub
grub, often appearing in the form of grilled
skewers), simply press a button at the edge
of the table. It summons the server, who
promptly appears as if from out of the ether.
The whole experience is confounding, in a
good way. Perhaps the most surprising twist
is that the transporting setting doesn't outshine
the equally enchanting food. We love nagoya
teba: fried-until-golden seasoned chicken wings
with "special" Japanese spices.
Zenkichi *77 North 6th St at Wythe Ave,
Williamsburg, Brooklyn (718-388-8985).*

444

Hear classical music under the stars

For nearly half a century, the New York
Philharmonic (nyphil.org) has run an annual
series of free concerts in the city's many parks
in late June. Sneak some beers in with a picnic,
kick back on your rug and soak up classical
sounds under the evening sky. If you're serious
about the music, get there early—and get as
close to the bandshell as you can. That's where
the audience is most reverential (and quietest).

445 See the circus animals come to town

The Ringling Bros and Barnum & Bailey
Circus Animal Parade (212-307-7171, ringling.
com) sees elephants, horses and zebras march
through the tunnel and on to the streets of
Manhattan, with midnight parades opening
and closing the circus's Manhattan run in
March each year. Follow the procession along
34th Street from the Queens Midtown Tunnel
to Madison Square Garden.

446 Drink to George at the Fraunces Tavern

This 18th-century tavern was Washington's
watering hole, the site of his famous farewell
to the troops at the Revolution's close. During
the mid to late 1780s, the building housed the
fledgling nation's departments of war, foreign
affairs and treasury. In 1904, Fraunces became
a repository for artefacts collected by the Sons
of the Revolution in the State of New York. You
can still get a beer in the tavern and restaurant
(212-968-1776), open for lunch and dinner from
Monday to Saturday, or see the collections
(admission $4; free-$3 reductions).
Fraunces Tavern Museum *54 Pearl St at Broad
St (212-425-1778/frauncestavernmuseum.org).*

Mob town

Tracing the physical history of New York's Mafia, **Richard Koss** *finds nothing is as it was.*

The underworld is in danger of overkill. The Mafia has well and truly entered pop culture, with Hollywood recycling its legends, gangsta rappers appropriating its aura and *The Sopranos* charming TV land with their inventive nicknames (although could they ever improve on the likes of real-life mobsters Otto "Abbadabba" Berman, "Louie Ha Ha" Attanasio or "Tony Tea Bags" LoPinto?). Well might a turn-of-the-century racketeer or 1920s bootlegger wonder what happened to *omertà*, the Mafia code of silence, before he reached for his gat.

Curiously, despite this plunge into the mainstream, Mafia landmarks in the city that brought the organization its greatest notoriety are being rubbed out faster than a stool pigeon. Take the barbershop at the old Park Sheraton Hotel (now the Park Central Hotel) on 56th St and 7th Ave. This is where Albert Anastasia was gunned down while getting a trim on October 25, 1957, by two affiliates of the Gambino family. For years after, the chairs were turned to face the door in honor of the

murdered "Lord High Executioner," who—desperate to defend himself—only managed to fire at his attackers' reflections in the wall mirror. Shots of espresso are all that fly around now, though, as the spot has been taken over by yet another of the city's ubiquitous Starbucks. Now there's nothing at all to mark the murder.

The Gambino family's former hangout has received a far more upscale makeover. The former Ravenite Social Club on 247 Prince St was the lair of the infamous John Gotti. It was here that he ordered numerous hits on his rivals in the 1980s over friendly games of dominoes, blissfully unaware that the FBI had tapped the joint and were building the case that ultimately sent him upstate. Today, it is home to the designer handbags of Amy Chan's boutique, and only paparazzi would dream of spying on the models and A-listers that pass through.

Gotti's most famous hit was made on rival Paul Castellano at Sparks Steakhouse (210 E 46th St). Though Castellano had just been made

a boss, he didn't quite fit in with Gotti's plans. Gotti had him and associate Thomas Bilotti killed in broad daylight while the streets were filled with Christmas shoppers.

Another mobster who didn't get to finish his last supper was Joe Gallo, who was celebrating his 43rd birthday on April 6, 1972 at Umberto's Clam House (129 Mulberry St on the corner of Hester St) with his wife and daughter. Members of the Colombo family, which "Crazy Joey" had crossed, dropped by to wish him happy birthday by shooting him three times. While the gruesome photo of his corpse that graced the front pages the next day is still fixed in the minds of many New Yorkers, Umberto's has since moved down the street to No.172, to be replaced by another Italian eatery, Da Genaro's.

Clearly, disloyalty carries the steepest price in the underworld, and the more toes an aspiring mobster steps on, the more bullets are likely to bear his name. Vincent "Mad Dog" Coll was such a loose cannon that just about anyone might have whacked him, especially after his accidental shooting of a child during a much-publicized shoot-out brought widespread attention and public indignation on the Mafia. Dutch Schultz was handed the pleasure of wiping out "Mad Dog," who had skipped a bail the former had been kind enough to pay. The inevitable shooting, by members of Schultz's gang, took place when Coll was in a phone booth in a drugstore (now a pizza parlor) on 314 W 23rd St on February 8, 1932.

The far more illustrious Arnold Rubenstein, who had fixed the 1919 World Series and is regarded as the basis for Meyer Wolfsheim in Fitzgerald's *The Great Gatsby*, got his comeuppance on November 4, 1928 after receiving a call inviting him to the same Park Central Hotel in which Anastasio would later be murdered. Entering Room 349, he was shot in the stomach; his assailant is still unknown, since, although Rothstein lived for several more days, he refused to reveal the name of his killer.

The Jewish mob mingled with surprising ease with the Italian Mafia, with Meyer Lansky and Bugsy Siegel's association with Salvatore "Lucky" Luciano dating back to their childhoods on the Lower East Side of the 1920s. Their hangout, Ratner's at 138 Delancey St, was one of the city's renowned Jewish delis. Sadly Ratner's closed in 2002. The place where they would convene in a back room to plot their

> "The chairs were turned to face the door in honor of the murdered 'Lord High Executioner,' who—desperate to defend himself— only managed to fire at his attackers' reflections in the barbershop mirror."

nefarious business activities has been converted into the über-trendy Lansky Lounge, designed— of course—to resemble a Prohibition speakeasy.

Needless to say, Brooklyn is not lacking in Mafia history. Indeed, the most famous of all gangsters hails from the borough. Before he moved to Chicago to run the Windy City and send out his inimitable Valentine's Day greetings, Al Capone spent his childhood in Brooklyn. He lived first at 95 Navy St near the Brooklyn Naval Yard, before his family moved to Park Slope. There's nothing to see at Nos.21 or 38 Garfield Place, which are private residences, but devotees can visit the St. Mary Star of the Sea church on Court Street in Carroll Gardens where he was married.

But the best way to pay your respects to the Mafia is a visit to St. John Cemetery in Queens (8001 Metropolitan Ave, Middle Village, Queens), which is sure to evoke the burial scene from *The Godfather*. Here such luminaries as Carlo Gambino, Vito Genovese, "Lucky" Luciano, Salvatore Maranzano and John Gotti rest in the peace they paid little attention to in life. It was Luciano who had Maranzano offed in 1931, and when he himself died 31 years later he was buried—a fine slice of Mafia irony—in the same section of the cemetery as his former foe.

448-454 *Become a tea gourmet*

Rebecca Flint Marx **finds a new generation of Gotham tea shops where the noble brew is no longer treated as coffee's wussy cousin.**

People have been drinking tea for about 5,000 years, but for most of us, the beverage is little more than a chaser for dry scones. A new crop of tea salons, however, is intent on changing that. Sleek and chic, they have more in common with wine bars than chintzy tearooms, right down to the tea sommeliers who will gladly help you distinguish, say, a fukamuchi sencha from a genmaicha matcha.

First, Dawn Cameron, the founder of Sanctuary T, guides us through a sampling of the five basic kinds of tea, from the mellowest to the most robust: white, green, oolong, black and pu-ehr. All teas, she explained, come from the same plant, *Camellia sinensis*. Herbal tea, along with tisanes such as mint and chamomile, is not technically tea but is instead derived from other plants. And while flavored teas are tasty, she says "unflavored tea is a real connoisseur's taste."

White tea, Cameron explains, is the mildest kind. Unlike other tea varieties, its leaves are unprocessed and unoxidized. Oxidation, or fermentation, Cameron says, "is where the real art" of tea making comes in—the maker must decide when to stop the oxidation by heating the leaves. It's just one of the many factors, which also include humidity and terroir, that affect the finished product. Green tea's antioxidant levels and other purported health benefits have made it a darling of the clean-living crowd. Like white tea, its leaves are unoxidized and steamed or pan-fired. A cup of green tea, says Cameron, should have a bit of a bite, and a "fresh, grassy" taste. Usually, it takes eight to ten months for tea to go from grower to retailer, though the leaves won't lose their pungency if stored correctly – away from strong odors, light, moisture and air.

Next in line is oolong, a traditional Chinese tea whose oxidation falls between that of green and black teas. Complex in taste and faintly redolent of chocolate, oolong is, says Sanctuary's manager and oolong expert, Aleksandra Milicevic, "a wine lover's tea," because of its complexity—the best is said to have a nuanced flavor profile similar to that in fine wines. In total contrast, the astringency of black tea is down to Empire: British colonialists favored fully oxidized leaves, since their tea had to be strong enough in flavor to stand up to the milk and sugar they liked to dump into their brew. Black teas grown on plantations in the Darjeeling and Assam regions of India are best known to Westerners; assams are generally used in breakfast teas.

The somewhat obscure and highly coveted pu-ehr is sold in cakes, rather than loose leaves, and has an odd yet intriguing aroma and taste that's reminiscent of a farm. No wonder it's sometimes referred to as "camel breath." Grown in China, pu-ehr is fermented and aged, sometimes up to 100 years. Also often likened to wine, its older vintages can sell for up to $3,000 per cake.

But where can you sample these marvellous brews? Tavalon Tea Bar (22 E 14th St between Fifth Ave and University Pl, 212-807-7027) offers more than 30 varieties of tea—and an on-site DJ. T Salon (75 Ninth Ave between 15th and 16th Sts, 212-243-0432) trumpets itself as being "the first environmentally sustainable tea bar-café-market in the world!" while Gramstand (214 Ave A between 13th and 14th Sts, 212-533-1934) boasts "Zen-like industrial design" and more than 50 types of leaf. Cameron's Sanctuary T (337B West Broadway at Grand St, 212-941-7832) provides a similarly mind-boggling array of tea, as well as full restaurant service in a spa-like setting, while Tafu (569 Lexington Ave between 50th and 51st Sts, 212-980-1310) brought premium Japanese teas—served by "tea concierges"—to midtown. In late 2007, Amai Tea & Bake House (171 Third Ave between 16th and 17th Sts, 212-863-9630), whose coveted sweets are sold at Takashimaya, became the latest to join the tea craze. Now, just remember 6.5 grams of leaves for every six ounces of water and you're good to go.

455-460 *Get some TLC... from students*

"Dental work," "cheap" and "performed by students"—six words that don't go great together. We test out some cheap options so that you don't have to.

L'Ecole

A five-course feast goes for $40 at the house restaurant of Soho's French Culinary Institute. But the wanna-be cooks are newbies in name only. Inside the serene, high-ceilinged eatery, black-clad servers (professionally seasoned, not students) dispense gratis canapés like fried corn fritters with fresh-made guacamole. The rotating selection of contemporary French dishes are spiked with global accents, such as curry-glazed scallops with baby beets and horseradish crème fraîche, a country pâté that comes with cherry chutney or passion-fruit cheesecake with a macadamia nut crust—each creation as tasteful to the eyes as it is to the tongue. If this is amateurs' work, every chef should be an amateur. If only wine—starting at $7 a glass—were included.
462 Broadway at Grand St (212-219-3300).

New York International Beauty School

Walk-ins are welcome here, where students practice on mannequin heads (just like on Shear Genius!). Licensed instructors supervise all work, and you can choose from a variety of styling and cut combinations for $10 and up. The studio is well lit and clean, with up-tempo Top 40 tunes blaring over the radio. We chose a wash, dry and set and found it well worth the $10, as did the other two customers in the salon. Shampoo and conditioner were massaged in and out under warm water, followed by a long, hot session under the dryer. Big bonus: The student stylists chat earnestly about your hair, but not much else. You'll notice, though, that we got our hair washed, not cut. While the service was flawless, we got an uneasy feeling walking in. Like Mom says, be careful of sharp objects.
500 Eighth Av at 35th St (212-868-7171).

New York School of Dog Grooming

Depressed that Rover's coif cost more than your own? This place offers cuts starting at $28 for smaller dogs and maxes out at $35 for larger pooches. If you happen to become enthralled by the art of canine cosmetology, pick up an application at the school, which has been training doggie beauticians since 1960. Christine Barci, who previously took her Pomeranian, Palmer, to a pro groomer in the East Village, maintains she had better results with the school. "I had him cut here last year, and I liked the way it looked. He doesn't seem to have any complaints," Barci says. "Palmer's got attitude. Now he's going to have a bigger attitude." Just make sure you have room in your apartment for your dog's ego after all is finished.
455 Second Av at 26th St (212-685-3776).

NYU College of Dentistry

Going to the dentist is painful for any nonmasochist (remember *Marathon Man*?), but the price of care can be worse than the throb of an abscessed tooth. The NYU College of Dentistry offers affordable checkups ($50) from dental students, with professors keeping a close watch over their charges and your mouth. "I feel very unworried here, because there are three, four people looking at you at the same time. At a private practice there is only one," says Gihan Sakr, 57, who makes the 80-mile commute from her home in Oxford, CT, for orthodonture that she says would cost her $20,000 at any other dentist. Sakr is paying only $2,000. Is it worth the risk? There's no risk, really—the students are supervised and the pain surprisingly un-*Little Shop of Horrors*.
345 E 24th St at First Ave (212-998-9800).

NYU Postdoctoral Program in Psychotherapy and Psychoanalysis

Like the dental school but for your brain, the practice here has postdocs treating you while being supervised by their teachers. Prices—as low as $5 in one case—are arranged according to a person's income. Our guinea pig signed up

after friends recommended it. "I had no idea there was anything affordable out there," says our wishes-to-be-anonymous friend. She's been coming here for more than a year. "It's amazing how much stuff you can explore if you have the opportunity and find somebody who's helpful, has empathy and can guide you a little bit." She continues: "I've been in this city eight years, going to this place for one and have seen concrete changes. It's helped me survive in New York."
240 Greene St, third floor, at Washington Pl (212-998-7890).

Touro College Acupuncture Clinic

Part of Touro's Oriental Medicine program, the clinic offers discounted treatments—$10 for the first visit, $25 for subsequent visits—performed by grad students working toward a masters of science in acupuncture. In the tradition of Chinese medicine, a diagnosis is made by asking specific questions about a patient's health, taking a pulse and examining the tongue. Our long-standing fear of needles was quickly allayed by the pleasant demeanor of the staff. Four student assistants (and one professor) questioned us; then, needles were placed in our body (left ear, elbows, ankles and knees). The pain was minimal; mostly we felt relaxed (though our ear got quite warm—a common reaction). Our diagnosis? We're "run-down." Before this experience, the thought of anyone poking us—professional or otherwise—was frightening. But in these hands and at this price, we'd be willing to give it another go.
33 W 23rd St, lower level, between Fifth and Sixth Aves (212-463-0400 ext 313).

461 Book ahead for the Lower East Side Tenement Museum

Housed in an 1863 tenement building (along with a gallery, a shop and a video room), this fascinating museum is accessible only by guided tour. The tours, which regularly sell out, explain the daily life of typical tenement-dwelling immigrant families. From April to December, the museum also leads walking tours of the Lower East Side.
Lower East Side Tenement Museum
108 Orchard St at Broome St (212-431-0233/tenement.org).

462 Order a Balkan burger

You'll need both hands to hold the massive pljeskavica—a "Balkan burger," or lamb-and-beef patty wrapped in pita-like flatbread—particularly if you've piled on the chopped cucumbers, homemade yogurt and ajvar, a zesty spread made with garlic, pepper and eggplant. Better come hungry.
Bosna Express *791 Fairview Ave at Putnam Ave, Ridgewood, Queens (718-497-7577).*

463 Join the adult-child bowling league at Rab's

When an adult-child bowling league started up some 13 years ago at Rab's, the owners were worried that no one would register for the Sunday 9am slot. But it proved so popular that a waiting list quickly formed. "Bowling with the family is a good laugh," says Staten Island mom Lori Buono, who's on a team with her husband, Patrick, and their children Karalyn and Kevin. "Besides," she says of the no-contact sport, "no one ever gets hurt at the bowling alley." It takes four people to make up a team, and at least one of them needs to be an adult—children as young as five are invited to play but, unfortunately, bumpers in the gutters aren't allowed. Bowling costs $15 per person per session, which includes league fee and shoe rental.
Rab's Country Lanes *1600 Hylan Blvd at Raritan Ave, Staten Island (718-979-1600/rabslanes.com).*

464 Shop for superhero supplies

When he's not busy writing his novels or helping to publish the *McSweeney* literary journal, Dave Eggers defends truth and virtue at this kitschy costume shop, where you can buy powerful anti-matter by the can. But beware: You must take the superhero pledge with every purchase.
Brooklyn Superhero Supply Co. *372 Fifth Ave between Fifth and Sixth Sts, Park Slope, Brooklyn (718-499-9884/superherosupplies.com).*

465 See New York in miniature

More than four decades back, Robert Moses commissioned an exact scale model version of New York City to serve as the centerpiece of an amusement park ride at the 1964 World's Fair in Queens. Visitors clambered aboard gondolas to gawk at Lilliputian versions of Gotham landmarks: the Statue of Liberty, the TWA terminal at JFK, the George Washington Bridge, the Cyclone roller coaster at Coney Island. "The Panorama of the City of New York" took 100 workers three years to construct, and attracted nearly six million people in its first two years.

Though the gondolas were eventually removed, the Panorama was regularly renovated through the 1960s (and integrated into the Queens Museum of Art when the institution opened in 1972). The last update occurred in 1992, when approximately 60,000 of the 895,000 structures were refurbished. After that, the Little Apple sat neglected, a half-remembered relic of civic pride.

But after being closed to the public for the latter half of 2006, the Panorama underwent a long-overdue upgrade: On guided tours (held Saturday and Sunday at 4pm) you'll see an updated lighting system that mimics the arc of the sun as it passes over NYC and a new audio track that includes a symphony of urban sounds—traffic jams, the rush of the subway, the orchestra tuning up at Lincoln Center.

Despite the improvements, one part of the Panorama remains decidedly untouched—the Twin Towers still stand proudly, albeit one twelve-hundredth their actual size. "We debated whether to keep them, but ultimately it's a historical representation from 1992," says QMA spokesperson David Strauss. "It gives people a chance to reflect on how things have changed."

David Lackey, who oversaw the Panorama's audio-video enhancements, is proud of how the project turned out, though he admits for a time it consumed his waking life. "One night I dreamt I was a giant, stepping over skyscrapers and walking between boroughs in a single bound," he says. "Of course, the next morning I was stuck in traffic for more than hour."

Queens Museum of Art *New York City Building, 111th St at 49th Ave, Corona, Queens (718-592-9700/queensmuseum.org).*

466

Park yourself on a barstool at the Grand Central Oyster Bar

Gotham was once a world-renowned oyster town, and this beloved 95-year-old landmark, nestled in Grand Central's lower level, reminds diners of that former glory. Two large rooms flank a white-topped counter where eaters can choose from more than 30 varieties of bivalve, including hard-to-find types like Chincoteagues from Virginia. They're all served with good old mignonette sauce. Since these little delicacies aren't terribly filling, O-Bar compensates with its famously gargantuan desserts: The apple pie bursts with so many razor-thin slices of fruit that it deserves landmark status all its own.

Grand Central Oyster Bar *Grand Central Terminal, Lower Concourse, 42nd St at Park Ave (212-490-6650).*

467 Get away from it all with Michelangelo and Mary Shelley

In April 2006, the expanded Morgan (designed by Pritzker Prize-winning architect Renzo Piano) reopened, doubling the amount of exhibition space and adding a number of new amenities. Thanks to the expansion, the museum is now able to display more of its 350,000 objects than ever. You'll see drawings by Michelangelo, Rembrandt and Picasso; a first edition of Malory's King Arthur tales from 1485; a *Frankenstein* annotated by Mary Shelley herself; manuscripts by Charles Dickens, Poe, Mark Twain, Steinbeck and Wilde; and sheet music drafts by the likes of Beethoven and Mozart.

The homey atmosphere of the Morgan, with its small, digestible galleries, unusual artworks (ancient Mesopotamian seals, anyone?) and historical display of Pierpont Morgan's home library is a rare treat. Pretty, warm and crowd-free, these buildings are a favorite we'd have been pleased to keep quiet about. Ah well.

Morgan Library & Museum *225 Madison Ave at 36th St (212-685-0008/themorgan.org).*

Grand Central Oyster Bar

468 *Meet an ancient Egyptian in Brooklyn*

Among the many assets at Brooklyn Museum (admission $8; free-$4 reductions) is the rich Egyptian collection. The 4,000 pieces include a gilded-ebony statue of Amenhotep III and, on a ceiling, a large-scale rendering of an ancient map of the cosmos. But the star of the show? A mummy, of course, preserved in its original coffin.

Brooklyn Museum *200 Eastern Pkwy at Washington Ave, Prospect Heights, Brooklyn (718-638 5000/brooklynmuseum.org).*

469 *Try Margon's cubano*

Join the midtown drones mobbing narrow lunch counter Margon (136 W 46th St between Sixth and Seventh Aves, 212-354-5013) and order a $5 cubano. Roasted pork, Swiss cheese, salami, ham, sliced pickles and mayo (ask for hot sauce) are toasted on a foil-covered sandwich press, creating a crusty gut-buster. Special.

470 *Explore Fort Wadsworth by lantern-light*

Explore the fortifications that guarded NYC for almost 200 years on an evening lantern-light tour, one of several popular themed tours of the Fort. Admission is free, tour or no, and the Fort is open every day.

Fort Wadsworth *At the east end of Bay St (718-354-4500).*

471  *Love Latino art*

Located in Spanish Harlem, the 8,000-piece El Museo del Barrio collection is dedicated to the work of Latino artists who reside in the US, as well as Latin American masters. Admission is $6 ($4 seniors) and the museum is open Wednesday to Sunday.

El Museo del Barrio *1230 Fifth Ave between 104th and 105th Sts (212-831-7272/elmuseo.org).*

A few of my favorite things

472-477

Marcus Samuelsson, chef

Dumpling House (118 Eldridge St, 212-625-8008) is a great spot. The value for money is incredible, and you can watch the women make the dumplings by hand. Bring a group of friends, eat like kings, and you'll still barely break $20. **For beer, I go to the otheroom (143 Perry St, 212-645-9758, theotheroom.com). It's a perfect little bar that always offers a good time without the total "scene," you know? Just a hot little bar.** One of the nicest places to go after hitting the museums is the Rose Garden on the east side of Central Park (105th St and 5th Ave). It's a masterpiece. It doesn't really matter when you go, it's always gorgeous. Great, too, for quirky people-watching. **Elephant (58 E 1st St, 212-505-7739, elephantrestaurant.com) is a small and quirky place in the East Village. It doesn't serve the best Thai food in town, but it has a perfect, inviting vibe. Prune (54 E 1st St, 212-677-6221, prunerestaurant. com) nearby serves a more refined meal.** Angel's Share (8 Stuyvesant St, second floor, inside Gyu-ya, 212-777-5415) is absolutely magical: a totally unexpected little spot perched above Third Avenue. Everyone behind the bar is Japanese and the cocktails are pitch-perfect. **I love vintage clothes and go to a lot of flea markets. There's the sweetest Ecuadorian couple that sells insane tamales near the Chelsea Flea Market (112 W 25th St) every weekend.**

Marcus Samuelsson is chef at Merkato 55, 55 Gansevoort St between Greenwich and Washington Sts (212-255-8555).

478

Admire great graffiti in Queens
5 Pointz (Jackson Ave between Crane and Davis Sts, Long Island City, Queens) is a gallery of a different sort. There's no art inside, but the façade of the block-long converted warehouse—visible from the 7 train—offers an evolving tableau of brilliant hued and wildly different tagging styles. If you're feeling as spry, scale the building's staircase to the roof for more graffiti and excellent city views.

479 Explore the Center for Architecture's headquarters

After five years of planning, the Center for Architecture opened to considerable acclaim back in autumn 2003. Founded in 1867, the organization languished for years on the sixth floor of a Lexington Avenue edifice, out of sight and mind of all but devoted architecture aficionados. In 1997, recognizing the center's isolation and perceived insularity, the American Institute of Architects (AIA) began searching Soho and the Village for new digs, finally opting for a vacant storefront in an early-20th-century industrial building. After a major design competition, Andrew Berman Architect was chosen to transform the space into a fitting home for architectural debate. The sweeping, light-filled design is a physical manifestation of AIA's goal of promoting transparency in both its access and programming. Berman cut away large slabs of flooring at the street and basement levels, converting underground spaces into bright, museum-quality galleries. He also installed a glass-enclosed library and conference room—open to the public—on the first floor, as well as a children's gallery and workshop on the mezzanine level. The building is New York's first public space to use an energy-efficient geothermal system: Water from two 1,260-foot wells is piped through the building to help heat and cool it. **AIA Center for Architecture** *536 La Guardia Pl between Bleecker and W 3rd Sts (212-683-0023/ aiany.org).*

480 Sit in Carnegie's garden

The only museum in the United States that is dedicated to domestic and industrial design—hosting a fascinating roster of temporary exhibitions—the Smithsonian's National Design Museum (2 E 91st St at Fifth Ave, 212-849-8400, cooperhewitt.org) was once the home of industrialist Andrew Carnegie. There is a still a lovely lawn behind the building, formerly the Scotsman's garden, that visitors can access.

481

Swim around the island

July's Manhattan Island Marathon Swim has to be the city's craziest annual sporting event. Having completed one of a range of punishing long-distance swims to qualify (see the website nycswim.org for details) and paid an entry fee of up to $1,415, you get to spend up to nine-and-a-half hours in choppy, 64°F salt water, amid the hurly-burly of NYC's commercial vessels. Still, there will be 25 solo swimmers and up to 18 relay teams to accompany you on the 28.5 miles counter-clockwise route around Manhattan Island. And if you're quickest back, you get the Gallagher Cup—it's from Tiffany's, dontcha know.

482 March along to Fleet Week

Around the last week of May each year, Navy vessels that have been deployed on active service overseas dock in Manhattan and their crews are let loose on the city. Which may not sound like a recipe for fun, but then you're forgetting the special openings and military demonstrations (impressively choreographed marines spinning rifles about the place like twigs, a big flypast, guided tours round imposing pieces of military hardware). To release your inner boy, just check the program details on cnrma.navy.mil/fleetweek/index.htm.

Want to raise a toast to a sailor? Our boys (and girls) in the Navy aren't so different from civilian tourists—they flock to Times Square. Maritime-themed Rum House (228 W 47th St between Broadway and Eighth Ave, 212-869-3005) welcomes sailors into the port with drink specials for guzzlers in uniform (a buck off drafts and well drinks at $6.75). Former serviceman David Sheeran offers seafarers a dollar-off deal on any drink at his midtown pub, Dave's Tavern (574 Ninth Ave between 41st and 42nd Sts, 212-244-4408), while at Bull Moose Saloon (354 W 44th St between Eighth and Ninth Aves, 212-956-5625), his bar and restaurant, service folk eat for half price.

483 *Warm up with Max's lasagne*

Generous and dirt cheap, the classic ricotta-free, molten lasagne at homey, low-ceilinged trattoria Max (51 Ave B between 3rd and 4th Sts, 212-539-0111) is the ultimate cold-weather comfort food—a perfect, tongue-scalding tower of fresh pasta, creamy béchamel and rich bolognese. A far cry from those tired Little Italy slabs.

484

Appreciate African-American art at the Studio Museum

When the Studio Museum opened in 1968, it was the first black fine-arts museum in the country. It remains the place to go for historical insight into African-American art and the art of the African diaspora. Under the leadership of director Lowery Stokes Sims (formerly of the Met) and chief curator Thelma Golden (formerly of the Whitney), this favorite has evolved into the city's most exciting showcase for African-American artists.

Studio Museum in Harlem *144 W 125th St between Malcolm X Blvd (Lenox Ave) and Adam Clayton Powell Jr Blvd (Seventh Ave) (212-864-4500/studiomuseum.org).*

485

Purchase a pour at the Pourhouse

Fans of exotic beers—and sports—can sip global finds like Hong Kong's Macau and Kalik, a Bahamian brew, while watching one of the 21 high-resolution televisions at this East Village tavern. Beers are around eight bucks, and a hearty menu (with entrees like chicken madeira) helps soak up the suds.

The Village Pourhouse *64 Third Ave at 11th St (212-979-2337/pourhousenyc.com).*

486-493

Play ping pong

Originally a lark for upper-crust Victorians, table tennis has since bounced its way into New York bars and basements. West Village's cavernous Fat Cat (75 Christopher St between Grove and W 10th Sts, 212-675-6056, $3 cover; $5 per person per hour weekdays; $6 per person per hour weekends) caters directly to that breed of gamer whose skills are directly proportional to their level of intoxication. Seven tables—surrounded by nets so players don't have to go chasing errant backhands—are set amid the shuffleboard, chess sets and billiards. Slate Plus (54 W 21st St between Fifth and Sixth Aves, 212-989-0096, slate-ny.com, $14-$17 for two people per hour) is a sort of upscale version of Fat Cat. The paddles are a bit worn, a favorable condition for the player who relies less on finesse and ball spin than crushing overhand winners. Located in the basement, its six tables sit alongside a variety of other gaming platforms. Be warned, though: Slate often hosts private parties at night. Southpaw

(125 Fifth Ave between Douglas St and Sterling Pl, Park Slope, Brooklyn, 718-230-0236, sps sounds.com) has only one table, but it's a good one. The staff rolls it out on Wednesday nights for an entertaining bout of neighborhood competition. It is free to play, so long as you're actively purchasing drinks. The wait is usually only about 20 minutes.

Perhaps you think you're good enough to test your skills against the best players in New York? Well, first you have to look the part. Once you figure out what style suits your game, order the corresponding blade at butterflyonline.com. Choose from the standard Shakehand or inverted Penfold, depending on your taste; beginner recreational paddles run from $16 to $60. For those rich dandies with too much time and floor space on their hands, pick up your own table at joolausa.com ($600-$1,500); plebs should opt for minitables ($160). Once confident that you won't embarrass yourself, join other New York table-tennis enthusiasts on Tuesday nights at Naked Ping Pong (487 Greenwich St between Canal and Spring Sts, nakedpingpong.com, $20 to attend, plus $10 to play). While you don't actually have to play naked inside the huge Tribeca loft, this

hip, weekly party serves enough booze to make it a distinct possibility.

Not serious enough for you? There are plenty of options for the most focused of competitors. Formerly the No.4 ranked player in the world, Wang Chen is better at table tennis than you could ever hope to be—much better. Enter Wang Chen's Table Tennis Club (250 W 100th St between Broadway and West End Ave, 212-864-7253, wangchenttc.com, $8 per person per hour, $75 monthly membership) and, in a case by the front desk, you'll not only find her many awards but also a picture of Wang with Keanu Reeves—who looks pretty sullen, probably because he just got his ass handed to him by a tiny smirking Asian woman. The three tables upstairs are generally only used by members and stronger players; the four downstairs are open to everyone. If a visit leaves you with any doubts as to how seriously some people take their ping pong, stop by the New York Table Tennis Foundation (384 Broadway between Walker and White Sts, 646-772-2922, nyttf.com, $9 per person per hour, $75 monthly membership), a spacious basement club in Chinatown—picture the secret army training scene in *Enter the Dragon*, but everyone is armed with paddles instead of swords. While they cater to more serious players, beginners are also welcome. The nine tables are in fairly constant use, but it usually doesn't take long to get on one (most games are played to 11). Head instructor Robert Chen gives lessons at a weekend workshop, Sat and Sun from 11am-2pm ($20). In Flushing, there's a state-of-the-art pong-nasium presided over by three-time Chinese table-tennis champion Yu Xiang Li and home court for Yan Jun Gao, currently the seventh-ranked player in the United States. The New York International Table Tennis Center (134-32 35th Ave, Flushing, Queens, 718-961-4208, nyittc.com, $6-$7 per person per hour; shoes and paddle rental, $1 each; $65-$299 monthly membership) has ten butterfly tables and, like the NYTTF, is open to novices and recreational players.

Finally, contrary to popular opinion, Coney Island is not just the home of circus freaks and competitive hot-dog eaters. No, it's also the oceanside locale of some of the city's most earnest players—who swarm all nine tables at the Brooklyn Table Tennis Club (1100 Coney Island Ave, Coney Island, Brooklyn, 718-421-2200, bttclub.com, $5-$6 per person per hour, $65 monthly membership). Come here for no-frills, hard-core pong at its best.

New York Table Tennis Foundation

494 Rummage for a bargain at Century 21...

A white Gucci men's suit for $300? A Marc Jacobs cashmere sweater for less than $200? Roberto Cavalli sunglasses for a scant $30? No, you're not dreaming—you're shopping at Century 21. The prized score is admittedly rare, but the place is still intoxicating: Savings range from 25 percent to a staggering 75 percent off regular store prices, making this a mecca for less-minted fashionistas. Century 21 (c21stores.com) has stores at 22 Cortlandt St (between Broadway and Church Sts, 212-227-9092) and 472 86th St (between Fourth and Fifth Aves, Bay Ridge, Brooklyn, 718-748-3266).

495-498

...or score loot for less at these well-curated consignment shops

Clothingline

This savvy company is like having a stylish best friend who knows when and where all the best sales are. And luckily, you needn't haul ass around town since Clothingline hosts its mark-down fests (usually 50 to 80 percent off) in one location, unloading goods directly from voguish labels including Helmut Lang and Theory. The warehouse can get pretty mobbed during lunch hours and after 5pm, so we recommend hitting it during off hours.

261 W 36th St between Seventh and Eighth Aves, second floor (212-947-8748/clothingline.com).

New and Almost New

Germophobes, you won't have to deal with strangers' cooties, as 40 percent of the goods at this resale shop is brand new. Owner Maggie Chan handpicks every piece hanging on the two color-coded racks serving up Prada, Chanel and Hermès garb ($15 and up). Fresh goods come in every week, with prices capped at around $600. But be warned—most of the clothes are sizes small and medium because they come from samples, magazines or skinny celebs.

166 Elizabeth St between Kenmare and Spring Sts (212-226-6677).

Outlet 7

Chained to your desk all day? Fortunately, this secret spot—a retail addendum to designer haven Showroom Seven—serves up goodies directly off the racks of more than 40 labels, seven days a week. Look for 40 to 70 percent off insidery brands including Benjamin Cho, Orla Kiely and Erickson Beamon, whose python bangles are currently halved to $90.

117 E 7th St between First Ave and Ave A (212-529-0766).

Samples for (eco)mpassion

Instead of a photo of a model who chooses to forgo food, an oversized pic of an impoverished girl drinking from a spigot greets customers at this charity-focused shop that opened in March 2008. Five percent of the proceeds are donated to a different nonprofit each month, such as kiva.org, which lends money to entrepreneurs in developing countries. Ike Rodriguez says the shop is a marriage of his defunct discounter Find Outlet and his earth-conscious e-tailer, greenfinds.com. Recent finds have included Lauren Moffat dresses (chopped from $400 to $150) and Linda Loudermilk tops (snipped from $150 to $50).

2 Great Jones St between Broadway and Lafayette St (212-777-0707).

499

Order a concrete at the Shake Shack

Danny Meyer's wildly popular Madison Square Park concession stand is mobbed during the summer; Gothamites line up in scores for excellent burgers and franks, served Chicago-style on poppy seed buns with a "salad" of toppings and a dash of celery salt. Frozen-custard concretes are our tip, though. Not only are the shake-like concoctions delicious (try the daily pie crust-infused special) but you can order the drink from a special express-lane part of the line, skipping the burger-hungry crowds entirely. Concrete good sense.

Shake Shack *Madison Square Park, 23rd St at Madison Ave (212-889-6600).*

500 *Visit Yoda in Queens*

The green puppet used in *The Empire Strikes Back* to portray the sage Jedi is on display at the Museum of the Moving Image (35th Ave at 36th St, Astoria, Queens, 718-784-0077, movingimage.us). Look out also for the chariot driven by the late Charlton Heston in *Ben-Hur*. Impressed you will be, young Skywalker.

501 *Sink your teeth into Kabab King*

You won't find more succulent Pakistani kebabs anywhere in New York that at Kabab King Diner (7301 37th Rd at 114th St, Jackson Heights, Queens, 718-457-5857)—in particular the so-hot-you'll-sweat beefbihari variety, which is marinated overnight in an incendiary red-yogurt rub. Ready those napkins.

502 *Ride the M4 bus*

No, really! Our favorite MTA route offers an engaging cross-section view of Manhattan. Pick it up in front of the Cloisters in Fort Tryon Park and gaze out the window as upper Broadway snakes through Washington Heights, skirts Harlem and turns at 110th Street to graze the top of Central Park. At Fifth Avenue, it veers south, passing the Guggenheim, the Met and the Frick, as well as numerous mansions along the boulevard. Midtown brings the Plaza, the department stores and the New York Public Library, before the bus turns on 34th Street and heads for Penn Station. We could ride this baby around all day.

503

Bypass the lobster rolls and get a bucket of Pearl's steamers

There are many excellent reasons to hunker down at the Pearl Oyster Bar (18 Cornelia St between Bleecker and W 4th Sts, 212-691-8211), a convivial, no-reservations, New England-style fish joint. Of course, everybody knows about the lemon-scented lobster rolls, probably the largest servings in the city, coming packed with sweet meat laced with mayonnaise and served on a butter-enriched bun with shoestring fries. And very fine they are too. But the real treat here is only found on the specials list: If you come here, you've got to try the steamers.

Don't take just our word for it. When we spoke to former *New York Times* food critic, editor-in-chief of *Gourmet* magazine and TV presenter Ruth Reichl in January 2008, she not only listed Pearl as one of her two favorite city restaurants—but specified that a bucket of steamers, a salad and a little lobster was her favorite meal here. The dish is presented as an ice bucket crammed full of giant, juicy clams, decorated with flat-leaf parsley and accompanied by the very necessary finger bowl: Getting messy with the steamers is a lot of the pleasure of this dish, especially the inky fingers you get from peeling off the dark foot that is attached to the flesh of each plump mollusk.

If you aren't stuffed after the clams, there are plenty of other options. You could wash them down with a bowl of clam chowder (the New England version, of course) or take on the bouillabaisse, a briny lobster broth packed with mussels, cod, scallops and clams, with an aïoli-smothered crouton balanced on top— great value at $18—while the supremacy of a bittersweet chocolate mousse topped by an enormous quenelle of barely sweetened whipped cream is a surprise at a spot better known for its sundaes.

All things considered, a restaurant that's truly worthy of its hype.

504-507
Rummage for goodies at a flea market

The Antiques Garage

Always a scene: LES bargain hunters compete with city antiques dealers every Saturday and Sunday. Offering more than 100 vendors on two floors of a parking garage, this market is perhaps the best known in the city—and for good reason. The prices here aren't the lowest you'll find, but the merchandise (deco and modern furniture, vintage sunglasses and eyeglass frames, prints and paintings, vintage clothing and accessories) usually hits the mark. It has its share of curio crap, but an early morning stake-out (get there before the post-brunch hordes) can be rewarding. It's operated by the folks behind the Hell's Kitchen Flea Market; a shuttle, costing just a buck, runs between the two spots.
112 W 25th St between Sixth and Seventh Aves.

Greenflea

Around the corner from the Museum of Natural History, this Columbus Avenue market sprawls out from the gymnasium and hallways of M.S.44 right across a large asphalt playground every Sunday. Hipsters and blue hairs mix with local families and regulars who munch on home-baked goodies while leafing through old encyclopedias and comic books. It's one of the kitschier markets in town: booths that are full of tie-dye creations, buttons and baubles from the attic stand side-by-side with troves of great vintage dresses and handmade quilts, contemporary handmade crafts and clothes.
Columbus Ave between 76th and 77th Sts.

Hell's Kitchen Flea Market

Tucked between the Lincoln Tunnel and Port Authority bus ramps, this unlikely slice of city street is closed to traffic every weekend when dozens of vendors unfold their tables and pile them full of goods. The newest of Gotham's fleas, this outdoor market moved from the long-running (albeit ill-fated—the lot was developed into condos) Chelsea spot The

Annex in 2005. Vendors tend to compensate for the out-of-the-way location by offering lower prices than you'll find in Chelsea, which can make it more than worth the trek. Look out for deco furniture, vintage housewares, kitchen accessories, glass doorknobs and crystals.
39th St between Ninth and Tenth Aves.

Park Slope

Battle the strollers that inevitably crowd the sidewalks around P.S.321 every weekend (weather permitting) for a peek at the vintage offerings and collectibles in this peanut-sized pocket frequented by Park Slope parents and post-grads. The address means it doesn't get the sorts of crowds that most of the city's other markets experience, which equals less pilfered pickin's for late-risers. It's been a neighborhood fixture for more than a decade, and some of the proceeds support the P.S.321 PTA. Look out for oriental rugs, furniture, vintage fashion accessories and costume jewelry.
P.S.321 playground, Seventh Ave between 1st and 2nd Sts, Park Slope, Brooklyn.

508
Admire the toys of bygone Gothamites

The lovely Museum of the City of New York contains a wealth of city history and includes paintings, sculptures, photographs, military and naval uniforms, theatre memorabilia, manuscripts, ship models and rare books. All of which are great—but it's the extensive toy collection, full of New Yorkers' playthings dating from the colonial era to the present, that really excites us.

Toy trains, lead soldiers and battered teddy bears share shelf space with exquisite bisque dolls (decked out in extravagant Paris fashions) and lavishly appointed dolls' houses. Don't miss the amazing Stettheimer Dollhouse, created during the 1920s by Carrie Stettheimer, whose artist friends re-created their masterpieces in miniature to hang on the walls. Look closely and you'll even spy a tiny version of Marcel Duchamp's famous painting *Nude Descending a Staircase*. Cute.
Museum of the City of New York *1220 Fifth Ave between 103rd and 104th Sts (212-534-1672/ mcny.org).*

509 Take the Multiethnic Eating Tour

On this semiregular culinary excursion run by Big Onion Tours (212-439-1090, bigonion. com), participants eat their way through the Lower East Side, at one time or another a haven for Jewish, Italian, German, Chinese, Irish and Dominican immigrants. Times have changed, but the influence of these communities can still be felt and, thankfully, tasted. On the two-hour, $20 eating tour, you'll try the likes of fried plantains from El Castilla de Jagua (113 Rivington Street) and full-sours from The Pickle Guys (49 Essex St), while sharing morsels from the area's sometimes seedy history. Often the food and the history overlap: While munching on summer rolls from Doyers Vietnamese Restaurant (11 Doyers St) on our tour, for example, we learned that 19th-century gang bangers chased their prey to the end of the street (then a dead end) to trap them in fights. It's just one of many bits of trivia you'll glean. Local lore and tasty snacks—now that's something we can sink our teeth into.

510-512
Drink a "pedigree punch"

The last time most of us sipped from a communal punch bowl, it was filled with an unidentifiable noxious liquid that left us nursing a bear of a hangover as we stumbled late to class. As it turns out, the punches that made us say "never again" at college parties are not that far removed from their potent brandy-and rum-based forebears, which got British sailors soused in the 17th century.

Punches have always been designed to render you blotto. In the past few years, pedigreed versions of these old-fashioned festive brews have been quietly making a comeback in New York bars. Try the signature Prohibition Punch at The Campbell Apartment (Grand Central Terminal, 15 Vanderbilt Ave, 212-953-0409): Appleton rum and Grand Marnier, mixed with passion fruit, cranberry and lemon juices, and topped with Moët & Chandon champagne (most punches combine at least five ingredients into a

dangerously smooth, alchemical blend). The drink arrives filled to the brim in a bulbous brandy snifter, but even more daunting are the punches offered for groups of two to six at Death & Company (433 E 6th St between Aves A and B, 212-388-0882) in the East Village. The cocktail geeks behind this speakeasy have gone to great lengths to replicate the sorts of elixirs Jay Gatsby might have served his guests. The recipe for their Fish House Punch, made with cognac and rum, dates to 18th-century Philadelphia (George Washington is said to have been a fan). Smooth and fruity, it's poured over a big block of ice into a porcelain bowl with matching cups.

Punches at the The Brandy Library (25 North Moore St between Hudson and Varick Sts, 212-226-5545, brandylibrary.com), meanwhile, are more modestly portioned. The tart, refreshing Mississippi Punch—made with Kentucky bourbon and Nicaraguan rum—is poured into a tumbler on the rocks. But yes, it still packs one hell of a punch.

513-515
Take the kids to a craft studio

Art projects are one of the best ways to keep kids' hands and brains busy, but when they do them at home you wind up scrubbing paint off the floor and glue off the ceiling, which adds a whole new level of misery to your day. Instead, visit a crafts studio, where you can paint a teacup for Grandma and still come home to a clean house. Drop in for some soothing pottery painting at Color Me Mine (116 Franklin St between Church St and West Broadway, 212-941-0120, colormemine.com) or Make (make meaning.com; 1566 Second Ave between 81st and 82nd Sts, 212-570-6868; 506 Amsterdam Ave between 84th and 85th Sts, 212-579-5575). If your kid is into beading, mosaics or T-shirt painting, check out the Little Shop of Crafts (littleshopny.com; 431 E 73rd St between First and York Aves, 212-717-6636; 711 Amsterdam Ave at 94th St, 212-531-2723). The Artful Place in Park Slope (171 Fifth Ave between Sackett and DeGraw Sts, 718-399-8199, theartfulplace. com) has open studio time on weekends for painting, collage making and drawing.

Lunch hour learning

Just got 30 minutes to spare? Let us show you how to get the most from New York's best museums in a serious hurry.

MoMA

Before you start, take a relaxing moment to gaze into the lovely sculpture garden. Ahhh. Now, go! Climb aboard the escalator to the fifth floor for paintings and sculpture from 1880 to 1940. Just off the escalator, hang a right and enter Gallery 1. You'll immediately see Paul Cézanne's *The Bather* but, before going for a closer look, peer into Gallery 2 for a second. The massive painting before you, *Les Demoiselles d'Avignon* by Picasso, is considered the single most influential work in the history of modern art. Now, wend your way through Gallery 5, taking in Gustav Klimt's *The Park*. Gallery 6 focuses on Matisse and includes the much admired *The Red Studio*, but breeze through Gallery 7 and into Gallery 14 for the artist's iconic *Dance (I)*. Then peek at Marcel Duchamp's amusing *Bicycle Wheel* (in Gallery 8) and a bounty of works by Piet Mondrian (Gallery 10). Gallery 12 allows quiet contemplation of the surreal: Salvador Dali's

The Little Theater. Exit (you've only got 17 minutes left), and head down to the fourth floor.

This area highlights works from the 1940s through the 1960s. Head straight for Gallery 17 and behold the work of Abstract Expressionist extraordinaire, Jackson Pollock. Tear yourself away from those enthralling drips and make your way to Gallery 19 to gaze upon the serene works of Mark Rothko. Stride past Jasper Johns' iconic *Flag* and Yves Klein (Galleries 20 and 21), preparing yourself for all things Pop in Gallery 23. The masterworks here by Andy Warhol and Roy Lichtenstein are as brilliant as ever. Minimalism (Gallery 24) doesn't get any better than Donald Judd's *Untitled (Stack)*. Now, with some seven minutes remaining, off you go to the third floor.

Again, bear right out of the escalator, head past the helicopter, and zip around this small gallery chock full of the very best of modern design. You'll be inspired by the wonderful collection of 19th- and 20th-century chairs, lamps, tables and posters.

The Met

If you haven't lingered for too long, you should have time left to pop into the museum's delightful shop just off the lobby. Treat yourself to something thoroughly modern.

Museum of Modern Art *11 W 53rd St between Fifth and Sixth Aves (212-708-9400/moma.org). Admission $20; free-$16 reductions. Free to everyone 4-8pm Fri.*

The Met

No time to waste—step to it and make a beeline to the Egyptian wing, on your right as you enter the building. Stay to your left and skip through roomfuls of stunning statues, jewelry, ornate coffins and elaborately carved reliefs. At the end of the long hall enter a giant room that houses the Temple of Dendur, the only Egyptian temple in the western hemisphere. Check out the fascinating 19th-century graffiti etched into the sandstone.

Ten minutes in, bid this little corner of Egypt farewell. Since much of the American wing is closed until spring 2009 (a selection of paintings from this section can currently be seen in the 19th-century European galleries), backtrack to the Great Hall. Head to the right of the main stairway and take a detour into the Arms and Armor Gallery to ponder the heavy metal.

Next, proceed to the medieval art room. Don't give the enormous choir screen a second glance and zip through the door on your left. Keep your eyes peeled for a statue of Perseus with the head of Medusa. Just beyond Perseus (the curious might want to steal a quick glance back at his handsome bum), you'll come upon the elevator. If it's May through October, ride up to the roof garden. Skip the wine bar (or you'll be here all day) and instead take a moment to drink in the stunning view of Central Park. You've got 13 minutes left.

Head back to the first floor, walk a few steps to the right, and ride another elevator to the second. Glide past a hodge-podge of 19th-century European goodies, including

MoMA

works by Renoir, Degas and a lovely collection of sculptures by Rodin. Hang a sharp left and dash past Cypriot pottery and sculptures. Don't trip! When you get to the balcony overlooking the main entrance look for the stairs down to the main floor. Three minutes to go.

For a dazzling finale, take a right into the new Greek and Roman Galleries. Pass through the Greek Sculpture Court and pause in front of the huge 300BC marble column from the Temple of Artemis, before admiring two larger-than-life statues of Hercules in the light-suffused atrium.

It's over. Catch your breath outside on the grand steps overlooking Fifth Avenue. Phew.

Metropolitan Museum of Art *1000 Fifth Ave at 82nd St (212-535-7710/metmuseum.org). Admission suggested donation $12; free-$7 reductions.*

American Museum of Natural History

The action starts the minute you walk into the main lobby, but our tour officially starts on the fourth floor. So be quick and hop the elevator to the right of the African Mammals Hall.

Nothing says *Jurassic Park* like a great big Tyrannosaurus rex staring down at you. Take a moment to appreciate your puniness. Good. Breeze around the hall to have a look at this awesome collection of dino fossils. Then zoom right back to the elevator and head back down to the first floor.

Go to your right and make your way into the North American Mammals Hall. Here you can get up close and personal to a pair of Alaskan brown bears, say "Hi" to some moose and tread lightly past the mountain lions. Exit into the lobby and bear to your right into the Hall of Biodiversity. That's 16 minutes gone already—quicken the pace.

Passing under a giant squid, plunge into the Hall of Ocean Life. Behold another behemoth: a 94-foot-long blue whale. The 21,000-pound model, based on a female found in 1925, is sculpted in fiberglass and polyurethane. Now go float past all the fish.

With eight minutes to go, leave the marine life in your wake and take a quick tour of the Dzanga-Sangha rainforest of the Central African Republic. See if you can catch a glimpse of a passing elephant through the trees.

It's time for something a little more out of this world. Head back into the main lobby of the first floor, pass through the Hall of Planet Earth, make the first left and enter the Hall of the Universe. Check out the impressive metallic iron meteorite: Weighing over 15.5 tons, this is the largest meteorite ever found in the United States. While you're here, find out what you weigh on the surface of various celestial bodies.

That's it, 30 minutes up. Come back down to earth and land in the Planetarium shop where you can reward your inner geek with a splurge on something spacey.

American Museum of Natural History/Rose Center for Earth & Space *Central Park West at 79th St (212-769-5100/amnh.org). Admission suggested donation $13; free-$10 reductions.*

519-522

Smoke in comfort in New York's puff-friendly bars

Snag that lighter and those cigs, you nicotine fiend, and follow the smoke clouds to Larry Lawrence (295 Grand St between Havemeyer and Roebling Sts, Williamsburg, Brooklyn, 718-218-7866), a cavernous, wood-paneled room offering a glassed-in upstairs alcove where you can spark up while sucking Smuttynose IPA pints ($5). You can also get your cigarette buzz on at multifloor Supreme Trading (213 North 8th St between Driggs Ave and Roebling St, Williamsburg, Brooklyn, 718-599-4224). Slurp a house whiskey-and-Pabst combo ($5) in secluded booths, shoot pool, then puff on the sprawling smoking patio. Jonesin' for a Manhattan alfresco smoke? Check out model-skinny Boxcar Lounge (168 Ave B between 10th and 11th Sts, 212-473-2830), where you'll dig two-for-one, 20-ounce drafts like Sixpoint Brownstone ($6 until 10pm) and blow rings in the verdant backyard (by law, only 25 percent of the space is smoking-permitted). Wait, what's that? Raindrops! No downpour can dampen your addiction. Scurry inside smoking-allowed, sofa-strewn hookah lounge Karma (51 First Ave between 3rd and 4th Sts, 212-677-3160), order a creamy, vodka-fueled Good Karma cocktail ($10), ask for an ashtray, then puff up with impunity—from the law, at least.

523 Visit New York's oldest museum

New York's oldest museum, founded in 1804, was one of America's first cultural and educational institutions. Highlights in the vast Henry Luce III Center for the Study of American Culture include George Washington's camp cot from Valley Forge, a complete series of the extant watercolors from Audubon's magisterial *Birds of America* and the single largest collection of Tiffany lamps in the world.
New-York Historical Society *170 Central Park West between 76th and 77th Sts (212-873-3400/nyhistory.org).*

524 Get your bicycle blessed

We're not making this up. Every spring, the bicycle season kicks off with a Blessing of the Bikes at the Cathedral Church of St John the Divine (1047 Amsterdam Ave at 112th St, 212-316-7540, stjohndivine.org). Take along your two-wheeler, and try not to snigger.

525

Check out the Harleys at Kiehl's

The 150-year-old store (109 Third Ave between 13th & 14th Sts, 212-677-3171) is, surprisingly, full of vintage Harleys. They're the owner's personal obsession.

526-531
Grab Gotham's best breads

Challah at Israel Beigel Baking Co.

Arrive after dark (any night but Friday—it's Shabbes!) and get warm challah for $2.25.

372 South 4th St at Hooper St, Williamsburg, Brooklyn (718-388-4031).

Ciabatta at Mazzola Bakery

We love this neighborhood mainstay for its porous, pillowy bread, jacketed in a hearty, flour-dusted crust ($1.90).

192 Union St at Henry St, Carroll Gardens, Brooklyn (718-643-1719).

Semolina raisin-fennel bread from Amy's Bread

Studded with golden raisins and fennel seeds and coated in cornmeal, this is bread that's as good as cake ($4.50).

amysbread.com; 250 Bleecker St at Leroy St (212-675-7802); 75 Ninth Ave between 15th and 16th Sts (212-462-4338); 672 Ninth Ave between 46th and 47th Sts (212-977-2670).

Everything bagel at Absolute Bagels

This family-run racket's everything bagel with scallion cream cheese? Don't mess around: Get the baker's dozen for $9.

2788 Broadway between 107th and 108th Sts (212-932-2052).

Croissants at Patisserie Claude

It tastes like butter, butter… and more butter in these delicious croissants ($1.70), which are made fresh daily.

187 W 4th St between Barrow and Jones Sts (212-255-5911).

Apricot-hazelnut parisienne at Silver Moon Bakery

A toothsome white-and-rye-flour flute ($4.25) gets an extra dose of goodness from hazelnuts and dried apricots. Subtle yet substantial, it's perfect for soaking up a café au lait.

2740 Broadway at 105 St (212-866-4717).

532 Mosey on down to Morris-Jumel Mansion

Built in 1765, Manhattan's only surviving pre-Revolutionary manse was originally the heart of a 130-acre estate that stretched from river to river (on the grounds, a stone marker points south with the legend "new york, 11 miles"). George Washington planned the Battle of Harlem Heights here in 1776, after the Brit colonel Roger Morris moved out. The handsome 18th-century Palladian-style villa offers fantastic views. Its former driveway is now Sylvan Terrace, which boasts the single largest continuous stretch (one block in total) of old wooden houses in all of Manhattan.

Morris-Jumel Mansion *65 Jumel Terrace between 160th and 162nd Sts (212-923-8008/ morrisjumel.org).*

533 Ride the Bronx Culture Trolley

The trolley in question is a replica of an early 20th-century trolley that shuttles you (for free!) around a whole host of galleries and performing arts venues across the Bronx. It also takes riders to the Artisans Marketplace, a giant craft fair that sells all manner of attractive handmade wares. Catch the trolley on the first Wednesday of the month (Feb-Aug and Oct-Dec) at 5:30pm, 6:30pm and 7:30pm from the Longwood Art Gallery at the Hostos Center for the Arts & Culture (450 Grand Concourse, Bronx). Visit bronxarts.org for a full schedule of seasonal events.

534 Visit the Bartow-Pell Mansion Museum

Operating as a museum since back in 1946, this impressive estate dates from 1654, when Thomas Pell bought the land from the Siwonay Indians. It was Robert Bartow, publisher and descendant of Pell, who added the Grecian-style stone mansion. Admission is $5 ($3 seniors).

Bartow-Pell Mansion Museum *895 Shore Rd North at Pelham Bay Pk (718-885-1461/ bartowpellmansionmuseum.org).*

535 *Experience the Cherry Blossom Festival*

Spring has its rites, even in the concrete jungle, and one of the more gorgeous ones is the Sakura Matsuri (Cherry Blossom Festival). This is the annual Japanese celebration of the cherry blossom (that country's national flower) and thus the arrival of spring. Each year, the Brooklyn Botanic Garden (1000 Washington Ave, Brooklyn, 718-623-7200, bbg.org), home to more than 200 frothy cherry trees, rejoices through April with the month-long *hanami* (cherry blossom-viewing season). Celebrations culminate with a festival of traditional taiko drumming and flute playing, tea ceremonies, flower-arranging, and the serving of an assortment of Japanese foods (usually on the last weekend of April or the first of May).

536

Listen to a free performance by Juilliard students

Inside the the bamboo-and-light-filled atrium of 180 Maiden Lane (180 Maiden Ln between Front and South Sts, 212-769-7406, juilliard.edu), catch a free hour-long concert by Juilliard students and alums on Tuesdays at 12:30pm. Some performances are by groups, some by soloists—all are exquisite.

537

Nosh while the kids play

Some pioneering lunch spots have figured out that if you give kids a place to play, their moms will show up in droves. Williamsburg's Mamalú Play & Munch Ground (232 North 12th St between Driggs and Union Aves, Brooklyn, 718-486-6312, mamalunyc.com) has an 800-square-foot play area, weekly toddler classes, organic baby food and Wi-Fi—not to mention tasty sandwiches and salads. Hopscotch Cafe (137 Ave A between E 9th St and St. Marks Pl, 212-529-2233, myspace.com/altdotcoffee) has a small playroom for tiny toddlers and sells kid fare like yogurt and juice boxes.

538 Churn butter at Lefferts Historic House

Located near the Prospect Park Zoo, this lovely 18th-century farmhouse once sheltered Dutch settlers and now helps to teach local history through its ongoing exhibit. Visitors can examine cooking tools in a Dutch kitchen, explore a Native American shelter, and try their hand at traditional farm activities such as sewing, churning butter and making candles.

Lefferts Historic House Museum *Prospect Park, Flatbush Ave at Empire Blvd, Brooklyn (718-789-2822/prospectpark.org).*

539 Shop underground at Nom de Guerre... if you can find it

Fitting in nicely with its revolutionary name, this upscale streetwear label's NoHo flagship is designed to resemble a bunker—albeit one where graphic T-shirts (around $50-$60) adorn white-painted walls. The average shopper would have to be sleuth-level perceptive to spot the faded stencil on the sidewalk in front of the forbidding, caged metal staircase that leads down to the store. A design collective founded by four New Yorkers, this understated label has a rugged look, encompassing upscale denim (around $230), Western-styled shirts, classic pullovers and collaborations with iconic outerwear company Mackintosh.

Nom de Guerre *640 Broadway at Bleecker St (212-253-2891/nomdeguerre.net).*

540 Catch Woody at Café Carlyle

This elegant boite in The Carlyle hotel, with its airy murals by Marcel Vertes, is the epitome of sophisticated New York chic, attracting such top-level singers as Eartha Kitt, Barbara Cook and Judy Collins. Woody Allen often plays clarinet with Eddie Davis and his New Orleans Jazz Band on Monday nights (call ahead to confirm). Don't dress casually—embrace the high life. The cover varies, but is usually $50-$125 (sometimes with compulsory dinner).

Café Carlyle *The Carlyle, 35 E 76th St at Madison Ave (212-744-1600/thecarlyle.com).*

A few of my favorite things

541-545

Race Taylor, DJ at 95.5 WPLJ-FM

Walking along Mulberry St in Little Italy is great in the summer. It's closed to cars and red, green and white lights and streamers hang above you. You can eat hot pasta, drink red wine and finish it all off with cold gelato—it's all straight out of *The Godfather.*

I love playing golf in the Bronx at the Van Cortland Park Golf Course (Van Cortland Ave South and Bailey Ave, Bronx, 718-543-4595). It's the country's oldest course, and every hole is beautiful and unique. Watching my ball hang in the air, I can almost hear the whispers of golfers past like Willie Mays, Babe Ruth and Sidney Poitier.

Belvedere Castle in Central Park is amazing. It's an old-fashioned castle right in the middle of the modern world. Anyone with interest in science or history should see it.

The Bohemian Hall & Beer Garden (29 24th Ave, Astoria, 718-274-4925, bohemianhall.com) is fantastic. You can sit down at any table on any night in the summer and you'll meet ten new thirsty friends. Beer, a garden... how can you go wrong?

Getting frozen ice is a must in the summer. You can find it on any city street corner with a frozen ice cart. My kids love it. Who knew $1 and a dixie cup full of frozen sugar water could bring so much joy?

546

Drink on the roof at 230 Fifth

Crowning a dreary Flatiron office complex, 230 Fifth (230 Fifth Ave between 26th and 27th Sts, 212-725-4300, 230-fifth.com) is a massive rooftop bar that offers stunning views of the Empire State, MetLife and Chrysler Buildings—and breathtaking views of the hordes of prowling hotties who've made it past the long, snaking lines outside. You'll find the door policy remarkably lenient (at 22,000 square feet, quantity over quality is the abiding theme—and they really pack them in). Just don't wear flip-flops.

547

Watch Asian film at The ImaginAsian

Since having been rechristened in 2004, this 300-seat movie palace has faithfully devoted itself to all things Asian or Asian-American. Typical fare includes jolting J-horror freak-outs, cutting-edge Korean dramas and the latest dance moves bustin' outta Bollywood. Tickets are $10 ($7 seniors and students).
The ImaginAsian *239 E 59th St between Second and Third Aves (212-371-6682/ theimaginasian.com).*

Make couscous the main event at La Maison du Couscous

Here, your usual side dish—with buttery grains of pasta, plump merguez sausage, seven vegetables, and falling-off-the-bone chicken and lamb—earns the right to be called "Couscous Royale."
La Maison du Couscous *484 77th St between Fourth and Fifth Aves, Bay Ridge, Brooklyn (718-921-2400).*

549

Enjoy opera on tap

Since 2005, a group of open-throated upstarts called Opera On Tap (operaontap.com) has been spreading the word of *Carmen* to a younger-minded crowd. How? By way of freeform shows (the singers barely rehearse, often improvise, and usually imbibe) in bars around the city, including a regular slot at Freddy's Bar and Backroom (485 Dean St at Sixth Ave, Prospect Heights, Brooklyn, 718-622-7035, freddysbackroom.com). The seemingly odd pairing of beer and baritones has been an unmitigated success, ushering in packed houses and helping founder (and lyric soprano) Anne Ricci to recruit an OOT

roster that now boasts more than 30 members. "I love the idea of bringing [opera] to normal people so they can experience the beauty of it," says Freddy's manager Donald O'Finn. "It's like bringing a Picasso to a small community gallery."

Party like a Motherfucker!

Roaming, polysexual trash fest Motherfucker—which has veteran NY-scenesters Justine D, Michael T, Georgie Seville and Johnny T at the helm—is generally considered the best bash going on in town right now. Held on the eves of major holidays at an array of the city's biggest nightspots, it features Justine, Michael and guests spinning an anarchic mix of sleazed-out electro, new wave and disco for the most utterly deviant menagerie of club freaks that you're likely to come across. In many ways, it's a throwback to the glory days of New York's once-decadent clubbing scene. See motherfuckernyc.com for details of upcoming parties.

551

Get a tat at New York Adorned...

Proprietor Lori Leven hires world-class tattoo artists to wield needles at her eight-year-old gothic-elegant establishment. Those with low pain thresholds can try gentler decorations such as henna tattoos, weirdly ethereal white-gold cluster earrings (crafted by Leven) or pieces by emerging body-jewelry designers.
New York Adorned *47 Second Ave between Second and Third Sts (212-473-0007/nyadorned.com).*

552

...or at Venus Modern Body Arts

Venus has been tattooing and piercing New Yorkers since 1992—before body art became de rigueur. The shop also offers an enormous selection of jewelry, so you can put diamonds in your navel and platinum in your tongue.
Venus Modern Body Arts *199 E 4th St between Aves A and B (212-473-1954).*

553 Kayak on the Hudson

So long as you know how to swim and show up in a bathing suit or shorts, the Downtown Boathouse (646-613-0740, downtownboathouse.org) will furnish you with a kayak, lifejacket, and paddle, and turn you loose in one of its enclosed bay areas on the Hudson for twenty minutes. There's no fee; just turn up from about mid May to mid October. Downtown Boathouse operates three locations: Pier 40 at Houston Street on the Hudson River (9am-6pm Sat, Sun); Pier 96, Clinton Cove at 56th Street and the Hudson River (9am-6pm Sat, Sun; also mid June-early Sept 5-7pm Mon-Fri); and at Riverside Park and 72nd Street (10am-5pm Sat, Sun).

554-559 *Find Australia in NYC*

Crocodile Dundee came and went, but Down Under dining is slowly but surely gaining a bit of traction on the city's culinary landscape. Here are some Aussie faves.

Eight Mile Creek

This slim, eight-year-old Nolita eatery has become popular with expats and New Yorkers for its authentic Australian ingredients (emu carpaccio, kanga skewers, rack of kiwi lamb), friendly service, and impressive, affordable regional beer and wine selection, including hard-to-find brews like Cooper's Ale and James Boag's premium lager. The lively Creek Bar downstairs doesn't hurt the approval rating either—what with its jukebox and regular, rowdy screenings of cricket, rugby and Aussie-rules football.
240 Mulberry St between Prince and Spring Sts (212-431-4635/eightmilecreek.com).

Bondi Road

Photos of Sydney's Bondi Beach, a projection screen playing movies of wave riders and a beach-style, fish-centric menu make the surfer theme obvious at this breezy nook. The laidback vibe continues with D.I.Y. ordering (diners pencil in their picks) and Aussie waitresses whose cheerful service is as refreshing as the bar's Bloody Mary oyster shooters, fueled with pepper-infused vodka.
153 Rivington St between Clinton and Suffolk Sts (212-253-5311/bondiroad.com).

Wombat

A no-frills space with stark metal tables and black walls, Wombat looks less like a restaurant than a bar. But the Aussie food, from chef Anders Goldkuhl (Patois, Caviar Russe), transcends the surroundings. You'll get such top tucker as an appetizer of rare, soy-cured venison medallions and crispy buckwheat fritters, perhaps followed by the chicken Wellington "Floater," a delectable piece of white meat poached in olive oil, wrapped in flaky puff pastry.
613 Grand St between Leonard and Lorimer Sts, Williamsburg, Brooklyn (718-218-7077/ thewombatbar.com).

Tuck Shop

Aussie transplants to New York seem to be on a never-ending quest to uncover authentic meat pies. They'll find them at Tuck Shop, an unpretentious Down Under café. The pies here, filled with minced beef, chicken or tofu, make an excellent midday snack or late-night booze sponge. Meat lovers can add a sausage roll, a light pastry shell filled with pork and sage. The grub is cheap enough that you can top off any meal with the requisite dessert— sticky-date pudding or a lamington, a tasty jelly-filled sponge cake rolled in chocolate and sprinkled with coconut.
68 E 1st St between First and Second Aves (212-979-5200/tuckshopnyc.com).

The Sunburnt Cow

The Sunburnt Cow puts together plates loaded up with inventive comfort food from Down Under. Peppery kangaroo sausage on buttery smashed potatoes and caramelized onions puts an Aussie twist on bangers and mash. Other highlights include emu burgers, barramundi and fish-and-chips battered with Coopers beer. The laid-back expat staff is eager to ply all visitors with Moo Juice, potent, fruity cocktails served in baby bottles.
137 Ave C between 8th and 9th Sts (212-529-0005/ thesunburntcow.com).

Sheep Station

At this Australian pub, with its lacquered wooden floors and tin-can lights, locals gobble down Aussie eats like burgers topped with beets, pineapples and fried eggs, but the real lure to the place is the international beer: New Zealand's Steinlager is on tap, as is California's Lagunitas IPA. Brews are dispensed in small, medium and large, helping you to pick a properly sized poison during happy hour (4-7pm Mon-Fri).
149 Fourth Ave at Douglass St, Park Slope, Brooklyn (718-857-4337/sheepstation.net).

560 Shop beneath street level

A chalkboard set next to an open metal hatch in the sidewalk in front of a nondescript hair salon is the only marker for the new subterranean outpost of this idiosyncratic menswear label. Chuck Guarino and Ryan Turner launched THECAST with a collection of artful T-shirts in 2004; at $40, these are still central to a collection that spans well-cut jeans in premium denim from one of South Carolina's oldest mills, dapper suits and soft, silk-lined leather biker jackets (from $375).

The space, with its raw concrete floors and crumbling brick ceiling, is about as far from a commercial showroom as you can get—instead of white minimalism, it's an anarchic jumble of Victorian-style wallpaper, candelabras and such gothic knick-knacks as a human skull (bought on eBay), mounted game trophies and a stuffed rattlesnake. Hardback copies of Dickens and Jules Verne are interspersed with the accessories, which include a 24-karat gold-plated, black-diamond-inlaid human jaw ashtray taken from a cast of the skull mentioned above ($3,250) and a snake's head tie bolo (from $650 for the silver-plated version), both made in collaboration with Derrick Cruz of cult line Black Sheep & Prodigal Sons.

"Smarter consumers don't want something everyone else has been wearing," says Guarino. "When they find places like this, they feel they've found their secret spot." Despite the macabre wares, the atmosphere is welcoming and unpretentious. Yet a visit is not without risk: Take care on exiting the hatch. "People are always banging their head," warns Guarino.
THECAST *119 Ludlow St, lower level (212-228-2020/thecast.com).*

Tuck Shop

561 Buy a New York scent at Bond No.9

Custom-blended scents that pay olfactory homage to New York City—Wall Street, Nouveau Bowery, New Harlem—can be purchased from this Manhattan perfumery (various locations; bondno9.com). Don't worry, there's no Chinatown Sidewalk.

562
Recite lines at Movieoke

Need to embrace your inner Travis Bickle or Mommie Dearest? Unfinished business with the Wicked Witch of the West? Re-enact your favorite movie scenes during movieoke (karaoke with movies instead of music) at The Den of Cin (44 Avenue A, 212-254-0800), every Wednesday from 9pm. Just pick your scene from the wide selection of DVDs, go up on stage in front of the screen, and mimic or reinterpret your role. There are subtitles to help you and a beer-guzzling audience to let you know exactly how good you are.

563 Play mini-golf

Any golfer worth their checkered knickers will tell you that putting is just as important as hitting the ball long off the tee. Mini-golf helped the heavy-handed Happy Gilmore learn to putt, and it can also help you become a regular Hale Irwin. With the closure of Coney Island's Batting Range & Go-Kart City, Randalls Island Golf Center (212-427-5689, randallsislandgolf.com) is home to the only decent local mini-golf tracks. Its two 18-hole courses ($4-$6) offer varying degrees of difficulty, with plenty of undulations and obstacles to help golfers hone their short game.

564 Laze around at Wave Hill House

This 28-acre former estate—overlooking the Hudson River at Wave Hill—once housed Mark Twain, Teddy Roosevelt and conductor Arturo Toscanini (at different times, natch). It's now a spectacular nature preserve and conservation center, where you can see art exhibits and dance and music performances. Admission is $4, unless you cleverly show up on Tuesday (all day) or Saturday (morning), when it's free.
Wave Hill House *W 249th St at Independence Ave, Bronx (718-549-3200/wavehill.org).*

565 Order mutton chop at Keens

Which New York era would you like to visit? The days of Tammany Hall, when cigar-smoking fat cats exchanged favors over mammoth cuts of meat and cold martinis? Earlier? How about a time when Sheep Meadow was an accurate description, and peasants cooked the unfortunate of the flocks over open fires across from what's now Tavern on the Green? Or what about earlier still—back to the period when nomadic hunters prowled what would later be called Manhattan, feasting on the haunches of deer? All of these eras and more can be imagined when you order Keens Steakhouse's famous mutton chop entrée—a glistening 26-ounce hunk of gamy flesh that is served with two strips of fat hanging from it like wings. The interior of this 123-year-old chop house is no less evocative, with its dark-wood paneling, collection of English pipes and private dining rooms that are as suitable for cutting a deal as they are for cutting loose the caveman within.
Keens Steakhouse *72 West 36th St between Fifth and Sixth Aves (212-947-3636/keens.com).*

566-570 Search out secret playgrounds

We love those sprawling monkey-bar villages, but at most of them you've got to trail your kid from the swings to the slide to the sprinklers to make sure they don't do a back flip off the fort ladder or start up a conversation with that guy in the trench coat. So skip the big ones like Harmony Playground, Hudson River Park and the Ancient Playground, and check out some of the more intimate neighborhood rec areas. Low-energy downtown moms gravitate toward the Downing Street Playground (Downing St at Sixth Ave) and the smaller toddler playground at Washington Square Park (Fifth Ave at Waverly Pl); Brooklyn Heights moms love the Harry Chapin Playground (Columbia Heights at Middagh St) for its sprinkler in the summer and manageable size. Upper West Side moms swear by Tecumseh Playground (Amsterdam Ave at W 77th St) and Hippo Playground (Riverside Drive at W 91st St).

571 Check out the Schomburg collection of black literature

An extraordinary trove of vintage literature and historical memorabilia relating to black culture and the African diaspora is housed in this West Harlem institution, founded in 1926 by its curator, the bibliophile Arturo Alfonso Schomburg. The center also hosts jazz concerts, film series, lectures and tours. Admission is free.
Schomburg Center for Research in Black Culture *515 Malcolm X Blvd (Lenox Ave) at 135th St (212-491-2200).*

572 Remind yourself which dogs rule West Village

Everybody knows about the dogs at Gray's Papaya—your senile aunt, out-of-towners, little green moon men—so why fixate? Why not buck the trend and head elsewhere? Don't get fooled: In this West Village Papaya war, there is but one tube-steak titan. Sure Papaya King at 14th and Seventh has great toppings, but alas, they do not conceal an inferior dog; Papaya Dog, on 4th Street and Sixth, comes closer. Slushes too. But get your teeth into the Recession Special—two franks and a 14-ounce drink for $3.50, including unlimited toppings—at one of three branches of Gray's Papaya (402 Sixth Ave at 8th St, 212-260-3532; 539 Eighth Ave at 37th St, 212-904-1588; 2090 Broadway at 72nd St, 212-799-0243) and you know you've got the best: flavorful, slightly charred, just perfect. But you can pass on the papaya drink.

573 See Spanish art

The Hispanic Society in Washington Heights has the largest assemblage of Spanish art and manuscripts outside of Spain itself. The quality is as high as the quantity is impressive. Look out for two portraits by Goya and the lobby's bas-relief of Don Quixote. The collection is dominated by religious artefacts, including 16th-century tombs brought here from the monastery of San Francisco in Cuéllar, Spain. Also on display are decorative art objects and thousands of black-and-white photographs that document life in Spain and Latin America from the mid 19th century to the present. Admission is free, but bear in mind that the library is closed on Sundays and Mondays.

Hispanic Society of America *Audubon Terrace, Broadway between 155th and 156th Sts (212-926-2234/hispanicsociety.org).*

574 Go for the cold stuff at the Brooklyn Ice Cream Factory

Manhattan views and proximity to Empire-Fulton Ferry State Park aren't the only draws for this old-fashioned parlor and longtime *Time Out* favorite. The all-natural goodies are prepared on the premises, including the hot fudge (a delicious, gooey dark chocolate unlike any plain ol' syrup we've tried) and the ice cream, which is made in small batches to ensure prime quality.
Brooklyn Ice Cream Factory *2 Old Fulton St at Furman St, Dumbo, Brooklyn (718-246-3963).*

575 Step into the wonderful world of Louis Armstrong

Jazz lovers will have little choice but to make the pilgrimage to Louis Armstrong House in Queens. Bear in mind that, although this was indeed the big man's house, it was actually his wife Lucille who dealt with its day-to-day upkeep—with the end result that her decor can somewhat overshadow the legendary life of Armstrong himself. Interesting nonetheless.
Louis Armstrong House *34-56 107th St between 34th and 37th Aves, Corona, Queens (718-478-8274/satchmo.net).*

576-587 Get to know Little Odessa

A Brooklyn boardwalk may not seem like an obvious place to pick up caviar, but you'll find plenty of fish eggs (and vodka to wash it down) in this enclave of Russian émigrés, Brighton Beach—also known as Little Odessa.

As you leave the F train at Neptune Avenue, nod to famous neighbor Coney Island, but turn resolutely left as you walk down the strand to the Boardwalk on the beach. First of a series of broad, open eateries is Tatiana (3152 Brighton 6th St at the Boardwalk, 718-891-5151), a lovely spot to sit and watch the world pass by while slurping up some borscht.

Walk down Brighton 6th Street to Brighton Beach Avenue, the main artery of this far-west outpost. Underneath the clattering elevated train, you can almost forget you're not in the mother country. Far less glitzy than Tatiana and serving good, cheap fare is Varenichnaya (3086 Brighton 2nd St, 718-332-9797)—note: In Cyrillic, a "V" looks like a "B," so don't let the awning throw you off. Equally unsnazzy yet excellent is Eastern Feast (1003 Brighton Beach Ave, 718-934-9005), an Uzbek house of kebabs. Next door is the Russian idea of a Western saloon, Baltika, named for the Russian beer.

Now for the shopping. Every three steps you'll find a Caviar Kiosk (like the one at 506 Brighton Beach Ave, 718-648-1174), selling small cans of black caviar at $14.95 and only

charging $45 for a tin the size of a wheel of brie. On the other hand, if you eat at Georgian Primorski (282 Brighton Beach Ave, 718-891-3111), crêpes with red caviar only run $9.50—however, enjoying the exuberant floor show might require several bottles of vodka. Rasputin (2670 Coney Island Ave, 718-332-8111) is another good bet. You can also buy interesting pickled foodstuffs to take home at the enormous M & I International Foods (249 Brighton Beach Ave, 718-615-1011), tasting the goods in advance at the upstairs café. Other food stores on the strip range from the posh Vintage Food Corp (287 Brighton Beach Ave, 718-769-6674), where you can pick up wonderful teas and baklava, to the more pedestrian Triple A Grocery across the street, where a little old man sits out front selling honey.

For non-perishable souvenirs, look into Russian-language specialist St Petersburg Books (230 Brighton Beach Ave, 718-891-6778) or Kalinka (402 Brighton Beach Ave at 4th St, 718-743-4546), which vends items from the kitschy to the sublime, including handpainted wooden boxes. End the day where you started: By night, Tatiana morphs into a club, featuring artistes like Magdalina, "the Russian Pamela Anderson." If that doesn't convince you the Cold War is over, nothing will.

588 *See the little doggies run!*

Tompkins Square Dog Run—or First Run—
was indeed the first off-leash area in New
York City. The run (or rather, pair of runs:
Large and small dogs have separate areas)
has been hugely successful. The organizers
even host a fund-raising party each Halloween
that attracts several hundred costumed dogs
and around 2,000 spectators, drawn by the
prospect of seeing dogs dressed for bar-mitzvah
or owner and pooch in matching cowboy suits.
Dog-owners with self-respect can benefit from
First Run's affordable obedience classes ($225
for a five-week course) and expert seminars.
For more information, see dogster.org.

589 Visit the Gracie Mansion Conservancy

The green-shuttered yellow edifice, built in 1799 by Scottish merchant Archibald Gracie, was originally constructed as a country house for the wealthy businessman. Today, the stately house is the focal point of tranquil Carl Schurz Park, named in honour of a German immigrant who became a newspaper editor and US senator. In 2002, Gracie Mansion's living quarters were opened up to public tours for the first time in 60 years. The site is hugely popular with the public, and reservations are a must. Tours last 45 minutes.
Gracie Mansion Conservancy *Carl Schurz Park, 88th St at East End Ave (212-570-4751).*

590 Make use of Public Toilet No.1...

Unless politicians are involved, public restrooms don't often make headline news. But the media had a field day when the first pay toilet to open in the city since 1975 (the year they were banned in the state of New York because coin-op stalls were said to discriminate against women) received its "first flush" by officials in a special ceremony in 2008. "Public Toilet No.1," as the *Post* christened it, is located in Madison Square Park (Madison Ave between 23rd and 24th Sts), and should be followed by around 20 across the city in the next two years.

It costs 25¢ to enter the large stainless steel and tempered glass box. Although the interior is stark (the shiny metal throne has no seat, just a wide rim that can be topped with paper covers), it's reassuringly sterile—the cubicle is automatically deluged with disinfectant after each use. Color-coded buttons flush, dispense toilet paper and call for help (yellow for assistance, red for more serious trouble). Dawdlers and OCD sufferers beware: The door opens after 15 minutes. Still, the new facility comes as welcome relief for visitors looking for a midtown rest stop, as well as particular sections of the city's population.

"I've had to have to resort to peeing in bottles while on the road," taxi and limo driver Josef Mullaev told us as he exited the restroom.

591-594 ...or go in style at these other fancy public restrooms

Bryant Park
The crème de la crème of park comfort stations, with mosaic tiles and cherry-wood framed mirrors.
455 Fifth Ave at 42nd St.

Henri Bendel
This pristine powder room is your best bet on Fifth Ave.
71 Fifth Ave at 56th St.

McNally Jackson Books
When nature calls in SoHo, this WC has woodland mural wallpaper and birdsong.
50 Prince St between Lafayette and Mulberry Sts.

The Solaire
This environmentally friendly apartment building in Battery Park City houses well-maintained public restrooms.
20 River Terrace at Warren St.

595 Find out exactly what "Happened in Brooklyn"

Founded in 1863, the Brooklyn Historical Society is located in a landmark four-story Queen Anne-style building and houses numerous permanent and ongoing exhibits, including "It Happened in Brooklyn," which highlights local links to crucial moments in U.S. history. A major photo and research library—featuring historic maps and newspapers, notable family histories and archives from the area's abolitionist movement—are accessible by appointment. Don't miss the boat tours of the waterfront, which take place in summer.
Brooklyn Historical Society *128 Pierrepont St at Clinton St, Brooklyn Heights, Brooklyn (718-222-4111/brooklynhistory.org).*

596-600

Wear the kids out

If your kids are at that stage when they're too old for epic naps but too young to sit through a movie or read a book, your best bet is to let them run around like banshees at a safe, padded play space until they pass out. The Toddler Adventure Center at Chelsea Piers is a bargain at $11 per session (Pier 62, 23rd St at the Hudson River, 212-336-6500, chelseapiers.com). Check the schedule at Baby Moves in the West Village for supervised open-play hours; it's $12 a session, or free if you're signed up for a class (139 Perry St Between Greenwich and Washington Sts, 212-255-1685, babymovesnyc.com). Apple Seeds (10 W 25th St between Broadway and Sixth Ave, 212-792-7590, appleseedsny.com) and Kidville (kidville.com; four locations in the city) have luxe play spaces with state-of-the-art climbing structures and toys, but you have to buy a family membership, ranging from $395 to $995 per year, to get in the door. The ultimate in relaxation can be had at Citibabes (477 Broadway between Grand and Broome Sts, third floor, 212-334-5440, citibabes.com)—pay for a massage or facial at the on-site spa, and a babysitter will supervise your toddler in the play space for free (all you have to do is pony up for the $2,000 annual membership fee).

601

Rent a rowboat from Loeb Boathouse and go rowing in Central Park

The Boathouse is open daily from April to October, weather permitting; boat rental is $10/hour plus $30 deposit. Head out on to the lake and admire gorgeous Bow Bridge.
Loeb Boathouse *Midpark at 75th St.*

602 Visit Flushing's Hindu Temple

Dutch colonists in the Flushing area who stood up for religious freedom in the New World back in the day would be at once surprised and satisfied to see this ornate stone façade dedicated to the Hindu deity Ganesh. This was the first Hindu temple in the United States. After visiting, try the dosas at next door's tiny Dosa Hutt.
Hindu Temple Society *4557 Bowne St between Holly and 45th Aves, Flushing (718-460-8484/ nyganeshtemple.org).*

603 Pick some pumpkins

A colonial era "living museum" with 15 restored buildings, Staten Island's Historic Richmond Town (441 Clarke Ave between Richmond Rd and St Patrick's Pl, 718-351-1611, historic richmondtown.org) includes residences, public buildings and a museum. Tours are available alongside a range of activities from quilting to, yep, pumpkin-picking. Check website for seasonal opening times.

604 Order olives at Sahadi's

Chaos gets itself a good name at Sahadi's, one of the handful of indispensable Middle Eastern grocers and bakers that are located in Brooklyn Heights. The powers that be at Sahadi's like to give the impression of order (a concept that becomes laughable just as soon as the place gets busy), so they'll scoop those capers, dried fruits, nuts and coffee beans for you. Just take a number, wait your turn, and make sure not to bypass the olives. Black, green or purple, pitted or otherwise, wrinkled or smooth, briny, garlicked, Sicilian or Greek—whatever your olive fancy. These treats surely justify waiting on line with every tenth Brooklynite on a Saturday afternoon.
Sahadi's *187 Atlantic Ave between Court and Clinton Sts, Brooklyn Heights (718-624-4550/ sahadis.com).*

605-607
Soothe your soul, Seoul-style

Bliss out with a steam 'n' soak at these late-opening Korean spas.

Aura Wellness Spa
The most exciting recent addition to the NYC spa landscape, this extremely slick, high-tech expanse feels more suited to Mars than its Herald Square surroundings. Treatments (which start at $70) include a turn in the grottoes: igloo-like, crystal-studded steam rooms that glow from within a pitch-black room in the center of the spa. Following Korean-spa tradition, the place offers insanely thorough body scrubs.
49 W 33rd St between Fifth Ave and Broadway (212-695-9559/spaaura.com).

Juvenex
An unassuming Koreatown building is home to this huge, soundproof, 24-hour oasis. Shy gals take note: Nudity is encouraged in the communal areas, full body scrubs are executed in shared, barely screened-off spaces, and the spa goes unisex after 7:30pm. The facilities are impressive, though: Lolling in one of the igloo-like saunas, made from 20 tons of jade stones and infused with Chinese herbs, is said to increase the metabolic rate, to improve the circulation and to detox the body. A basic Purification Program costs $115.
25 W 32nd St, fifth floor, between Fifth Ave and Broadway (646-733-1330/juvenexspa.com).

Perfect Spa
Not in Koreatown, but equally popular with steam-and-massage devotees, this one-stop salon offers everything from pedicures to waxing in its frill-free treatment rooms. The main attraction is the super-thorough trad soap body scrub, which kicks off with a drenching from the Vichy shower (a ceiling device with eight faucet heads) and costs from $80 for 40 minutes or $145 for 70 minutes with a full-body hot apricot oil massage.
1100 Second Ave between 57th and 58th Sts (212-752-8880).

Gotham's fowl fans are sticklers for Japanese yakitori: grilled chicken skewers, served sizzling with salt or painted with sweetened soy sauce. Lately, Manhattan has seen a lot of this affordable finger food (skewers average $2). Yakitori is the star at sleek, new izakayas like Union Square's Ariyoshi (806 Broadway between 11th and 12th Sts, 212-388-1884), where diners devour juicy chicken meatballs, kawa (fatty, gooey skin crinkled onto the skewer in accordionlike folds) and, for hale eaters, salted chicken hearts. Likewise, midtown's Yakitori Totto (251 W 55th St between Broadway and Eighth Ave, 212-245-4555) celebrates organic chicken's beak-to-tail grandeur (innards included). Amid the smoke plumes, chefs meticulously grill gizzards and knee bones alongside more conventional victuals like chicken breasts with wasabi, delivered piecemeal in a cavalcade of two-bite portions. Totto's avian-temple sibling, Yakitori Torys (248 E 52nd St between Second and Third Aves, 212-813-1800), serves Totto's skewers, but also gives fowl the ceviche treatment. Dime-thin slices of "sashimi" marinate in a bath of salmonella-killing citrus and sesame oil, imbuing firm, pink flesh with eye-opening astringency. Don't be chicken and deprive yourself of poultry in its rarest form.

611 Feel sheepish at Philipsburg Manor

Laraine Perri takes the kids to watch master barbers at work.

Your kid may love her Uggs, but she probably doesn't know how they came to be so cozy. No need to book a trip to Australia for the revelation—it can be found about 40 minutes from midtown. Sleepy Hollow's Philipsburg Manor (admission $12, children free-$6) is the oldest working farm in the metropolitan area and a picturesque historic jewel. Clichés be damned: Entering the compound is like stepping back in time. One minute you're on a typical suburban-Westchester street. The next, you've crossed a wooden bridge and are standing in front of a working 18th-century mill, an idyllic vista with a stone manor house, gabled barn and 25 bucolic acres. My son, Timothy, was three years old when we first visited Philipsburg Manor. Although he was too young to take an interest in the workings of a gristmill, his delight in jumping into a pile of hay was off the chart—and all my husband and I needed to feel glad we'd made the trip.

Since that visit, we return every April for the Sheep-to-Shawl festival (generally on a Saturday and Sunday at the end of the month, call for details), during which workers in period garb relieve sheep of their bulky winter coats by hand. Little ones can't help with the shearing, but since Sheep-to-Shawl covers the entire process of making woolen cloth, kids can participate in many of the activities that follow. Timothy was four when he first helped with the "picking and carding" of the wool, which entails removing bits of straw and combing the bunched fleece to straighten it. Older children can spin and dye the yarn, and then weave it into cloth.

Spring is also birthing season: Last year saw the arrival of a dozen lambs, and my son got a real kick out of watching them frolic. Kids also can meet Josh and Jake—not twins from a Park Slope pre-school, but a pair of three-year-old oxen. Children and adults alike will marvel at the herding abilities of Scottish border collies and the way the water-powered mill grinds grain into flour. If your tween overloads on pastoral fare, let him or her try stilt-walking—a slice of recreational life from a definitively pre-Wii era.

Philipsburg's charms are hardly limited to festival days. Interactive tours of the newly renovated 1680 manor house include a stop at the "touch room," where kids can handle everything from bells and brooms to fur pelts and sugarcane; Timothy especially enjoyed wielding the baking utensils in the open-hearth kitchen. Visitors also can explore the mill, barn and slaves' garden. Originally a vegetable patch for the Africans enslaved on the farm, the slaves' garden now grows scarlet runner beans, black-eyed peas, sweet potatoes and more for the cooking demonstrations held in the manor house. Costumed tour guides tell stories of the site's history as a farming and trading center, as well as sharing illuminating facts about slavery in colonial New York.

Farm life fuels a farmer-worthy appetite; Timothy was ravenous after the morning's activities. Break for lunch at the site's new Mint Café. No ordinary museum cafeteria, the café is operated by Mint Premium Foods, a specialty market and caterer in nearby Tarrytown. Choices such as the antibiotic-free prosciutto and Grana Padano panini or a salad of Japanese calamari, seaweed, lemongrass and ginger (both $8.50) are solidly 21st century but so scrumptious you'll pardon the anachronism. Options for young gourmands abound—the panino with all-natural turkey, brie and apple ($8.50) is a luxe spin on a kid classic. You're also welcome to BYO: Picnic tables overlook the Pocantico River and mill.

Don't head home before stopping at the gift shop. The selection includes items you'd never find at Toys "R" Us: Think hand-carved wood flutes modeled on those the enslaved Africans fashioned for themselves, and colonial games such as nine pins. Pick up a bag of cornmeal ground at the gristmill, and your farm-fresh tyke can have a "Mill-to-Muffin" experience back in your big-city kitchen.

Philipsburg Manor *381 N Broadway, Sleepy Hollow (914-631-8200 Mon-Fri/914-631-3992 Sat, Sun/hudsonvalley.org).*

612-615

Watch "football" with expats in New York's soccer bars

Whether you prefer Juventus or Spurs, Barcelona or Celtic, here are a few sure spots for watching your team play live.

Brass Monkey

With its beautiful wooden booths, exposed brick walls and a menu featuring Irish stew and bangers and mash, there's arguably no other place in the city that makes you feel more like you're watching "footie" in a London pub. Plus the Meatpacking District location puts you in prime shopping position post-game— assuming thoe four pints of Boddingtons haven't gone to your legs.
55 Little West 12 St (212-675-6686/ brassmonkeynyc.com).

11th Street Bar

The official home of the Liverpool FC New York Supporters Club, this beautiful bar is always jam-slammed with city-dwellers sporting red shirts. Even if you don't support the team, it's worth stopping in to grab a beer and watch a match with the jovial, soccer-loving crowd. You might want to be wary, though, of wearing blue on the day Liverpool play local rivals Everton in the infamous "Merseyside derby."
510 E 11th St (212-982-3929/11thstbar.com).

Floyd

True, with its over-sized couches and indoor bocce court, Floyd gives off a laid-back, playful vibe when you first walk in. But don't be fooled into thinking it's all fun and games come kickoff—especially when Tottenham take the pitch. The Brooklyn bar is the official home of the New York Tottenham Hotspur Supporter's Club and you'll be made quite aware of this when you try to get a beer and are accosted by Spurs fans who want to know one thing only: Do you support Spurs? (We recommend answering in the affirmative.)
131 Atlantic Ave between Clinton and Henry Sts, Cobble Hill, Brooklyn (718-858-5810/floydny.com).

Nevada Smith's

Apparently "the planet's most famous live football venue" (we think administrators at the Nou Camp might have something to say about that), Nevada Smith's is Mecca for NY soccer fans. There's not a direction you can look without seeing a TV showing anything from EPL, La Liga and Bundesliga to American college soccer. Just be prepared to pay a $20 cover and to stand—the bar gets pretty packed.
74 Third Ave between 11th and 12th Sts (212-982-2591/nevadasmiths.net).

616

Discover Snug Harbor's Secret Garden

The Staten Island Botanical Garden in Snug Harbor boasts more than 20 themed gardens, from the White Garden (based on Vita Sackville-West's creation at England's Sissinghurst Castle) to the tranquil, pavilion-lined Chinese Scholar's Garden. Our favorite of all these wonderful places, however, is the delightful Secret Garden, complete with its child-size castle, a maze and a secluded walled garden. The Secret Garden is open dawn to dusk daily, and admission is free to everyone.
Staten Island Botanical Garden *Snug Harbor Cultural Center, Building H (718-273-8200/ sibg.org).*

617

Munch the best movie theater popcorn in NY

Organic kernels at the IFC Center (323 Sixth Ave between Third and Fourth Sts, 212-924-7771) are popped in canola oil, lightly salted and bathed in real melted butter. Not in the mood for a movie? Top a pot off with a shake of Old Bay seasoning and be on your way— you don't have to be a ticket-holder to score this $4.75 snack.

618

Order the custom-made stationery from Bowne & Co

An authentic re-creation of the original 1875 print shop, Bowne & Co Stationers (211 Water St between Beekman and Fulton Sts, 212-748-8651) not only looks the part—with all those vintage gaslights and its carved mahogany shelving—but this South Street Seaport landmark acts it too. Printing presses and type settings manufactured between 1844 and 1901 are used to create fine-art prints, stationery (with custom-order letterheads) and wedding invitations.

A few of my favorite things

619-623

Dave Martin, executive chef

MoMA (11 West 53 St between Fifth and Sixth Aves, 212-708-9400, moma.org) has a great program, beloved of those in the know, called "Target Free Friday Nights," where you can get in for free from 4pm to 8pm. I usually have some great wine and snacks at the bar at MoMA's restaurant, The Modern (themodernnyc.com), then roll over and wait in line for a free night at the museum. Doesn't get better than that. **Having brunch at The View restaurant at the Marriott Marquis (1535 Broadway, 212-398-1900) is amazing. Yes, it's a hotel chain, but sitting on the 48th floor overlooking the city is great for tourists and locals alike. The restaurant actually spins, so you get a real bird's-eye view of the city. Food is in the old-school buffet-** brunch style (not half bad, with dishes like large Thai water prawns and jumbo sea scallops) and there's all-you-can-drink Cava—a steal at $60 per person.
On my occasional day off, I like to head down to the West Village and have a late lunch, maybe a pulled-pork sandwich at Blue Ribbon Bakery (35 Downing St, 212-337-0404, blueribbonrestaurants.com), which is always bustling with energy. Afterwards, I head across the street to their Downing Street Wine Bar (34 Downing St, 212-691-0404) for some fun wine flights and a tasty cheese plate that comes with killer Mexican honey.
I know that the cupcake thing has been talked about to death over the last couple of years, but I have to be honest, I've tried them all over the country and Billy's Bakery (184 9th Ave, 212-647-9956, billysbakery nyc.com) wins my cupcake race hands down. They do other baked goods, too— the banana cake with cream-cheese frosting is yummy.
Down in Tribeca, I frequent Landmarc (179 W Broadway between Leonard and Worth Sts, 212-343-3883, landmarc-restaurant.com), which has incredible wine prices that you won't find anywhere else. They have another location in the Time Warner building (10 Columbus Circle, 3rd floor, 212-823-6123), but the original location definitely has more of a comfy vibe. The global wine list has so many choices; I'm always a sucker for the Oregon pinots.

Dave Martin is executive chef at Crave on 42nd, 650 W 42nd St between 11th and 12th Aves (212-564-9588/craveon42nd.com).

624-625

Suck in the smells of Curry Row

Madhur Jaffrey is no fan of the inauthentic, "generalized curry" on East 6th. But Curry Row is still a must-see—and must-smell. Barkers lure diners into jewel-box eateries with begging eyes and the puissant promise of cardamom and curry. Rent hikes have eradicated many of the originals, but those that remain—we've had good feeds at Taj Mahal (318 E 6th St between First and Second Aves, 212-529-2217) and Banjara (97 First Ave at 6th St, 212-477-5956)—stay true to the raga-bacchanalian spirit of the place.

626

Shop secondhand at Beacon's Closet

At some vintage boutiques prices come close to those at major fashion labels. Not so at this bustling Brooklyn favorite, where not only are the prices great, but so is the Williamsburg-appropriate clothing selection—from iconic T-shirts and party dresses to sneakers, leathers and denim, alongside some second-hand CDs. Beacon's Closet (beaconscloset.com) has two locations, one in Williamsburg (88 North 11th St between Berry St and Wythe Ave, 718-486-0816) and the other in Park Slope (220 Fifth Ave between President and Union Sts, 718-230-1630).

627

Play chess in Washington Square Park

The old stone tables in the park's southwest corner are popular with chessmen honing their game. Amateurs and five-bucks-a-game hustlers still gather to take on all-comers in what they call "the snake pit."

628

Wonder at New York City Waterfalls

Until mid October 2008, you won't have to make the trek up to Niagara to see spectacular cascades. New York is gaining four monumental (from 90 to 120 feet high) waterfall installations. One is at Pier 35 in Lower Manhattan, another by the Brooklyn anchorage of the Brooklyn Bridge, a third between Piers 4 and 5 in Brooklyn and the fourth on the north shore of Governors Island. Commissioned by the Public Art Fund, they're the creation of Danish artist Olafur Eliasson, known for works inspired by natural elements: His 2003 *Weather Project* for London's Tate Modern transformed the echoing Turbine Hall into a sultry microclimate with a huge 'sun' made from 200 lamps. *The New York City Waterfalls* will operate betweem 7am and 10pm each day, illuminated after sunset. Viewed by land or boat, they'll provide a dramatic contrast with the urban landscape. Circle Line Downtown (866-925-4631, circle linedowntown.com) is offering dedicated 30-minute boat trips from South Street Seaport for $10, and the free Governors Island and Staten Island ferries will also provide good vantage points. See www.nycwaterfalls.org for more information.

629

Sup rye whiskey

Once a favorite spirit of the (original) speakeasy set, rye whiskey is experiencing a comeback. East Village bar Death+Co. (433 E 6th St between Ave A and First Ave, 212-388-0882) has a collection of nearly a dozen varieties (some, like the Hirsch 21-year-old, go for over $20 a shot). Barkeep Philip Ward also mixes the hard stuff in inventive cocktails, like the Monongahela Mule—Old Overholt rye with fresh lemon juice, homemade ginger beer, mint and raspberries. The Whiskey Ward (121 Essex St between Delancey and Rivington Sts, 212-477-2998), a Lower East Side saloon, stocks the hard-to-find Van Winkles 13-year-old family rye among its 40-large whiskey collection. New Williamsburg BBQ joint Fette Sau (354 Metropolitan Ave between Havemeyer and Roebling Sts, 718-963-3404) has an eight-seat bar and a more than a dozen ryes—ranging from $5-$35—including two from local producer Tuthilltown Spirits.

630
Find funky furniture at Las Venus

Island hipsters all head to this center of 20th-century pop culture to feed their need for a kitsch furniture fix. Vintage pieces by the greats—Miller, McCobb, Kagan—are flanked by reproductions and the overall collection creates an artfully cluttered reservoir of affordable finds. There are two Las Venus locations, one at 163 Ludlow St (between Houston and Stanton Sts, 212-982-0608), the other at 888 Broadway (at 19th St, 212-473-3000 ext 519).

631
Get bulletproof

Spy wannabes and budding paranoids love Q Security (240 E 29th St between Second and Third Aves, 212-889-1808) for its body armor and high-powered bugs. We can't get over the fact the store can custom-bulletproof your favorite jacket. Take that, gun crime!

632
Give the little diva a manicure

Dashing Diva (dashingdiva.com; five locations in the city) offers "Little Diva" manicures ($8) and pedicures ($20) for kids under eight. The best part is that, while your daughter is being doted on by the adoring staff, you can catch up on Britney's latest exploits as someone soaks, rubs and beautifies your aching arches. Now that's what we call parenting.

633

Take comfort in congee

There is a wonderfully starchy comfort in congee, and bamboo-laden Congee Village (100 Allen St between Broome and Delancey Sts, 212-941-1818) is a great place to find it. The Cantonese rice porridge, cooked to bubbling in a clay pot over a slow fire, is best early in the day; pick a chunky version, such as the treasure-laden seafood, the chicken and black mushroom, or the sliced fish. The truly adventurous can tuck into the snail-and-frog congee. Reserve a basement room and you also get a karaoke machine, ready and loaded with a mix of Chinese and English pop tunes.

634 Eat and drink your way along pretty Stone Street

A mini cobblestone street closed to vehicular traffic, historic Stone Street, between Broad and Whitehall Streets, is not only a model of what a little civic restoration can achieve, but an ideal place to barhop and restaurant graze as well.

Stone Street Tavern (52 Stone St, 212-785-5658) is an unassuming watering hole in an 1836 building, with a comfort-food menu, friendly staff and rustic decor. Brighter and more boisterous is relative old-timer Ulysses (58 Stone St, 212-482-0400), whose ginormous wraparound bar (the city's longest) is packed even on weekends.

Across the street, tiny newcomer Smorgas Chef (53 Stone St, 212-422-3500) is a laid-back bistro featuring signature Swedish meatballs and other Scandinavian staples such as gravlax and herring. Chef Michael Sullivan's outstanding eatery, Brouwers of Stone Street (45 Stone St, 212-785-5400), offers rotating gnocchi specials, pan-seared sea scallops and an Angus New York strip steak in a countrified yet elegant living-room-like setting. Sought out equally for its bar and its kitchen, Adrienne's Pizza Bar (54 Stone St, 212-248-3838), owned by Ulysses creator Petter Poulakakos, prepares savory and authentic Italian fare in a cheery old-world atmosphere.

635 Befriend the chef at Sushi Yasuda

Even in the best restaurants, waiters can sometimes mangle a chef's good intentions. The antidote: a seat at the bar at Sushi Yasuda (204 E 43rd St between Second and Third Aves, 212-972-1001), in front of head chef Naomichi Yasuda. With only a small counter separating customers from the affable master, Yasuda develops an uncanny understanding of each person's preferences. "Small mouth, yes?" is his greeting to a woman for whom he always makes his pieces of sushi a bit smaller. "Bigeye!" he says to another as she sits down—the nickname refers to her favorite tuna. Express enough admiration and you might get a nickname too.

636 Acquire antique jewelry at Doyle & Doyle

Whether your taste is Art Deco or Nouveau, Victorian or Edwardian, gemologist sisters Pam and Elizabeth Doyle, who specialize in estate and antique jewelry, will have that one-of-a-kind piece you're looking for, including engagement and eternity rings.

Doyle & Doyle *189 Orchard St between Houston and Stanton Sts (212-677-9991/doyledoyle.com).*

637 Listen to cars you can't see on Brooklyn Heights Promenade

Everyone knows that the Brooklyn Heights Promenade offers spectacular waterfront views of Manhattan. But our favorite aspect of a stroll along its third of a mile length is the fact that car noise, infuriating in any other context, becomes amost emollient when issuing from an unseen Expressway beneath your strolling feet. Go again. Tell us if we're wrong.

638
See a puppet show in the park

Tucked just inside the western boundary of Central Park is a curious old wooden structure that seems mysteriously plunked down, like Dorothy's house in Oz. Inside is one of the best-kept secrets in town: a tiny marionette theater with shows performed daily. Designed as a schoolhouse, the building was Sweden's entry in the 1876 Centennial Exposition in Philadelphia, before being moved to NYC a year later. It was eventually restored by the City Parks Foundation in 1990. You'll feel as though you've stumbled upon Hansel and Gretel's hideaway.

Central Park Swedish Cottage Marionette Theatre *West Side at 79th St, Central Park (212-988-9093/cityparksfoundation.org).*

639 Drink sweet tea, Southern-style

Until Gotham's wave of barbecue openings in 2006 and 2007, finding decent sweet tea this far north of the Mason-Dixon Line was about as likely as stumbling across a ten-gallon hat at Barneys. No longer. Stop at Georgia's Eastside BBQ (192 Orchard St between E Houston and Stanton Sts, 212-253-6280) for a brew that most closely resembles what you'd sip in the Deep South: a blend of Irish Breakfast and Assam that holds up nicely to the simple syrup. The appearance of the beverage is near-perfect at Virgil's Real Barbecue (152 W 44th St between Sixth Ave and Broadway, 212-921-9494), where the tea heads into Arnold Palmer territory with the addition of lemon juice (and a large citrus wedge garnish). And for extreme sweet-tooth types, Pies-n-Thighs (351 Kent Ave at South 5th St, Williamsburg, Brooklyn; 347-282-6005) goes to town with a cuppa that's got about four teaspoons of sugar per serving.

640 Exchange folding stuff for folding stuff at Kate's Paperie

Kate's is the ultimate paper mill. You can choose from more than 5,000 kinds by mining the rich vein of stationery, custom-printing services, journals, photo albums and creative, amazingly beautiful gift wrap. There are Kate's Paperie store located throughout the city, see katespaperie.com for details.

641 Ride the bull at Johnny Utah's

The $25,000 mechanical bull at this midtown cowboy spot, incongruously located inside the Rockefeller Center Hotel, was the first to begin operations in Manhattan (it is still one of only two on the entire island). The bull is free to ride, so saddle up.

Johnny Utah's *25 W 51st St between Fifth and Sixth Aves, (212-265-8824/johnnyutahs.com).*

Things not to do

Wanna stay in bed this weekend? *Drew Toal* ***discovers that might not be the worst idea.***

Ask most of you what not to do on weekends, and likely as not you'll answer, "Step out of my front door." The main reason for this reluctance to engage with the greatest city in the world is *them*. The slow-walking, picture-taking, dumb-question-asking tourist sporting the "I ♥ New York" t-shirt and the goofy grin. They're all just so helpless and get in the way so much that us locals would prefer a visit to the Sunni Triangle to spending a Saturday afternoon anywhere near midtown. It does get one to wondering, though. What is the appeal of these tourist-sucking swill heaps that dot the cityscape? I decided to find out, so that you never have to.

Before entering the lion's den (Times Square, natch), I decided a few side-trips were in order. Hopping off the L train at Union Square, my senses were immediately assaulted by the thick crowds, hordes of protestors (apparently, they prefer peace to war), the huge metronome defacing the side of the building at the corner of Broadway and 14th, and any number of gauche consumerist depots tailored to bedazzle visitors

with much of the same crap they can get at home in the suburbs, but at higher New York prices. Even the Strand, magnificent bookstore though it may be, is difficult to appreciate properly when weekend cultural warriors are out shopping for books to impress their friends.

The next item on my list required me to trek further downtown to Canal Street's purveyors of the world's finest, fakest handbags and high-end imitation jewelry. In my opinion, paying $1,800 for a bag is more criminal than fashionable—early 20th-century economist Thorstein Veblen was the first fully to explore this notion of "conspicuous consumption," whereby fools and braggarts pay exorbitant prices for commodities in order to increase their social standing. Buying designer knock-offs is almost worse, begging the question: Who would want to impersonate someone shallow enough to spend that kind of money on an accessory?

OK, enough messing about: It's time to face my fear and go to midtown. Looking out on the slavering masses, I decided that I needed both

Westin Hotel

a drink and a television to watch some March Madness college hoops. The obvious choice, in the context of my mission, was the ESPN Zone. Walking in, I was chagrined to discover it would be a $10 minimum to sit down at a table during the tournament (anything more than ten bucks represented an afternoon drinking investment that I wasn't yet ready to make). My attitude shifted slightly as I watched the teams I had bet on as sure-things get knocked over like dominoes by small, unheralded schools. My tourney bracket in ruins, I vowed never to return to this depressing place.

It was then off to Madame Tussauds. I had been to the one in London and, frankly, the New York branch was no less stultifying. To be sure, the figures are skillfully made, but the ungrammatical signage was irritating and for a $29 entrance fee there's really no justification for a serious lack of effort in the lame Chamber of Horrors. I've seen greater terrors in my toilet after a hard night on the sauce.

On that note, it was time for lunch. I had passed the large rotating lobster many times, but had never thought to stop in the Times Square Red Lobster before today. With all the amazing culinary options available in town, there was never any reason to. I had assumed—erroneously, it turns out—that most rational people would share this view. In fact, there was a 20-minute wait for me to get a table for one. As preposterous as that sounds, it was no zanier than the huge portion of crab fettuccini alfredo ($15.50) that was put in front of me. If you want some insight into how we became the fattest country on Earth, try out the Red Lobster experience.

In truly American fashion, instead of walking off my food, I opt to jump on the New York Sightseeing bus right outside the restaurant. This two-hour loop around southern Manhattan isn't too cheap at $49, but isn't actually all that bad. Traffic is usually bad, but if you aren't in a rush, the trip isn't horrible. My main gripe with the bus stems from my ardent belief that walking or biking are much better ways to see the sights. After all, most of us locals don't ride the bus—at least in Manhattan—and there are plenty of scenic, accessible places that are much better appreciated from a lower vantage point.

Heeding my own advice, I step off the bus and walk a few blocks in order to evaluate the architectural atrocity better known as the Westin Hotel. This seriously ugly building was designed by a Miami-based firm, and it sure looks the part. Granted, it is hardly the city's only vertical faux pas, but this one has the particular effect of making me barf in my mouth a little. To be fair, that might have been the Red Lobster.

As evening approached, I considered getting tickets to see the lowly Knicks finish out their dismal season at Madison Square Garden. Isiah Thomas has brought the once-proud franchise so low that tickets are practically being given away, but just because a guy is handing out anthrax pellets for free doesn't mean you should take them. I decided to abort this mission until better players are hired or the $8 beers go down in price—heavy drinking is really the only way to make that awful team palatable and that price, frankly, is prohibitive to inebriation.

> *"If you want some insight into how we became the fattest country on Earth, try out the Red Lobster experience."*

A quick aside, if I may. New York City has a strange infatuation with Irish culture (or, more specifically, the Emerald Isle's many pubs). This is not to denigrate Ireland; I have enjoyed that country's hospitality several times. It's just that our St. Patrick's Day parade dwarfs any celebration that you'd likely see even in Dublin, and our thousands of Irish bars attract only the worst casualties of the human condition. After opting against the game, I went across the street to Tir na Nog for a pint of Stella ($6.50) and some chicken fingers ($10). As if to illustrate my point, not 20 minutes after I set down on a stool, a few bridge and tunnel heroes walked in and started regaling the polite bartender with stories of their recent beer pong tournament. The leader then proceeded to order a round of Smithwicks, of course pronouncing it phonetically. Pbfff… tourists!

643 *Try a Frito pie*

A neighborhood fave that is also one of those rare spots that successfully appeals to both adults and children, Cowgirl (519 Hudson St at 10th St, 212-633-1133) maintains its appeal with hearty southwestern-style food and kitschy 1950s-era ranch decor. Heartiness and kitsch meet with Cowgirl's signature Frito Pie, an opened bag of Fritos filled with hot chili, cheese, onions, jalapeños and, yep, Frito chips. You don't have to eat the bag.

644 *Ride the Astroland rides... before it's too late!*

They said it was over. Heck, we said it was over. But, in March 2008, Astroland rose from the ashes for another year, kicking off its season in traditional fashion when Miss Cyclone Angie Pontani broke a bottle chocolate egg cream across the lead car of the Cyclone rollercoaster. How long will Coney's legendary theme park last? At the time of writing, its future is still uncertain. Want to ride the Log Flume, the Top Spin, Dante's Inferno and—of course—the Cyclone one last time? Don't wait around too long.

645 *Keep the kids interested at MoMA*

Parents of Gotham, alert. Everyone knows how relaxing it can be to wander through the galleries at the Museum of Modern Art (11 W 53rd St between Fifth and Sixth Aves, 212-708-9400, moma.org), contemplating the Lichtensteins and Warhols, but it's even more relaxing if someone else holds your kids' attention. Show up at the museum by 10am on a Saturday or Sunday, and you can snag four free tickets to the Ford Family Programs. In Tours for Fours, A Closer Look for Kids (ages five through ten) and Tours for Tweens (11- to 14-year-olds), museum educators lead the kids on age-appropriate treks and keep them inspired and busy with art projects. Visit MoMA's website for schedules.

646 Shop for gefilte fish at Domino

Lacking the carby, easy-to-love virtues of challah, kugel and even matzo ball soup, gefilte fish is perpetually cast as the ugly stepchild of the Jewish holiday food family. It's too often associated with mass-produced store-bought varieties, pale cutlets suspended in a gray-tinted jelly. Despite its unpalatable reputation, the holiday dish—traditionally made from freshwater fish like carp or pike that is ground with eggs and bread or matzo meal—does have devoted fans. It's sure to win more among those willing to trek out to Domino (1824 Kings Hwy between 18th and 19th Sts, Midwood, Brooklyn; 718-627-4008), a Russian store whose eye-popping array of edible delights includes a gefilte fish that will finally put its unsavory status to rest. A sliceable loaf that's sold for $5.49 per pound, Domino's gefilte is moist, dense and manages to taste like fish without being fishy. According to one salesclerk, who spoke to us through a translator, their version is made of carp that is ground together with milk-soaked bread, then stuffed back into its skin, "like my grandmother used to make it."

647 Browse boarder gear at Dave's Quality Meat

Dave Ortiz—formerly of ghetto/urban-threads label Zoo York—and professional skateboarder Chris Keefe stock a range of top-shelf streetwear in their wittily designed shop, complete with meat hooks and mannequins who are sporting butchers' aprons. Homemade graphic-print Ts are wrapped in plastic and then displayed in a deli case.

Dave's Quality Meat *7 E 3rd St between Bowery and Second Ave (212-505-7551/davesqualitymeat.com).*

648 Sit in quiet solidarity with the white statues of Sheridan Square

These queer couples from 1980 may not be the hottest representations, but George Segal's *Gay Liberation* sculpture in Sheridan Square Park (Seventh Ave at Grove St) has been a quietly powerful image since its 1992 installation. Sit beside them and reflect on the city's huge role in the fight for gay rights—the reborn Stonewall Inn (thestonewallinn.net), where the famous riots began in 1969, is on Christopher Street close by.

649 Order veggie dogs at F&B

Any vegetarian who's ever answered the craving for a dirty-water dog by indulging in a condiment-stuffed, frankless bun should hightail it to F&B (Frites & Beignets, roughly "fries and doughnuts" in French). At this European-inflected fast-food eatery, six of the ten wiener options—from the traditional mustard-and-kraut Champion Dog to the rémoulade-and-onion-smothered Great Dane—can be ordered with a smoky-tasting tofu pup instead of the standard beef or pork. And in a city where veggie burgers can be found at any grungy diner but veggie franks never seem to make it out of the doghouse, F&B's offerings are enough to make you sit up and beg.

F&B *269 West 23rd St between Seventh and Eighth Aves (646-486-4441/gudtfood.com).*

650

Feed your TV addiction at the Paley Center

The Paley Center (formerly the Museum of Television & Radio; admission $5-$10) is nirvana for boob-tube addicts and pop-culture junkies. It contains an archive of more than 100,000 radio and television programmes, which can be searched on a computerized system in the fourth-floor library. Once you've found your favourite *Star Trek* or *I Love Lucy* episode, just walk down one flight to take a seat at your assigned console. (The radio listening room operates the same way.) There are also cartoon screenings, public seminars and special presentations.

Paley Center for Media *25 W 52nd St between Fifth and Sixth Aves (212-621-6600/paleycenter.org).*

651 *Shop for candy*

Aji Ichiban

If you're looking for unconventional candy, try this Hong Kong snack minichain (there are five outposts in Manhattan), which bills itself as a "Munchies Paradise." Some items will disappoint sweet-tooth cravings (such as, say, the spicy dried fish, the "supreme salted kumquat" and the "black glutinous rice cake"), but adventurous candy lovers will appreciate a break from the mini-Musketeer dominion while sampling popular Thai coconut-milk candy and delicious lychee gummies (both $5/1/2lb). We also like the Chinese pop music.
167 Hester St between Elizabeth and Mott Sts (212-925-1133/ajiichiban.com.hk).

Dylan's Candy Bar

This riotous, three-story, 5,500-square-foot sugar emporium is a danger zone for the ADD-afflicted. Opened by Dylan Lauren (daughter of Ralph), it has towering larger-than-life lollies, vintage candy commercials on a constant video loop, an ice-cream bar, an M&M bar (with 21 colors!), and an 11-foot-tall chocolate bunny statue (don't worry about a meltdown—it's fake). Beware a sugar hangover at the register: Bulk candy runs $10.99 per pound.

Dylan's Candy Bar

1011 Third Ave at 60th St (646-735-0078/ dylanscandybar.com).

Economy Candy

Walking into this LES shop, family-run since its opening in 1937, is like entering a time warp. The store is stacked, nearly to the ceiling, with old-school favorites like Abba-Zaba, Lemonheads and Mary Janes. What's more, Economy lives up to its name, underselling every candy outpost in the city except for maybe Costco. Bulk bins run $1.79-$6 per pound, and bags of Pixie Stix sell for $1.49.
108 Rivington St at Essex St (800-352-4544/economycandy.com).

Hershey's Times Square

If classic chocolate's your thing, head over to this paean to the most middlebrow of American candies. While bags of mini-Mounds cost considerably more here than at Duane Reade and you'll have to dodge a few pokey tourists, where else can you buy cartons of Milk Duds and Whoppers ($2.95), and every kind of Hershey's Kiss known to man (caramel-filled, white-striped, and peanut butter)?
1593 Broadway at 48th St (212-581-9100/ hersheys.com).

The Sweet Life

Those overwhelmed by the size and selection at Dylan's and Economy will enjoy the Euro-feel of this cozy store, which opened 26 years ago and is now run by a brother-and-sister team. Serge Gainsbourg serenades from the speakers as you peruse a modest but sophisticated assortment of Italian "Glitterati" candy ($11/lb), salty Dutch licorice ($6.99/lb), and an absolute rainbow of licorice sticks in flavors like green apple and watermelon ($3.50/lb). While you're here, be sure to check out those 60¢ Softy-Pops (chocolate-covered marshmallows on a stick) and seasonal fudge ($10/lb) in flavors like chocolate and pumpkin, all made on the premises.
63 Hester St at Ludlow St (212-598-0092/ sweetlifeny.com).

652 *Play skee-ball*

All the fun of Coney Island, without having to leave the bar: Skee-ball has made itself at home in the East Village with Brewskee-Ball (brewskeeball.com), the world's first beer-fueled skee-ball league. Thirty-two teams—boasting such colorful monikers as Skeezy Like Sunday Morning or the BREW-nettes—battle Mondays, Wednesdays and Sundays at Ace Bar (531 E 5th St between Aves A and B, 212-979-8476), for the honor of quaffing triumphantly from the Brewskee-Ball Mug at the championship game in late August. Need to sharpen up those skee-lls before you take part? Head to Times Square and the lanes at Dave & Buster's entertainment restaurant (234 W 42nd St between Seventh and Eighth Aves, 646-495-2015), where you're sure to find your 40.

653 *Eat shrimp and grits, South Carolina-style*

This basic pairing entered the Southern-food pantheon courtesy of Carolina fishermen, but the classic combination isn't just for breakfast any more. A menu staple from Charleston to Raleigh, the comfort dish is rumored to have made its upscale debut at Crook's Corner in Chapel Hill, North Carolina, where extra-creamy grits showered in shrimp, chopped bacon and scallions are served come dinnertime. In New York, you'll find a similar version at Bobby Flay's Bar Americain (152 W 52nd St between Sixth and Seventh Aves, 212-265-9700), where a museum-quality replica is presented as an elegant starter under a porcelain dome.

An entrée version at the Clinton St Baking Company (4 Clinton St at Houston St, 646-602-6263) adds a spicy Creole kick to the shrimp, cheddar cheese to the grits and cornmeal-crusted fried green tomatoes on the side. But the brunch at Geoffrey Zakarian's Café at Country (90 Madison Ave at 29th St, 212-889-7100) offers New York's richest rendition: a two-inch-deep casserole of butter-drenched grits topped with a handful of spicy shrimp, green onions, a soft-boiled egg and a healthy—well, maybe not healthy, but certainly tasty—heap of sticky pulled pork.

Dave & Buster's

654

Drink before a fire

The back room of Art Bar (52 Eighth Ave between Horatio and Jane Sts, 212-727-0244) is a mellow spot decked out with a hearth, chandeliers, leather couches, and a pop-culture rendition of *The Last Supper*. At beer garden Soho Park (62 Prince St between Crosby and Lafayette Sts, 212-219-2129), you can enjoy frosty brews in front of the toasty flames, while at warm, crimson-hued Keybar (432 E 13th St between First Ave and Ave A, 212-478-3021) shadows from the bar's central fireplace play on the wall among lanterns, candles and artwork. In Williamsburg, head to Metropolitan (559 Lorimer St between Devoe St and Metropolitan Ave, Brooklyn; 718-599-4444), a gay bar that's small but boasts two fireplaces and ski-lodge decor. And finally, at Moran's Chelsea (146 Tenth Ave at 19th St, 212-627-3030), the dark, wood-paneled tavern room's two fireplaces and seasonal cognac-laced martinis may inspire you to toast a new holiday tradition.

655

Stroll Brooklyn Bridge

If the last time you walked across this most hallowed and beloved of bridges was during the 2003 blackout, for shame. It takes only about 40 minutes—okay, 60 minutes if you're slow—to traverse the mile of pedestrian-friendly wood-planked pathway perched just above the road. No matter which way you look (up at the web of steel cables, out at Manhattan or Ellis Island or Brooklyn Heighs) a postcard-worthy vista awaits.

656

Shop for records in the best jazz store in town

The Jazz Record Center (236 W 26th St, Room 804, between Seventh and Eighth Aves, 212-675-4480, jazzrecordcenter.com) is the city's finest, stocking both current and out-of-print records, as well as books, videos and other jazz-related merchandise.

Keybar

657

Watch champion eaters stuff down far too many dogs

What could be more American than July the Fourth and a surfeit of hot dogs? Mull it over at Nathan's Hot Dog Eating Contest (nathans famous.com/nathans/contest), a competitive-eating contest held at Coney Island landmark Nathan's Famous (1310 Surf Ave at Stillwell Ave, 718-946-2202). Each year, a field of 20 or so diet-disdaining souls strives to consume—and, of course, keep down—as many hot dogs (with buns) as possible over a 12-minute period. The record is a terrifying 66.

658

Take them to a show at one of the city's great kid theaters

There are great ones all over the city where tickets cost $25 or less. Check out timeoutkids.com to see what's playing at Symphony Space (2537 Broadway at 95th St, 212-864-5400, symphonyspace.org), the 13th Street Repertory Company (50 W 13th St at Sixth Ave, 212-675-6677, 13thstreetrep.org), the New Victory Theater (209 W 42nd St at Seventh Ave, 646-223-3020, newvictory.org), Manhattan Children's Theatre (52 White St between Church St and Franklin Pl, 212-226-4085, mctny.org), the Lucille Lortel Theatre (121 Christopher St at Bedford St, 212-924-2817, lortel.org) and the Brooklyn Center for the Performing Arts (2900 Campus Rd at Hillel Pl, Flatbush, Brooklyn, 718-951-4600, brooklyncenter.org).

Move to the
music

Cristina Black takes a walk through downtown Manhattan's peerless musical history

Plenty of Manhattan's music landmarks lie in midtown and on the Upper West Side. John Lennon was shot at the Dakota at 72nd Street and Central Park West, Carole King and Gerry Goffin wrote "The Locomotion" in the Brill Building music publishers' enclave at 1619 Broadway, and the Hit Factory, a now-defunct studio at 421 W 54th Street, hosted sessions for *Born in the U.S.A.* But downtown has the maximum density of sites relevant to NYC's sonic history. Tompkins Square Park is a good place to start a musically themed tour of the city. The street that runs along the eastern edge of the East Village green space is officially known as Avenue B, but the three-block stretch was named Charlie Parker Place in 1992: The jazz saxophonist lived in the ground-floor apartment at 151 Avenue B (near the corner of 10th Street) from 1950 to 1954. During that time, he recorded "Autumn in New York" and "Round Midnight" (with Miles Davis). Cut through the park to Avenue A and head south. On your left, just before 6th Street, is Sidewalk

Café (94 Avenue A), hub of the antifolk scene that spawned Regina Spektor, Nellie McKay and the Moldy Peaches, among others. Pop in for a two-drink minimum to take a chance on the venue's current crop of ramshackle songwriters. Then keep going south until you reach Houston Street, where Avenue A turns into Essex Street. The Mercury Lounge, near the southwest corner (217 E Houston St), is a small room for indie-rock hopefuls; the Strokes played here before they got big.

Ludlow Street is a half block east off Houston. Turn there and walk south, passing the clubs Pianos, Living Room and Cake Shop, all on your left between Stanton and Rivington. This is pretty much the center of the live rock scene that sprung up in the early 2000s—watch out for drunken, puking college kids. They're all here to soak up the kind of historic NYC cool that emanated from the Beastie Boys' late-1980s masterpiece *Paul's Boutique*. That panoramic foldout picture from the CD's booklet? It's the intersection of Ludlow and Rivington. Walk

one block south and you'll see the Williamsburg Bridge rising to the east from Delancey Street. Sonny Rollins named his 1962 album, *The Bridge*, for his famous practice sessions on the busy thoroughfare, which leads to the Brooklyn hipsterville that nurtured TV on the Radio, Interpol, Clap Your Hands Say Yeah, Animal Collective and many other revered indie-rock bands of the 2000s. (Also: Barry Manilow grew up there.) Before all the members of those bands were born, Lou Reed and John Cale formed the Velvet Underground while living in a loft at 56 Ludlow (a couple blocks south of Delancey near Grand) in 1965. Go one block further and make a right on Hester, following it to Chrystie. No.59 housed the first Beasties practice space, hence the track name "59 Chrystie Street" from *Paul's*.

After a one-block walk west, you're on the fast-gentrifying punk boulevard of dreams: The Bowery. If you want an effete symbol of the punk rock spirit, turn right and walk six blocks north to the recently shuttered CBGB

at No.315. This is where Patti Smith and Lenny Kaye watched Television play during a residency in 1974. Soon after, Blondie, the Ramones and Talking Heads joined the party. In the 1980s, hardcore bands like Agnostic Front and Sick of It All took the reins. The club stayed a sanctimonious shithole until it closed in 2006. Despite its newfound fanciness—high rents, boutique hotels—the area remains a punk monument, immortalized by the renaming of the corner of 2nd Street and Bowery as Joey Ramone Place. The block, where Joey and Dee Dee Ramone resided, was the backdrop for the band's first album cover.

If you think the Ramones were awfully loud and obnoxious, skip the Bowery side trip and keep walking west on Hester. Turn right when you hit Mulberry and check out Angelo's at No.146, the titular establishment from Billy Joel's "Scenes from an Italian Restaurant." Head north on Mulberry until you reach Houston again. No.47 (half a block east) is the site of the old Knitting Factory. Now an all-purpose rock club located on Leonard Street in Tribeca, the legendary spot was a haven for experimental sounds from the late 1980s through the early '90s, hosting performances by such notables as Sonic Youth, Cecil Taylor and John Zorn.

Now turn around and head back west toward Greenwich Village, the center of the 1960s folk scene. From Houston, make a right on MacDougal and walk two blocks north. There, on the corner of Minetta Lane is the old beatnik hangout Café Wha?, where Peter, Paul & Mary, Bob Dylan and Bruce Springsteen all played in their salad days. Make a left on 3rd Street and you'll see the Blue Note at No.131, which has hosted virtually every big name in jazz, including Dizzy Gillespie, Sarah Vaughan

> ## "On the corner of Minetta Lane is the old beatnik hangout Café Wha?, where Bob Dylan and Bruce Springsteen both played in their salad days."

Cake Shop

and Tito Puente. Keep going north and you'll reach the southwest corner of Washington Square Park on W 4th Street, to which Dylan refers in his song "Positively 4th Street," widely regarded as a bitter backlash against the Village scenesters who disapproved of his departure from traditional acoustic folk. You might even catch some of those purist types strumming away in the park.

To see another legendary jazz establishment, head west to Seventh Avenue (the street Simon & Garfunkel made famous for wayward women in "The Boxer"). Just before W 11th Street, you'll see the red marquee of the Village Vanguard (178 Seventh Avenue South). The Weavers played here on New Year's Eve 1949, but the club has been a jazz spot since the 1950s, featuring residencies by Bill Evans and John Coltrane in 1961, and by Wynton Marsalis in the early 1990s. Make a left on W 11th, then another left on Hudson. After yet another left on W 10th, you'll pass by Seagull (240 W 10th), the tiny, pink-decored hair salon owned by Johanna Fateman of Le Tigre. Clients include Genesis P-Orridge and Lady Jaye of local industrial band Psychic TV, and Régine Chassagne of Arcade Fire. At the end of the block, make a right on Bleecker, walk south to Commerce and make another right. Now strut-dance down the sidewalk to the corner of Barrow, just as Tina Turner did in the 1985 video for "What's Love Got to Do with It?" If any of the gawping passersby has got a cellphone camera, you should be able to assess your performance the following week on YouTube.

660

Get yourself the greatest grilled cheese in town

A grilled cheese sandwich should be foolproof: After all, it's just American cheese melted between two slices of bread. But so much can go wrong. Soggy or burnt toast, undercooked cheese or a downright skimpy portion can utterly ruin this perennial comfort fave. That's never the case at Astoria's Cup Diner & Bar, right across the street from the American Museum of the Moving Image and two blocks from the Kaufman Astoria multiplex. The generous slabs of sourdough bread soak up butter without being overpowered by it, and are nicely browned by a flat-top Salamander grill with a nifty overhead flame.

The bustling space is bright and airy, with large windows up front, massive sepia- and blue-toned murals, and an exposed kitchen in the back. Cup Diner's manager-chef Jerry Feidner describes the look as "retro, but from no particular period." In other words: classic. Kind of like grilled cheese.

Cup Diner & Bar *35-01 36th St at 35th Ave, Astoria, Queens (718-937-2322).*

661

Take the Water Taxi to let river breezes riffle your hair

In their kitschy and instantly recognizable "New York cab" livery, Water Taxis set sail from more than a dozen piers, combining direct commuting routes down the East River, to South Brooklyn or to Yonkers, with more entertaining hop-on/hop-off weekend loops (two boats an hour; one-day pass $15-$20). They've got a snazzy interactive map of all the routes and stopoffs (nywatertaxi.com/map), and also run a few specialist tours.

662 *Visit Alice's statue*

To join the throngs paying homage to Alice, the Mad Hatter and the White Rabbit, head to the eastern flank of Central Park (East 74th Street park entrance). Just north of the Conservatory Water—that's the Boat Pond to any Manhattan children, past and present, who've sailed a toy ship there—the statue has been clambered over by kids since 1959, on the instructions George Delacorte who commissioned it to honor his late wife.

663 *Grab a dumpling from the Sun Dou Dumpling Shop*

Proudly fatty pork-and-cabbage dumplings star at this Chinatown takeout-window shack (214-216 Grand St between Elizabeth and Mott Sts, 212-965-9663). One buck buys four fried-before-your-eyes beauties or a scallion pancake, while a scant 65¢ scores you an impossibly fluffy steamed pork bun—a bit of heaven for penny-pinching mortals.

664

Watch soccer over a steak at Boca Juniors Steakhouse
The New York rage for Argentine steak meets the Argentine mania for futbol at Boca Junior Argentinian Steakhouse (81-08 Queens Blvd at 51st Ave, Elmhurst, Queens, 718-429-2077). Sure, it's a parrillada serving juicy filet mignon, skirt steak (entraña) and tenderloin steak (lomo) topped with garlicky chimichurri, but even the beef takes second seat when Boca Juniors, the most popular soccer team in Argentina, come on the restaurant's plasma TVs. Such is the allegiance to Boca that the waiters' outfits, the napkins, the walls and even the carpet sport the team's blue and yellow colors. Don't even think of asking them to change the channel.

665

Shop the world at Kiosk

If the most traveling you've done of late has been in a taxi, the internationally sourced goods at Salvor Kiosk can at least make it appear as if you've been racking up mileage points. Sourced by the proprietors of Soho's Salvor Studio—known for their silk-screened T-shirts and pillows, sold at both Bloomingdale's and Paul Smith, among others—the kiosk stocks a cache of international items that changes every few months. The emphasis is on gorgeously designed mundane goods (rulers, slippers, glasses), all of which are rare, and, like an open exit-row seat on an international flight, fleeting. Think: Finnish tar candy and Japanese bike baskets, an intriguing blend that mirrors the city's own multicultural melange.

Kiosk *95 Spring St, second floor, between Broadway and Mercer St (212-226-8601/ salvorkiosk.com).*

$20

666 Be afraid, be very afraid at Blood Manor

Located on the fifth floor of a clubby West Chelsea high-rise, Blood Manor is a 5,000-square-foot haunted house, with 20 themed rooms—some inspired by classic horror flicks (*Hostel, From Dusk Till Dawn*)—and a labyrinth of blackened and black-light passageways. Forty gored-out actors work the set, amid body bags, gutted pigs, epileptic strobes, and bile and blood by the gallon. There are blood-splattered holding cells, a pit crawling with rubber snakes, rats the size of bull mastiffs, a gory lobotomy lab and a framed portrait of Abe Lincoln with a bullet in his forehead. Animatronics howl, thunder crashes, teens squeal, pots clang, air cannons fire and a coffin-lounging nun demands *Exorcist*-style lovin'. Beware of the chain-saw-wielding maniac in tightie-whities and tube socks, and the electrocutionee who occasionally pops out his (real) glass eye. There's only one bathroom in the whole joint: Behold a severed head in the toilet, a mass murderer hidden behind the shower curtain and a drippy blood manor scrawled across the mirror. The line can take up to two hours to navigate, although RIP skip-to-the-front tickets are sold at a premium ($45). "You picked a baaad night to come," warns an Uncle Fester-ish door bitch once you reach the cobweb-laced gates. The trek lasts about 20 minutes, depending on how long you gawk at the zombie strippers. And drunken visits are highly discouraged.

For the real stuff of nightmares, though, you could as easily join the tangle of tawny limbs, sparkly belts, oil-slick lips and shabby-lookin' B&Ters in open-toe sandals at Guest House (homeguesthouse.com), the bottle-service sperm bank downstairs. Expect to pay $350 for a bottle of Grey Goose.

Blood Manor *542 W 27th St between Tenth and Eleventh Aves (212-290-2825/ bloodmanor.com).*

667 Take a picture with the Naked Cowboy

Don't sneer, you've always been tempted. Naked—a.k.a. Robert Burck—can be found in Times Square almost every day. Ask.

668 Glimpse the Bronx's prehistoric past

One of the world's oldest formations is in the Bronx: The Fordham gneiss came into being 1.1 billion years ago when a landmass collided with North America. You'll be able to see the black-and-white-banded rock if you gaze across Spuyten Duyvil Creek from Inwood Hill Park.

669 See where 40 percent of us came from

On the way back to Manhattan from a visit to the Statue of Liberty, the ferry makes an unsurprisingly popular stop—after all, the NPS point out that "over 40 percent of America's population can trace their ancestry through Ellis Island." Once a depot through which more than 12 million people entered the country between 1892 and 1954, the Ellis Island Immigration Museum (212-363-3200, nps.gov/elis) is a moving tribute to the people from so many different countries who made the journey to America, dreaming of a better life. The $6 audio tour, narrated by Tom Brokaw, is informative and inspiring.

670 Visit the Apple Store at 3am

Recession or not, the Apple Store Fifth Avenue (767 Fifth Ave between 58th and 59th Sts, 212-336-1440, apple.com/retail/fifthavenue), NYC's subterranean mecca for all things Mac, is an absolute mob scene during the day, thronged with gawking tourists, frenetic techies and assorted timewasters. Inside a bunker marked by a 32-foot-tall glass entrance, aisles are lined with test-drive-ready iPhones, MacBooks, iPods and all manner of accessories. Many flock to the 45-foot-long Genius Bar, where the earnest staff offers assistance with the most annoying of computer problems. The crowds can be avoided, however, if you're prepared to come at night, for the store is open 24 hours. Can't fall asleep because your computer's acting up? Haul it in for a 3am checkup.

671

Practice your swing at a Gotham driving range

Chelsea Piers Golf Academy

This is an expensive but kick-ass practice facility. There's a three-tier driving range, golf simulators and plenty of personal instruction available.
23rd St and Hudson River.

Golden Bear Golf Center

Always super-busy, perhaps because it was in *Golf Range* magazine's top 100. A large bucket of range balls runs about $10.
232-01 Northern Blvd, Queens.

Flushing Meadow Park Pitch & Putt

Night golf! The lights don't shut off until 1am, and the entire course can be negotiated with a wedge and a putter.
Passarelle Ramp at Willets Point Station.

Randalls Island Golf Center

The facility has a nice two-tiered range. If you get too frustrated with your crappy swing, head over to the batting cages and work out some of that aggression.
1 Randalls Island, Manhattan.

Breezy Point Executive Golf Course

The longest hole on the course is 150 yards. No need to bring the 2-iron, killer.
155th Street and the Boardwalk, Far Rockaway.

672 Order a 100-cheese fondue

Artisanal is the best place in town to find an authentic Alpine bowl of hot dipping cheese ($24-$30). Options include one remarkably harmonious version that combines 100 cheeses of wonderfully varied stink.
Artisanal *Park Ave between 32nd and 33rd Sts (212-725-8585).*

673 Visit Titanic Joe's house

For more than 20 years, Joe Colletti ("Titanic Joe") has bedecked the front windows of his brick row house at 11th Street and 47th Road in Long Island City with memorabilia surrounding the ill-fated RMS *Titanic*. The display includes newspaper clippings, movie posters, signed letters from survivors (he claims to have met nine of them), and even a photograph of the rescue attempt at sea. He started assembling his collection in 1984, after seeing *Raise the Titanic*; he also felt Gotham needed a formal tribute to the voyage. The material visible from the street is only the tip of the iceberg, with far more inside. As far as seeing it, Colletti says, "Sure: if you knock, and I happen to be home."

New York Transit Museum

674 *Take a bus, train or taxi to the Transit Museum*

Sure, it looks like an entrance to the subway. But your MetroCard's no good here: those stairs at the corner of Boerum Place and Schermerhorn Street lead down to the New York Transit Museum (718-694-1600, mta.info/mta/museum; open 10am-4pm Tue-Fri; noon-5pm Sat, Sun). The straphanging's more leisurely in this restored 1930s station (abandoned in 1946), where you'll find old subway cars and turnstiles, as well as bus steering wheels and seats for children who want to play at being a bus driver. Well-presented photos and videos afford an excellent look at the city's transit history and rush hours past.

675 *Dare yourself to try a pork margarita at Porchetta*

It's fitting for an eatery that puts pig on a pedestal to attempt to make quaffable swine. Behold: the pork margarita. At aptly named restaurant Porchetta (241 Smith St at Douglass St, Boerum Hill, Brooklyn, 718-237-9100), chef Jason Neroni and bartender Adam Kane choose cracklings over kosher salt to coat the cocktail's rim. Neroni dries out salted slabs of pigskin for his homemade pork rinds, which Kane then pulverizes in a food processor with even more salt and dried chilies. To finish, two ounces of Don Julio añejo tequila is shaken with a squeeze of lime, orange liqueur and a splash of fresh blood-orange juice, ensuring that lard and salt aren't the only flavors left on your lips. Porky!

676 *Take a midnight stroll*

Who needs sleep? Become a night crawler and take to the streets after dark to enjoy some of New York's best sights.

New York after dark doesn't have to be X-rated to be interesting. In many of the city's neighborhoods the late-night hours are monumentally serene—a time when the city relaxes and opens itself up to exploration. Chinatown and the Financial District, which teem with shoulder-to-shoulder bustle during the day, are peaceful by moonlight—not to mention steeped in rich city history. Start at the South Street Seaport (Fulton St at South St, Pier 17, 212-732-7678). Its annoying mall-ness fades at night—even the mime knocks off around 10pm—and it's easier to enjoy the docked schooners and views of the illuminated Brooklyn Bridge. From there, walk up Fulton Street and take a right on Front, where inviting bars and restaurants are nestled in old brick buildings. Around the corner on Dover Street, the Bridge Café (279 Water St at Dover St, 212-227-3344) occupies the site of the city's oldest continuously operating bar. Along with a drink, try the blue-cheese soufflé.

Continue up Dover and hang a right on Pearl, which takes you into Chinatown. Bear right at St. James Place. Whiffs of seafood and overripe lychee signal the change of 'hood. At 88 East Broadway, stop at White Swan Bakery (at Forsyth St, 212-226-5333) for Asian pastries and all your fish-oil needs. Keep chugging up East Broadway and you'll reach 169 Bar (169 East Broadway between Jefferson and Rutgers Sts, 212-473-8866), formerly known as the "Bloody Bucket" for its frequent fisticuffs. These days the crowd is docile and eclectic, and there's live music every night. Next head west toward Bowery and start walking downtown. Only on Pell Street can you get a "foot rub" as late as 1am, at Foot Heaven (16 Pell St between Bowery and Mott St, 212-962-6588). It requires a modicum of preparation, though: You must call before 11pm to line up your appointment.

Take a quick right onto Mott, then a quick left onto Bayard. Linger for a moment by karaoke bar Winnie's (104 Bayard St between Baxter and Mulberry Sts, 212-732-2384); across the street on Baxter, you might see perps getting dragged into a police holding cell by the fuzz. After that, wander south and west to Centre Street and walk downtown to City Hall Park. The southern gates are open all night, offering visitors surprisingly scenic respite amid the soft glow of oil lamps above the fountain.

With its screened fences and ultrasanitized memorial photos, Ground Zero is no longer the emotional gut-punch it once was. Still, if you want to remember and reflect, this is the time to walk over to Church Street and do it. One block east on Broadway, behind the Century 21, is an area that was the Fifth Avenue of its day—a snazzy commercial stretch frequented by the finest turn-of-19th-century ladies. Now, it has a Burger King.

Now walk south on Broadway, passing by Trinity Church (74 Trinity Place, 212-602-0800) and the graveyard where Alexander Hamilton is buried. Challenge him to a duel and feel superior. Across from Trinity, Wall Street at night is an urban canyon, and wears its history proudly (Washington, memorialized in sculpture, took his first oath of office here). Say hello to the security guard who stands watch at The New York Stock Exchange (11 Wall St at New St, 212-656-3000) from 6pm to 6am—he's lonely—then meander leisurely south (glancing at Fraunces Tavern, where George Washington bid farewell to his soldiers during the Revolutionary War), taking care to traverse the tight cobbled streets that evoke the small trading-post town of 200 years ago. End at South Ferry, at the tip of the island. Hard-core insomniacs should take the Staten Island Ferry over and back. It runs every half hour (or every hour from 1:30am to 5:30am), and from the water the skyline rises right in front of you, a cheesy New York cliché that's really worth it.

677

Chomp a Super Heeb sandwich

It's tough to say what's best about the Super Heeb sandwich at Russ & Daughters (179 E Houston St between Allen and Orchard Sts, 212-475-4880). Is it the rich, nearly impossibly fluffy whitefish salad? The subtle kick of the double-whipped horseradish cream cheese? The reassuring chewiness of the hand-rolled, boiled bagel? Or the sinus-clearing pop of the wasabi-flavored flying-fish roe?

Taken alone, each of these ingredients is cause for gastronomic celebration. United, they form a sandwich of such sublime power it could very well reform our health care system, lower the divorce rate, and achieve peace between—if not warring nations— then at least Yankees and Red Sox fans.

So you can love the $9.45 sandwich, but can't quite wrap your head around the name? Its somewhat provocative moniker, explains fourth-generation Russ Niki Russ Federman, comes from *Heeb* magazine, which ranked the sandwich as the world's second-best food (and that was before the addition of wasabi roe). It's one of the store's more popular bites, especially, Federman says, among young Jews who "find the word sort of empowering." Not exactly what bubbe intended, but her grandkids certainly seem to approve.

678

Visit the grave of Bill the Butcher

William Poole, a.k.a. notorious Bowery Boys gang leader Bill the Butcher (in terms of *Gangs of New York*, that's Daniel Day-Lewis), was at the Stanwix Hall saloon on February 24, 1855, when Tammany Hall enforcer John Morrissey had him shot. Poole died on March 8 and was buried in an unmarked grave in Green-Wood Cemetery (Fifth Ave at 25th St, 718-768-7300, green-wood.com). A headstone was added in 2003 with his famous departing words: "Good-bye, boys, I die a true American."

Harlem nights

The neighborhood known for its capital-R Renaissance keeps transforming and rejuvenating itself. Richard Koss says that's good news for New York nightlife.

Decades after the 1920s stopped roaring and the Depression consumed the '30s, stories still periodically break about a "New Harlem Renaissance." As with most rumors of second comings, it's often driven by wishful thinking. After all, Harlem has had as many downs as ups since its golden age, when jazz was king and the neighborhood's clubs and ballrooms were the most throbbing in the city.

Yet Harlem's stock has risen noticeably in the past decade. The infusion of money is obvious just from a walk along 125th Street, where the sidewalk vendors have (for the most part) been supplanted by chain stores, and there is an increasing number of refurbished brownstones. This financial jolt has also invigorated the neighborhood's nightlife, as seen in the variety of bars and clubs that have opened, reopened or been renovated in the past few years. Anyone who feels hemmed in by the Meatpacking District's velvet ropes or has grown weary of Williamsburg as NYC's "alternative" stomping

ground should investigate these spots from Sugar Hill to Spanish Harlem.

One of the true jewels in Harlem's crown, Minton's Playhouse (208 W 118th St between St. Nicholas Ave and Adam Clayton Powell Jr. Blvd [Seventh Ave], 212-864-8346, uptownat mintons.com) reopened in summer 2006 after being boarded up for more than 30 years. Few clubs in the city can boast as rich a history as Minton's—Miles Davis dubbed it "the black jazz capital of the world." Belly up to the long wooden bar for the nightly shows, but don't disturb the jazz pilgrims. A two-drink minimum is always in effect, though you'll pay a $10 cover from Wednesday through Saturday.

Subterranean St. Nick's Pub (773 St. Nicholas Ave at 149th St, 212-283-7132) hasn't undergone anything like Minton's makeover; aside from the name, it has barely changed since the '40s when Duke Ellington urged a visit to Sugar Hill in "Take the A Train." The place is all low ceilinged,

St. Nick's Pub

neighborhood vibe, with unpredictable free food and reliably cheap drinks.

An intimate, red-accented boîte that opened in 2004 on the ground floor of a brownstone, The DEN (2150 Fifth Ave between 131st and 132nd Sts, 212-234-3045, thedenharlem.com) lures Harlemites and downtowners with a variety of DJ sets. A Thursday night (no cover charge before 9pm, $5 after) catches the DEN (an acronym for dining, entertainment and nightlife) at its mellowest, while Saturday night's new-school R&B set (beginning at 11pm) draws the most sweat. But the virtuosity on display here owes more to mixology than music. The innovative cocktail menu titillates with names like Sex in the Inner City, Uncle Tom Collins (accompanied by an Oreo cookie), Foxy Brown and Jungle Fever (with equal parts Bushmills Irish Cream and Kahlúa). You can grab a stool by the sleek copper-topped bar or sink into one of the comfy banquettes.

Neighborhood professionals and tourists wandering Harlem's main drag cool their heels at MoBay's Uptown (17 W 125th St between Fifth Ave and Malcolm X Blvd [Lenox Ave], 212-876-9300, mobayrestaurant.com), a small, lively restaurant-bar that features local musicians performing gospel, R&B, jazz, reggae and African rhythms Tuesday through Saturday (no cover charge). The highlights on the Caribbean-inflected soul-food menu include corn bread (garnished with a coconut-pineapple-cream sauce) and catfish—or if you're not that hungry, have a seat at the thin bar that puts drinkers right across from each other and try one of MoBay's concoctions. The Harlem Mojito is made with cognac, while the Triple Threat mixes three 150-proof rums in a pint glass ($18)—lethal.

One of Harlem's most famous landmarks, the 1939-vintage Lenox Lounge (288 Malcolm X Blvd [Lenox Ave] between 124th and 125th Sts, 212-427-0253, lenoxlounge.com) trades so heavily on its past, that you might feel you've arrived too late and everyone's moved on. This is where Billie Holiday sang, John Coltrane played, the young Malcolm X hustled and James Baldwin held court. The Art Deco lounge (tastefully restored in 1999) has served as a backdrop in numerous films evoking the Harlem of yesteryear (among them *Malcolm X* and the 2000 remake of *Shaft*), which only reinforces the place's nostalgic aura. The fabled Zebra Room at the back of the bar hosts jazz outfits, but the $20 cover for weekend shows isn't always warranted; drinks can get expensive and service sometimes verges on the catatonic.

While the celebrated Alhambra Ballroom, restored to its swanky, chandeliered majesty in 2003, is now given over to weddings, fund-raising banquets and political functions, Harlem Lanes (2116 Adam Clayton Powell Jr. Blvd [Seventh Ave] at 126th St, 212-678-2695, harlemlanes.com) right above it caters to the general public, particularly children. Harlem's first bowling alley has 24 well-maintained lanes, open till 2am on Fridays and Saturdays; on those nights, a DJ commands the lounge area. Once the weekend's over, head to either of two small sports bars with flat-screen TVs and Monday Night Football drink specials. On other evenings, the bars can be very quiet.

Old school's in session at Showman's (375 W 125th St between Morningside and St. Nicholas Aves, 212-864-8941), which was founded in 1942 and is now frequented by a mature crowd that settles quietly at the long bar or the adjoining tables to enjoy the free hors d'oeuvres. This establishment's claim to fame (or perhaps just distinction) is Thursday's Tap Dance Night—probably the only such weekly event in town—and its house organ, a Hammond B-3. The rest of the week offers three nightly sets of either jazz, gospel or blues, and there's never a cover, just a two-drink minimum per set.

The plush Moca Restaurant and Lounge (2210 Frederick Douglass Blvd [Eighth Ave] at 119th St, 212-665-8081, mocabar.com) has firmly staked out its turf on this up-and-coming stretch. Its casual bar and cushy sofas are ideal for an aperitif before moving on to the restaurants that have sprung up nearby, or for a nightcap after savoring some live music. DJs spin hip-hop and R&B on weekends for an upscale, mixed crowd. Mondays you'll find a comedy show whose raunchiness carries over into Red Room Erotica poetry the following night.

In Riverbank State Park (a complex made up largely of track fields and other athletic facilities), the River Room (Riverbank State Park, 145th St at Riverside Dr, 212-491-1500, theriverroomofharlem.com) is a spacious,

modern hall with a high, vaulted ceiling. The haute Southern cuisine is pricey, though not prohibitively so, and floor-to-ceiling windows afford sublime views of the Hudson, the Jersey Palisades and the George Washington Bridge. On Tuesdays, there's salsa dancing ($10 cover), while Friday and Saturday nights showcase jazz (no cover). The view can be savored from either the small bar or, weather permitting, the patio, particularly at sunset.

LGBT Community Center

There are more eggs to be found beyond Manhattan. In Queens, the Barnyard Easter Egg Hunt (Queens County Farm Museum, 73-50 Little Neck Pkwy, Floral Park, Queens, 718-347-3276, $4 admission) takes place in the orchard, but the kids will likely be distracted by Whiskers, the resident bunny, or the joy of bouncy hayride. Brooklyn's Spring Fling Egg Hunt (Brooklyn Bridge Park, Main St at Plymouth St, Dumbo) begins promptly at 11am, but there's plenty of child-focused entertainment to follow—perhaps tunes from the Deedle Deedle Dees or Care Bears on Fire, plus games with prizes (winners in previous years have got to scoff baskets from master chocolatier Jacques Torres).

692 *Walk the drawbridge at Ninja*

Stylish restaurantgoers always strive for the grand entrance, but at Ninja (25 Hudson St between Duane and Reade Sts, 212-274-8500), you're more likely to be… entranced. A lowered drawbridge lets you descend into a subterranean 6,000-square-foot labyrinth that's supposed to resemble a Japanese mountain village. Servers wear black robes and begin some of the courses with "ninja magic" tricks that involve glowing fingers and bursts of smoke and flame. Don't say you haven't been warned!

688-691 *Don a bonnet, find an egg*

Easter weekend? Check. Bored kids? Check. Just as well New York plays host to some serious festive fun. On the East Side, the annual Easter Parade and Easter Bonnet Festival (Fifth Ave between 49th and 57th Sts, nycvisit.com) is a loose-knit gathering more than a formal procession, with participants meandering about in their madcap millinery. Station the family just outside St. Patrick's Cathedral for the best view of the inspired headgear. Fort Tyron's Spring Festival (Anne Loftus Playground at Fort Tryon Park, Broadway at Riverside Dr, 212-333-2552) is the best Easter event uptown: expect storytelling, face painting, stilt walkers and, of course, an egg hunt.

693 *Love the LGBT Community Center*

Many seasoned queers take this place for granted, but without the largely volunteer-operated support system, there would be no Gender Identity Project, no Center Kids program or National Archive of LGBT History, no Promote the Vote campaign, no Lesbian Cancer Initiative or Center Voices Presents series—not to mention no venue for the 300 or so groups that meet here every week. The Center is, quite simply, a labor of love. So love it back, queen!
LGBT Community Center *208 W 13th St between Seventh and Eighth Aves (212-620-7310/gaycenter.org).*

694 *Get New York's best pizza at Di Fara...*

Pizza is the great equalizer. Everyone likes the stuff: food snobs, undiscerning drunks, old folks, picky kids, carnivores, vegetarians. But no one can agree on who makes the best slice. Ask your friends to name their favorite pizzerias and they'll likely either rattle off the classic joints or tell you about some hole-in-the-wall down the block.

We're going to let you in on a secret. The perfect pizza is made in a one-room pizza shop by a man named Domenico DeMarco. He was born just outside Naples and has been making pies here for more than 40 years (he is now 71). His movements are slow and deliberate: He stretches the dough into an irregular, oblong shape; dresses it with sauce he makes from both fresh and canned San Marzano tomatoes; carves his own slices of mozzarella over each pie;

then eases the uncooked pizza onto a wooden paddle and into the heat. When it's ready, DeMarco pulls the pie out with his bare hands. Then he shreds nuggets of fior de latte and grates grana padano on top, drizzles some olive oil and adds a few pinches of fresh herbs (basil and oregano). One bite reveals a harmony of textures and flavors atop a complex and nutty, charred, crisp crust. Prepare to wait for a slice: He's been perfecting his art for decades, and he's not about to rush things now.

Di Fara Pizza *1424 Ave J at 15th St, Midwood, Brooklyn (718-258-1367).*

695-698 ...then compare it to classic NY pies

The city's legendary pizza joints are not necessarily the best these days, nor the oldest—but they're still popular and should all be visited once. Make your own mind up... and expect long lines.

Grimaldi's Pizzeria

This pizzeria was founded in 1990 by Patsy Grimaldi, a nephew of Patsy Lancieri (the man behind Patsy's). Some critics say that standards have dropped, but this joint remains crowded and its coal-fired oven issues a nicely charred pie topped with fresh mozzarella and basil.

19 Old Fulton St between Front and Water Sts, Dumbo, Brooklyn (718-858-4300).

John's of Bleecker Street

This place was established in 1929 by John Sasso, who worked at Lombardi's, but nowadays it's hardly worth the wait to get in. They pump out mediocre pies with goopy cheese and sauce. The slightly charred crust, however, is a great echo of better times.

278 Bleecker St between Sixth and Seventh Aves (212-243-1680).

L & B Spumoni Gardens

Opened in 1939 by Ludovico Barbati, this pizzeria is also a spumoni shop, takeout operation and full-service restaurant. Sicilian-style pie lovers come for the fluffy square slices draped with mozzarella and dusted with pecorino romano.

2725 86th St between 10th and 11th Sts, Bensonhurst, Brooklyn (718-449-1230).

Lombardi's

Supposedly, this is where it all began: Gennaro Lombardi opened the shop in Soho in 1905—the first pizzeria in the U.S. We can't vouch for how the pizzas tasted a century ago, but the current product is inconsistent: It can be delightfully balanced, or may be oversauced and undercooked, with a gummy, droopy crust.

32 Spring St between Mott and Mulberry Sts (212-941-7994).

699 *Get rescued by a real fireman*

The New York City Fire Museum (278 Spring St between Hudson and Varick Sts, 212-691-1303, nycfiremuseum.org, suggested donation $1-$5), a former fire station in SoHo, now houses a collection of antique engines and other historic gear. Interesting in itself (moving, too, given the permanent exhibit commemorating firefighters' heroism after the attack on the World Trade Center), but one of the hour-long tours is even better. You'll need to get together a group of at least 20 friends, each paying five bucks. For that, retired NYC firefighters will guide you round the apparatus room on the first floor and, magnificently, give you an interactive fire safety presentation. Sound like high school? Forget it. We're talking full-on laser, black light and safe smoke simulation in a mocked-up apartment. Not one for asthmatics—and the museum recommends everyone wears comfortable clothes. Call in advance on 212-691-1303 ext.13.

700-706 *Buy international fashion— without boarding the airplane*

You might curse French women for their louche glamour, but you don't have to leave home to beat them at their own game. Provençal native Ludivine Grégoire's charming eponymous boutique (172 W 4th St between Cornelia and Jones Sts, 646-336-6576) provides an excellent arsenal of sweetly chic labels such as Vanessa Bruno, Les Prairies de Paris and Noro, which uses *très raffiné* fabrics like muslin and cotton sateen. Sticking with the Romance languages, get all Hispanic without having to endure the flamenco flounces at Lola y Maria (175 Rivington St between Attorney and Clinton Sts, 646-602-9556). Owner Gina Pagano fills the racks of her tiny shop with edgy Latin brands, including surreal creations by designer David Delfin (Spain's answer to Alexander McQueen) and Brazilian fave Coven—all scouted from Pagano's trips to Madrid and Buenos Aires.

Scandinavia is hardly well known for flamboyant couturiers, but it is thanks to Denmark that we have—along with supermodel Helena Christensen—floral designer Lief Sigersen's shabby-chic emporium Butik (605 Hudson St between Bethune and Little W 12th Sts, 212-367-8014). The shop features, among other enticements, Copenhagen-based designer Mads Norgaard's striped, maritime tees ($105) and Stories by Rikkemai's patchwork purses ($358). And forget about H&M and ABBA when thinking about Sweden's contribution to fashion: Copenhagen-born Steen Knigge's slick boutique Hus (11 Christopher St at Gay St, 212-620-5430) shows off the region with a slew of coveted lines including Nudie Jeans and Tretorn. You'll also find Filippa K's minimalist pieces and hard-to-find Tiger of Sweden.

Insufficiently exotic for you? It's time to ride the subway to India. Unable to find non-Bollywoodesque South Asian options in the city, sisters Selima and Karima Popatia opened Indömix (232 Mulberry St between Prince and Spring Sts, 212-334-6356) in 2004. While some goods, like crystal bangles ($45–$50 each), are sourced from Bombay markets, the Popatias also hit India's Fashion Week for coveted, girly lines like Kavita Bhartia.

Finally, when one country simply isn't enough, you need Kiosk (95 Spring St between Broadway and Mercer St, 212-226-8601). Like a shopper's version of a world tour, Alisa Grifo's well-curated boutique shifts its focus to wares from a particular nation every four months (Mexico, Sweden, Japan and Germany have all been featured). Don't worry about DVT, all you're risking here is burning a hole in the plastic.

707-708 *Find beauty freebies*

Shore up your vanity with some posh loot from the basement-level counters at Bergdorf Goodman (754 Fifth Ave at 57th St, 212-753-7300). Otherwise, local skin-care brand Kiehl's is legendary for its generously sized—but still TSA-friendly—freebies (109 Third Ave at 13th St, 212-677-3171; 154 Columbus Ave between 66th and 67th Sts, 212-799-3438). You can also sample ribbon-wrapped scents at the French fragrance house L'Artisan Parfumeur (see artisanparfumeur.com for locations).

709

Shop for sneakers at Alife Rivington Club

Sneakers are a religion at Alife Rivington Club (158 Rivington St between Clinton and Suffolk Sts, 212-375-8128), a tiny hole in the wall, which is the city's hub for hard-to-get treads. The store, like its wares, has a definite exclusive vibe: There's no sign, no street number—in fact no indication at all that the joint even exists from the outside. Look closely and ring the bell to enter, then check out the rotating selection of 80 or so styles. If you're smitten, don't dawdle—Alife doesn't restock, so once that fly pair of Adidas has sold out, those shoes are gone.

710

Sweat over delicious dandan noodles

Heat-seekers: Trek to a fluorescent-lit mall in Flushing, Queens, and locate the stand slinging chewy dandan noodles at $3 a pop. They're chockablock with pickled vegetables, crumbled pork, peanuts, fiery chili oil and fragrant Szechuan peppercorns. Ouch.
Sichuan Chengdu *Inside J & L Mall, 41-82 Main St between Maple and Sanford Aves, Flushing, Queens (no phone).*

711

Cheerlead yourself fit

Like, omigod! The three-part class at New York Health & Raquet Club (1433 York Ave at 76th St, 212-737-6666) combines cardio and dance training with intense body-conditioning exercises. "It's a hugely good workout, with a lot of core and upper-body work," says course creator (and former cheerleader) Andrew Gray. "We're not gonna be building pyramids, but we'll be conditioning the body as if preparing for that." Each class culminates, of course, with a big ol' cheer. Gym membership costs $125 per month with a $500 initiation fee.

712-719

Get a cheap Manhattan manicure

Artisan Spa

Although only a glass door separates this space from the maddening crowd of Union Square, it's like a different dimension inside: Porcelain vases overflow with cherry blossoms, fountains bubble, and plush chairs make for a blissed-out climate. A rainbow selection of Essie nail polish—and a widescreen TV—keep things interesting.
143 Fourth Ave between 13th and 14th Sts (212-260-1338).

Bellagio Nail & Spa

Clean and low-key, this salon furnishes perfect-ten manicures, delivered by some of the nicest employees in the city. Plenty of tables ensure you'll never have to wait more than 20 minutes: By the time you choose your polish, they'll be ready to seat you.
10 E 23rd St between Broadway and Madison Ave (212-505-6100).

Charming Nails

Ladies who lunch and their youthful prep-school counterparts frequent this small UES salon, where attentive staff live up to the name. Call in advance.
212 E 87th St between Second and Third Aves (212-987-7239).

CoCo Nails

Waltz into this churn-'em-out, no-frills joint at any hour (it's open until 8:30pm on weeknights) for immediate attention and perfectly turned-out fingertips.
164 E 33rd St between Lexington and Third Aves (212-684-7880).

Go Girl

This sunny nook—complete with pink-pillowed window seats, girly wall illustrations and an indie-music soundtrack—is a haven for pooch-lovin' LES chicks. Make an appointment to secure a seat at one of two manicure tables.
193 E 4th St between Aves A and B (212-473-9973).

Nails & More

Columbia kids flock to this unadorned space, where a friendly staff—clad in matching lavender aprons—ensures that all clients are in and out in 15 minutes (unless they stick around to watch soaps on the TVs). A luxurious hand massage is a welcome highlight.
267 Columbus Ave between 72nd and 73rd Sts (212-787-2444).

Nails on 54th

Smack in the center of midtown and roughly the size of a small apartment, this spot may not appeal to those with delicate tastes, but skilled, efficient service keeps lunchtime professionals coming back for more.
133 E 54th St, second floor, between Park and Lexington Aves (212-223-0650).

SoHo Nail

Two flights up, this sunny, bare-bones aerie offers over 360 hues of polish and, at $7, one of the cheapest manis in SoHo. Be prepared to wait for a turn at one of its ten stations. And be warned that it lacks dryers (and AC).
458 West Broadway, third floor, between Houston and Prince Sts (212-475-6368).

720 Go underground for sake

On weekends a wait is almost guaranteed for a seat at mini basement bar Decibel (240 E Ninth St between Second and Third Aves, 212-979-2733, sakebardecibel.com). What's the big deal? This Japanese spot has got a helluva sake selection. Most of the staff speaks little to no English, so be prepared to get lost in translation, especially when it comes to the snacks: They can be as mundane as rice crackers or as outré as jellyfish.

If you can't cram in at Decibel, try the midtown sake den Sakagura (211 E 43rd St between Second and Third Aves, 212-953-7253, sakagura.com). It's difficult to find—through the unmarked lobby of an office building, down some stairs and along a basement corridor—but there's a worthy prize at the end of the journey, in the form of more than 200 varieties of the Japanese rice wine.

721 Take cake and coffee at Café Sabarsky

Come for the *Kultur*, stay for the *Schlag*. The Neue Galerie's Café Sabarsky (1048 Fifth Ave at 86th St, 212-288-0665) offers a slab of Old Vienna and the perfect pre- or post-gallery restorative. Viennese cream-topped coffee is served from silver tray to marble tabletop, Adolf Loos designed the chairs, and Kurt Gutenbrunner (Wallsé) has seen to the menu. The desserts are to die for—apple strudel swaddled in fabulously flaky pastry, quark cheesecake with pears, and *faschingkrapfen* (a sort of doughnut with apricot confiture). Work it off viewing the small but exquisite collection of German and Austrian art upstairs.

722 See a multimedia show at 3LD

In spring 2007, the veteran downtown theater group 3-Legged Dog inaugurated its new mothership: a sinuous, space-agey two-stage complex off the beaten path in the Financial District. Equipped with top-shelf video, light and sound technology, the space has quickly become the hot venue for multimedia auteurs who want to push their theatrics into the 21st century. Particularly impressive is the use of use Musion Eyeliner, a technology that allows video projections to appear as if they're floating in space alongside actors onstage.

3LD Art & Technology Center *80 Greenwich St between Edgar and Rector Sts (212-388-7371/ 3ldnyc.org).*

723 Relish a roti at Nio's

This Trinidadian canteen has mastered the roti, a dinner-plate-size flatbread stuffed with split peas ($4.50). Request baby-soft potatoes and *channa* (chickpea curry) for one fine mess.

Nio's Trinidad Roti Shop *2702 Church Ave at Rogers Ave, East Flatbush, Brooklyn (718-287-9848).*

A few of my favorite things

724-729

Marty Markovitz, Mayor of Brooklyn

I love walking along both the Coney Island and the Brighton Beach boardwalks: There is nowhere better to capture the character—and characters—of Brooklyn.

The best Nova lox in New York is at Barney Greengrass (541 Amsterdam Ave at 86th St, 212-724-4707, barneygreengrass.com). I always order "The Sturgeon King"—it's the epitome of Jewish breakfast soul food.

I love eating at Junior's (386 Flatbush at Dekalb Ave, 718-852-5257, juniors cheesecake.com) because it defines "Brooklyn attitude." Alan Rosen and his family really know how to satisfy a Brooklyn appetite, too. It's the first place I go when I fall off the diet wagon.

If you're a lover of our fine-feathered friends like I am, Birdcamp (150 E 58th St, 212-935-5033) is the place to go. Once in a while, you'll catch me there boarding my eight-year-old African grey parrot, Beep, or buying his favorite toys and food.

Visiting the Museum of Jewish Heritage (36 Battery Place, 646-437-4200, mjhnyc.org) is an incredible experience. It's a living, breathing memorial to the depravity of human nature, but also to the hope, heroism and survival of the Jewish people.

Lastly, I love strolling the Brooklyn Promenade. It has the most breathtaking views of Manhattan.

730

Make yourself at home among 52 acres of flora

Since it opened almost a century ago, the Brooklyn Botanic Garden (900 Washington Ave at Eastern Pkwy, Prospect Heights, Brooklyn, 718-623-7200, bbg.org) has provided a relaxing haven for stressed New Yorkers. Don't miss the Osborne Garden at the Eastern Parkway entrance, spanning three acres.

731 Take in the Fab Four (kinda) over brunch

Doors open at 11am on Saturdays for the Beatles Brunch at BB King's Blues Club and Grill (237 W 42nd St between Seventh and Eighth Aves, 212-997-4144, bbkingblues.com), where you can munch on a classic all-you-can-eat buffet to the strains of Strawberry Fields, a look-alike, sound-alike Fab Four tribute band. Brunch is $42 ($39.50 advance) and the band takes to the stage at noon.

732-736 Get over yourself and relax into the luxury of a guy pedicure

When your best foot is forward, but it's hangnail-flecked and just plain nasty, head to one of these guy-friendly spots for help.

Jin Soon Natural Hand & Foot Spa

All three locations of this nail haven present minimalist decor—and a cast of generally gorgeous female patrons. While the menu presents seven varieties of pedicure, the staff recommend "The Balm of Purity" ($40) for men, which softens tough calluses via essential oils and includes a trance-inducing foot massage.
56 E 4th St at Bowery (212-473-2047); 23 Jones St between Bleecker and W 4th Sts (212-229-1070); 421 E 73rd St between First and York Aves (212-249-9144).

Renew & Relax

Outfitted with white-and-beige polka-dot walls, this spot boasts a regular influx of male clients. And no wonder: A basic 35-minute pedicure is just $23, and, since no polish application is involved, men benefit from an extra ten minutes of foot and calf massage. For $6 more, the staff spend extra time whittling away toughened heels and calluses.
50 Third Ave between 10th and 11th Sts (212-388-9821).

Nickel Spa for Men

Utilitarian decor and a laid-back vibe define this guys-only space. Two variations are on offer at the semi-enclosed nail station: The Spa Pedicure ($30) includes a seaweed-mask exfoliant, while the Deluxe Pedicure ($35) involves a hot paraffin treatment.
77 Eighth Ave at 14th St (212-242-3203).

Avalon Salon & Day Spa

Tucked away on a quiet street, this unisex spot offers private rooms complete with two chairs (so you can bring a friend). While they don't offer extravagant treatments, their basic pedicure ($27) meets the needs of even the most neglected feet.
112 Christopher St between Bleecker and Hudson Sts (212-337-1966).

Paul Labrecque Salon & Spa

Two variations are available at this full-service day spa (which houses a private gentleman's barbershop): the Classic Pedicure ($65) and the Deluxe Pedicure ($85), which starts with a salt scrub and ends with a high-gloss finishing buff. Afterward, grab a cup of coffee at the salon's complimentary espresso bar.
171 E 65th St between Lexington and Third Aves (212-988-7816).

737 Go gnudi at The Spotted Pig

While New York's first London-style gastropub makes a very fine burger, it's chef April Bloomfield's feather-pillow-light gnudi that you need. The plump, sage-butter-slicked gumdrops of sheep's ricotta are the Pig's most sought-after dish.
The Spotted Pig *314 W 11th St at Greenwich St (212-620-0393).*

738 Visit a very literary brownstone

Arthur Miller wrote the play *All My Sons* (1947) and Norman Mailer wrote his novel *The Naked and the Dead* (1948) while living in the same brownstone in Brooklyn Heights. Find it at 102 Pierrepont Street, between Clinton and Henry.

739

Order a stout float at Back Forty

Any great dish usually amounts to more than the sum of its parts, but rarely have we stumbled across such an alchemical marvel as the stout float ($8) at Back Forty (190 Ave B between 11th and 12th Sts, 212-388-1990). Dubbed a "dessert for people who don't want dessert" by chef Shanna Pacifico, it's a hearty muddle of malty O'Reilly's Stout from Pennsylvania brewery Sly Fox and creamy vanilla ice cream from Il Laboratorio del Gelato. Forget port and pie—in one bold stroke, this grown-up float sates desires for both an after-dinner drink and dessert.

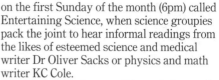

740-745

Release your inner dork

If you think this is a joke, think again—New York is a hotbed of bespectacled smartypants. Don your best pocket protector and check out one of the city's many geeky gatherings. The monthly gatherings at Café Scientifique (Rialto, 265 Elizabeth St between E Houston and Prince Sts, 212-334-7900, sciencecafenyc.org) see speakers from one of New York's many research institutions dazzle the crowd with their latest and greatest findings; the best bit is often the lively Q&A session that follows.

If the idea of "people doing strange things with electricity" appeals to you, then check out Dorkbot-NYC, a monthly meeting of designers, engineers, students and science boffs (see dorkbot.org for schedule and locations). Over at Cornelia Street Café (29 Cornelia St, 212-989-9319, corneliastreetcafe.com), Nobel laureate Roald Hoffmann curates a monthly gathering

on the first Sunday of the month (6pm) called Entertaining Science, when science groupies pack the joint to hear informal readings from the likes of esteemed science and medical writer Dr Oliver Sacks or physics and math writer KC Cole.

Nerds looking for something a little out of the ordinary won't want to miss the monthly concert party featuring "chiptune" sounds derived from rewiring hacked Nintendo gaming consoles. "It's the folk music of a new digital era," enthuses organiser Mike Rosenthal. "A lot of experimental music is hard for people to get into, but this has a real playful element to it." Tribeca's media venue the Tank (279 Church St at Franklin St, 212-563-6269, thetanknyc.org) plays host.

Not afraid to show off your high I.Q.? Join the throng of know-it-alls who know how to spell really hard words at the Williamsburg Spelling Bee in Pete's Candy Store (709 Lorimer St between N 10th and 11th Sts, Williamsburg, 718-302-3770). Compete for prizes such as Broadway show tickets or the chance to be included in one of two prestigious finals.

Strand Bookstore

Rather than single-error elimination, "it's three strikes and you're out," says comedian/host Jennifer Dziura. "It's a little less pressure." Whether you are competing for free booze, prestige or serious prizes, quiz nights are the perfect outlet for your inner dork. The gold standard in useless trivia is the Big Quiz Thing (bigquizthing.com), held every other Monday at the Slipper Room (167 Orchard St at Stanton St, 212-253-7246, slipperroom.com). It's one of the few places where you can see cool brainiacs vie for cold hard cash—and the occasional cookie. You've got to love any competition where you can earn Smart-Ass Points for a wrong answer that makes the host laugh.

And now for something completely different. Thanks to Nasty Canasta, Jonny Porkpie and the Pinchbottom crew (pinchbottom.com), your perverted genre fantasies could be about to come shimmying to life. The Pinchbottom dancers have served up such delights as the unforgettable boobified Godzilla, and the group promises 'more geektastic burlesque', including nights devoted to superheroes.

746

Browse 18 miles of books

Boasting an extraordinary 18 miles of books, the Strand Bookstore (828 Broadway at 12th St, 212-473-1452, strandbooks.com) offers a mammoth collection of over two million discount titles, made all the more daunting by its chaotic, towering shelves and surly staff (Patti Smith found fuel for her punk angst while working here). Reviewer discounts are in the basement, while rare volumes lurk upstairs. If you spend enough time here you can find just about anything you want (or don't want), from that out-of-print Victorian book of manners to the kitchiest sci-fi pulp.

747
Give a "Yee-haw!" when the bull riders come to town

Every January, Madison Square Garden hosts the Professional Bull Riders, Inc. (PBR) in the Versus Invitational—a three-day competition that pits the sport's best riders against its roughest buckers. According to PBR livestock director Cody Lambert, the "bulls make up half the athletes here; they're as special as the guys that ride them." See pbrnow.com for details.

748-750
Grab a two-buck beer. Hell, grab a one-buck beer

If you're on your uppers and need to drown your sorrows, chart a course for Welcome to the Johnsons (123 Rivington St between Essex and Norfolk Sts, 212-420-9911), a dive that masquerades as a 1972 rec room, tabletop Pac-Man and shopworn pool table included. Until 9pm nightly, icy Pabst cans are $1.50 ($2 afterward) and the $2 cocktails ($4 afterward) are brawny enough to double as antiseptic. Thus emboldened, embrace your inner collegian at NYU-centric sports haven Bar None (98 Third Ave between 12th and 13th Sts, 212-777-6663), where you can chug $2 drafts and drinks from 11am to midnight daily—and possibly booty-dance with an undergrad. If you're craving economical sustenance to sop up all the cheap booze, pop a squat at Anytime (93 N 6th St between Berry St and Wythe Ave, Williamsburg, Brooklyn, 718-218-7272) and order a mound of crunchy Tater Tots ($3.50), paired with $1 PBRs (6-8pm, 11pm-1am).

751
Time it right for taro-and-turnip cakes

Crispy on the outside and smooth as butter inside, the taro-and-turnip cakes ($4) at dim sum palace Golden Unicorn (18 East Broadway at Catherine St, 212-941-0911) are sweet with thick tamarind sauce—but available only on the weekends from noon to 3pm.

752
Learn judo with a movie legend (kinda)

Shiro Oishi, owner of Oishi Judo Club (547 Greenwich St between Charlton and Vandam Sts, 212-966-6850) has been busting out martial arts moves for a while—he played a henchman in 1989's *Black Rain*. For the last 20 years Oishi has offered straightforward lessons in judo to "everyone, from five-year-olds to old people—as long as they can still walk—and of all nationalities and skill levels," first on Leonard Street and now at this new studio on Greenwich Street. A block of 20 classes costs $450, and ten classes costs $225.

753
Listen to the word of mouth—get a table at A Voce

The name of last year's runaway hit translates to "word of mouth," but it wasn't just the glowing reports of Andrew Carmellini's refined Pan-Italian meals that persuaded readers of *Time Out New York* to vote it best new restaurant of 2007. Formerly of Café Boulud, Lespinasse and Le Cirque, the chef rebelled against his Francophilic stomping grounds, using the stylish, modern dining room (who can forget those Eames swivel chairs?) as a backdrop for imaginative Italian cuisine tempered with old-world touches. In Carmellini's hands, the traditional is elevated to the sublime: "My grandma's" meat ravioli—ground veal, pork and beef folded into al dente pasta kerchiefs and bathed in a confitlike tomato sauce—are a far cry from coarse red-sauce eats. French cuisine's loss is your gain; go there tonight.

A Voce *41 Madison Ave, entrance on 26th St between Madison Ave and Park Ave South (212-545-8555/avocerestaurant.com).*

754-756

Skate New York's iconic rinks...

Rockefeller Center

Admit it, just twirling on the ice in front of gawking tourists has enormous appeal. But how 'bout learning to skate first? Olympic gold medalist Jojo Starbuck holds group lessons at the rink—which turned 71 in 2008—twice a week. Or you can wing those triple lutzes on your own. Admission costs from $7.50.

600 Fifth Ave between 49th and 50th Sts (212-332-7654/rapatina.com/iceRink).

Trump Wollman Rink

Go for a glide at this romantic Central Park spot (admission $4.75-$12), which has been open for over 50 years. Night skating makes an especially good outing in the longish days of early spring: The rink is open until 11pm on weekends.

830 Fifth Ave, enter at Central Park South and Sixth Ave (212-439-6900/wollmanskatingrink.com).

The Pond at Bryant Park

The city's finest in free ice skating, on 17,000 square feet of temporary rink. Drawback? Free means crowds, by day or by night. But you can always watch the gliders while sipping a Mountini at Canadian-themed bar Celsius.

Sixth Ave between 40th and 42nd Sts (212-382-2953/thepondatbryantpark.com).

757-761

...then twirl on less crowded ones

Abe Stark Rink

This jumbo indoor rink near the Coney Island boardwalk (admission $8, skate rental $4.50) is out of the way for most New Yorkers. But its size—about four acres—makes the long trip on the F train worth it. Besides hosting open skate sessions on the weekends, there are also weekly youth hockey games.

Surf Ave at 19th St, Coney Island, Brooklyn (718-946-6536/nycgovparks.org).

Rockefeller Center

Sky Rink at Chelsea Piers

Kate Wollman Rink

Bet you didn't know New York City has a second Wollman Rink. Located next to the lake in Brooklyn's Prospect Park, the facility has 26,600 square feet of ice, which means it's one of the most spacious skating spots in the city (admission $3-$5). After a long day on the ice, chow down on casual fare—hot chocolate, hot dogs, pizza—from Kate's Corner, a snack bar conveniently located next to the rink.

Prospect Park, enter park from Ocean Ave at Parkside Ave, Brooklyn (718-287-6431/ prospectpark.org).

Riverbank State Park

Located about 85 blocks north of the midtown mayhem, the covered rink at Riverside Drive—which is part of a 28-acre recreational facility—provides some of the least-crowded weekend skating to be had in the whole of upper Manhattan (admission $3-$5). Thanks to the local kids who frequent Riverbank, the rink has a true community feel—something you won't find at Bryant Park.

679 Riverside Dr at 145th St (212-694-3642/ nysparks.state.ny.us/parks).

Sky Rink at Chelsea Piers

At the indoor Sky Rink at Chelsea Piers, you'll find the city's best-kept ice, with an admission price to match ($9-$12.50, skate rental $7). It's worth it, though: the glassy surface makes this an ideal spot for any budding Tara Lipinski or Brian Boitano to test out their skills. While the rink does have open skate times, it's best known for its stellar schedule of classes; see the website for details.

Pier 61, Hudson River between 17th and 23rd Sts (212-336-6100/chelseapiers.com).

Trump Lasker Rink

Central Park's other outdoor rink (admission $2.25-$4.50) is about the same size as attention-hogging Wollman, but without the long lines. Lasker's space is divided into two sections, one for public skating and one for hockey; kids as young as three can sign up for competitive team play. Adults will enjoy the picturesque view of the park's nearby pond. For an après glacé treat, head up to Harlem's yummy dessert café Make My Cake (121 St. Nicholas Ave at 116th St).

Midpark between 106th and 108th Sts (917-492-3857/wollmanskatingrink.com/main_lasker.htm).

Mission
Accomplice

Timothy Benzie **gets into character on a Gotham walking tour with a difference.**

You're somewhere in the heart of Little Italy on a chilly Sunday afternoon when you make contact with "the Russian." He's waiting for you nervously, and quickly shepherds you through the busy kitchen of a Sicilian restaurant into an unused dining area. A nod by the gangster to one of the staff means food and wine are quickly produced. It's down to business. He doesn't mince words: Do I have what he's looking for?

Make no mistake, Accomplice: New York is not like any other walking tour. For one thing, participants only learn where the tour begins the day before, via a paranoid phone call from a stranger. The tour also tells you almost nothing about Manhattan the way other jaunts do. There's no time in Accomplice for anyone to point out where James Dean had his second apartment or where Patricia Field buys her bagels. There's no time because you have to complete a "mission," during which you are most definitely being watched, and maybe even followed, in an experience that feels close enough to a real adventure to raise jittery giggles from the most jaded participant.

For those who came in late, the first of the Accomplice tours began in 2005 and was so successful it spawned the follow-up Accomplice: West Village; more variations are on the way. If you live in Little Italy, SoHo or the West Village you probably know the drill, but for anyone else the tours have achieved that rare cultural balance: They're cool enough to be a best-kept secret, successful enough to thrive.

It's all thanks to brother and sister team Tom and Betsy Salamon. "We were on a walking tour with our parents around all of those neighborhoods, and while it was sort of interesting and we'd lived in New York for a long time, and we'd seen stuff we'd not seen before, it was very dry and kind of like a heightened field trip," Tom explains. "We were talking about it a couple of days later and laughing about how dull it was, and thought it would be really fun to have a sort of game that took place in those neighborhoods.

"We thought that it would be fun to have actors along the way who would jump out at you… Then we thought what if there was a purpose behind it, a story, and that maybe we could write a story about why a group of people would be doing this," Tom chuckles. "So we thought a crime story would be fun."

The first tour Accomplice: New York was the result of six months' planning. Set downtown around Chinatown and Little Italy, it involved the incident with the "Russian mafia" mentioned above, as well as… but to give anything else away would be churlish. Part of the joy of the tours is an ongoing uneasiness Hitchcock would have loved. Is this an actor, or a local ready to clean your clock? (The cast, with brag sheets full of Broadway credits, are really very good.)

> *"Part of the joy of the tours is an ongoing uneasiness Hitchcock would have loved. Is this an actor, or a local ready to clean your clock?"*

The tour also works because the specific tasks feel less like orienteering challenges and more like inevitable steps in a narrative. Heather Pilkington, taking part in the tour, is thoroughly taken in. "It was like being Robert De Niro in a gangster film," she laughs, after being as floored as everyone else by the tour's shock ending.

Tom admits that the movies have had some influence. "I have a background in film and Betsy has a background in psychotherapy, and those two elements together I think enabled us to really figure out a way to mess with people—in a theatrical way.

"We had sort of envisioned it as having stepped into the middle of movie. But we were also really into reality TV at this time, which was just getting started, like *Survivor*.

So it was going to feel a bit like a reality show… but it was before reality shows are like they are now, which is totally ridiculous." (Thankfully the tours are nothing like reality TV, but it's nice to know Jeff Probst inspired somebody in a positive way.)

The other element that makes the tours work is that the tasks aren't that easy. Participants are given a cell number in case they get lost or make a mistake, which happens with some regularity. Being a local is not considered an advantage. Tom is full of stories, including one where a team had to be prevented from stealing a painting from a building because they thought it was a clue.

Nearing the conclusion of Accomplice: West Village, one team is feeling very cocky. They reckon they spotted the twist a few blocks back, although it turns out they were only half right. One of the posse is David Mills, an editor and writer, who began the experience a little reticent but is now smiling. "The old cliché holds true: the more you put into it, the more you get out of it," he admits. "I went from being bemused by what I was experiencing, to amused by it, and fully participating in it. I mean, I wouldn't say it was a great way to learn about the history of the Village, but as a thing to do, it was thoroughly kooky and a lot of fun."

Franchising is such an ugly word, but Accomplice: Hollywood premieres in the spring (and no, participants won't be given a car to drive around in), while September 2008 will see the proposed launch of Accomplice: San Francisco. For the moment, though, the enterprise is small enough for Tom and Betsy to appear regularly at the tour's concluding venue to talk to participants. It's a nice touch. If you complete the tour later in the day, actors from the experience turn up to take their bow, with some real surprises.

So did I have what "the Russian" wanted, huddled in the back of the Italian restaurant, in that totally alien yet oddly familiar cinematic scenario? Of course. I just made him an offer he couldn't refuse.

Accomplice: New York is a three-hour experience (1-5pm Sat and Sun) for eight people, costing $65. Accomplice: West Village is a two-and-a-half-hour tour (1-3pm Sat and Sun), also for eight people, costing $55. For more information, visit accompliceny.com.

763

...or tour with the guide who literally wrote the book

Venerated historian Justin Ferate wrote the book on Gotham walking tours. No, really—the city commissioned him to pen the NYC tour-guide licensing exam, which he designed to educate, as well as assess, would-be guides. In addition to a regular roster of tours covering everything from midtown murals to Green-Wood Cemetery to the quaint attractions of City Island, Ferate leads a free 90-minute trek through Grand Central every Friday at 12:30pm. Visit his website, justinsnewyork.com, for more information.

764

Sample the PB at Peanut Butter & Co

Bully stole your lunch again? Replace it at Peanut Butter & Co: The staff use eight types of peanut butter to create over 15 different goopy pacifiers, such as the popular Elvis—the King's famous favorite of peanut butter, bacon, banana and honey, grilled. The warm cinnamon-raisin-flavored peanut-butter sandwich with vanilla cream cheese and tart apple slices is good taste and texture rolled into one. Death by Peanut Butter is a landslide of ice cream, Peanut Butter Cap'n Crunch and peanut-butter chips. Goober-free items bolster the brown-bag theme: tuna melt, bologna sandwich… Better get a lock for your Speed Racer lunch box.
Peanut Butter & Co *240 Sullivan St between Bleecker and W 3rd Sts (212-677-3995/ilovepeanutbutter.com).*

765
Get a free ride… or become a designated driver yourself

Women-run nonprofit RightRides (718-964-7781) wants you to get home safely. They invite women and trans people to call for a free ride in a Zipcar within 19 neighborhoods of Brooklyn and Manhattan, from Greenpoint to the East Village, on Saturday nights. Those who want to volunteer as designated drivers can sign up for an orientation session at rightrides.org.

766

Try two classic dishes in the place of their invention

Located in a spectacular, triangle-shaped, 1837 building on a corner where three streets meet, Delmonico's has a long, illustrious history. It was the city's first fine-dining institution, and is credited with having invented lobster Newburg and baked Alaska. Both are still served.
Delmonico's *56 Beaver St at William Sts (212-509-1144).*

767-770

Cringe and purge

It's never been easier for therapy-obsessed New Yorkers to unload the lurid details of their lives. Perhaps it's the high rent that's leaving them cash-strapped, but growing numbers of Gothamites seem to be substituting more traditional therapy for more public forms of unburdening—for example, sharing some of their more salacious sexual escapades with roomfuls of eager strangers. Whether your aim is to spout off, shock or just live vicariously, there is now a slew of open mics and public readings—even a game-show-style event—where you can let your slip show, Freudian or otherwise.

Fahrenheit

Hosts DanTagonist and Brad Ackerman first met in April 2007 and decided to run this spin-off of the Antagonist Movement (first Sunday of every month, 9pm); tales range from guys beating off and bestiality to liaisons with congressional leaders, but our favorite performer has to be septuagenarian D'yan Forest, who strums a ukulele and sings songs about her juicy, senior, uh, sex life. You'll also get to enjoy details of event regular "Brother" Mike Cohen's junior-high-school blow-job sessions—and how he once let a dog lick food from his penis. Brrrr.
Black and White 86 E 10th St between Third and Fourth Aves (uncoolkids.com).

In the Flesh

Rachel Kramer Bussel formed this monthly erotica reading in October 2005 as a way for published writers to share their humorous, porny works with a captive New York crowd. Readers have included *Playboy* model and Washingtonienne sex-blogging scribe Jessica Cutler and erotic novelist Gael Greene, and among the prize tales are comedian Dan Allen explaining to eager listeners that he lost his virginity at the age of 16 to a hooker—one of the first times he'd revealed the incident.
Happy Ending Lounge 302 Broome St between Eldrige and Forsyth Sts (inthefleshreadingseries. blogspot.com).

The Liar Show

Started in August 2006, this event asks the audience to listen to four explicit performers, then vote on which one of the storytellers is lying. Not so easy, when you're listening to stories of this caliber—perhaps the one of Christen Clifford's that involves her trying to masturbate while breastfeeding, then getting locked out in her hallway (with her vibrator) when the FedEx guy shows up. If you spot the fib, you'll win a free "I can tell a lie" T-shirt.
Comix Comedy Club 353 W 14th St between 8th and 9th Aves, (212-524-2500/ theliarshow.blogspot.com).

Storyhole

Joan Vorderbruggen held her first naughty open mic in February 2007, as a raunchy option for hipster Brooklynites who wanted filthy talk without having to take the L train into Manhattan. You might encounter a poet or health-care provider telling the crowd about, say, her butt plug "slipping in" and the attendant fears of having to go to the emergency room. And for your honesty? Win a new chastity belt, some Punky Brewster undies, or maybe a free beer.
The Palace Cafe 206 Nassau Ave between Humboldt Ave and Russell St, Greenpoint, Brooklyn (storyhole.com).

771 Nibble a potato knish at Knish Nosh

The hefty pastries ($2.50) from this stalwart are commendable for their floury, elastic dough and the homespun mashed-potato-and-onion filling. (You'll catch Knish Nosh employees peeling their veggies in the back daily.)
Knish Nosh 100-30 Queens Blvd at 67th Ave, Forest Hills, Queens (718-897-4456).

772 Visit the site of Son of Sam's first murder

Around 1am on July 29, 1976, a postal worker named David Berkowitz fired five shots into a car parked on Buhre Avenue, between Mayflower and Pilgrim Aves in the Bronx. One woman died and the Son of Sam was born.

113 Shop at Union Square Greenmarket

We can't vouch for the latte-sipping owners of little yippy dogs who seem to make up the regulars at this weekly foodfest (Mon, Wed, Fri and Sat), but for locavores and Gristedes-goers alike the supreme visual appeal of comestible flora, fauna and baked deliciousness here is undeniable. Plus, free samples always make our pupils dilate.

774-778

Eat the finest chocolate

A wave of new premium chocolate shops has provided ample choice for chocoholic Manhattanites looking for a fix. Legendary chocolatier Jacques Torres has unveiled his most irresistible creation yet: Chocolate Haven (350 Hudson St between Charlton and King Sts, entrance on King St, 212-414-2462, jacques torres.com), an 8,000-square-foot factory that serves as the Manhattan hub for the pastry chef's growing chocolate empire. The space features a cocoa-pod-shaped café overlooking the candy-making facilities, so visitors can indulge in treats and watch as cocoa beans are transformed into exquisite chocolate bars.

West Village sweet boutique Chocolate Bar (48 Eighth Ave between Horatio and Jane Sts, 212-366-1541, chocolatebarnyc.com) carries only candies, cookies and brownies from local makers of the highest caliber. Check out the shop's mojito truffle, flavored with rum, lime and mint. If that's not enough, then simply stroll down to No.80 Eighth Avenue at West 14th Street and load up on more dark stuff at Li-Lac Chocolates (212-274-7374, li-lacchocolates.com). This neighborhood institution has been sweetly pushing delectable treats on locals since 1923, but in 2005 they upped and moved into this cute corner shop, painted lilac of course.

Boozehounds, on the other hand, will fall head over heels for Chocolat Michel Cluizel (chocolatmichelcluizel.com). The fine French chocolatier opened his first stateside shop inside the Flatiron's ABC Carpet & Home (888 Broadway at 19th St, 212-473-3000), and even managed to score a liquor license. His "adult" bonbons, wrapped in foil, contain premium hooch. Smooth, top-quality chocolate is spiked with tipples such as rum, cognac, calvados, vodka or whisky.

If you like chocolate on your candies, then check out Divalicious (365 Broome St between Elizabeth and Mott Sts, 212-343-1243). Here, you'll find chocolate-covered everything—fortune cookies, graham crackers and pretzels—as well as chocolate lollipops and charming chocolate hearts.

Union Square Greenmarket

A few of my favorite things

779-783

Hedda Lettuce, drag queen

I love the Clearview Classics at the Chelsea Cinemas (260 West 23rd St, 212-691-5519, clearview cinemas.com). Every Thursday night, straight, gay, old and young come to watch classic camp films on the big screen. I host, doing a commentary to allow some audience participation in old faves like *Queen of Outer Space, Mommie Dearest, Showgirls* and *Valley of the Dolls.* **Payless Shoe Store (payless.com) at 484 Eighth Avenue has come a long way over the years—they have so many fierce heels now, I could cream myself. Even Pat Fields designs for them! They love a fashionable girl with big feet, so I can always find my size.** Garo Sparo is one of the most talented designers on the scene and he is still an underground sensation. He designs for every burlesque act under the sun (as well as a host of Upper East Side society matrons) and he has a wonderful little studio in the East Village (by appointment only, 212-255-0383, garosparo.com). **I always eat at the Ukrainian East Village Restaurant (140 Second Ave, 212-614-3283). The food is delicious, cheap, portion-heavy and great quality; it is jam-packed on weekends and you can watch Ukrainian performers dancing along to guitars and tambourines in colorful skirts.** Mo Jo's Coffee Shop (128 Charles Street, 212-691-6656) is a sweet little cafe that looks like you stepped into a scene from *Little House on the Prairie*—log-cabin walls, wooden details, and the best stack of blueberry pancakes for just $4.

784

Sample the cuisine of Iacopo Falai—and don't miss his bombolini

He slices. He dices. He tempers chocolate. He rolls pasta. He makes the dough rise, and ensures that the soufflés don't fall. Ice creams and éclairs? They were done this morning. And don't forget all those savory dishes: octopus with celery and caviar, seared foie gras with chestnuts, braised short ribs... This isn't an informercial. We're talking about none other than Iacopo Falai, the onetime Le Cirque pastry chef who has slowly built himself a mini hipster-café-and-restaurant kingdom south of Houston Street—Falai (68 Clinton St between Rivington and Stanton Sts, 212-253-1960), Falai Panetteria (79 Clinton St at Rivington St, 212-777-8956) and the most recent, Caffe Falai (265 Lafayette St between Prince and Spring Sts, 917-338-6207). His entrepreneurial skill impresses, but what really gets us is that, in a city of specialists, Falai, a chef-owner-baker-pâtissier, does it all.

Our favorite Falai creation? His vanilla-specked, brioche-like *bombolini* doughnuts, filled with cream or jam and rolled in sugar. The heavenly pastries are sold at the Panetteria and Caffe locations for $2.50 each, a price slashed in half after 7pm.

785
Sit in the front row at the opera for $25

Front orchestra seats at New York City Opera can be had for $25, as part of its Opera-for-All program. Tickets go on sale at nycopera.com on Mondays at 10am; they sell out in 24 hours-ish.

786
Visit the country's first sushi bar

In 1963, at 145 E 52nd St, Nobuyoshi Kuraoka opened sushi bar Restaurant Nippon: America's first. Nippon is still dishing the fish, but up the street at No.155.

787 Play badminton

Flip the bird to your opponents at the New York City Badminton Club in Manhattan ($25 per day for nonmembers and $15 for members, 646-271-3228, nycbadminton. com). The club is open year-round, shuttlecocks are provided, and rackets can be rented for $3 a day.

788 See the subway's best views

Riding the subway may not be the most relaxing way to get around when you're packed in with the puffy-coated throng during rush hour, but hop aboard an N train on a Saturday afternoon and be treated to an awe-inspiring skyline view as the train hits the elevated tracks in Queens. Other transfixing views can be seen from the L to Canarsie, the 7 to Shea Stadium, and the B or Q to Coney Island. If you have an entire afternoon to kill, ride the A train all the way out to Far Rockaway—you'll pass by Jamaica Bay, where you can try to spot geese, warblers and woodcocks from your seat.

789 Dance at Camaradas El Barrio

Spanish Harlem's most vibrant nightspot, Camaradas El Barrio (2241 First Ave at 115th St, 212-348-2703, camaradaselbarrio.com) is a Puerto Rican tapas bar, whose wooden benches, exposed brick, and modest gallery create a casual hang for kicking back over a pitcher of sangria. Camaradas has an irresistible menu of small plates (try the root and vine chips), a loyal clientele of young Boricuas, and a throbbing music scene. On Thursday nights, the Afro-Rican rhythms of local band Yerba Buena fill the bar; Fridays see a DJ spinning salsa, hip hop and 1980s dance hits; and Saturdays host a rotation of Latin funk and jazz bands.

790

Visit the
Folk Art Museum

The stunning eight-floor
American Folk Art Museum
(45 W 53rd St between Fifth
and Sixth Aves (212-265-1040/
folkartmuseum.org) celebrates
traditional craft-based work,
but one of the best ways to
explore the collection of pottery, trade signs, delicately stitched
log-cabin quilts and wind-up toys is on one of the Free Music
Fridays (5:30-7:30pm). Not only do you get a chance to explore the
exhibits for free, but there is free music in the magnificent atrium.

791 Plump for plov at Vostok

Forgo the smoky kebabs at this Jewish-Uzbek eatery for a taste of better-than-it-sounds plov. The heaping rice dish ($6.50) is cooked in lamb fat with onion and carrot, and dotted with chunks of meat. Mop up what's left with a hunk of lepushka—tandoor-baked bread sprinkled with nigella seeds.
Vostok *5507 13th Ave at 55th St, Borough Park, Brooklyn (718-437-2596).*

792 Swing, midsummer

With more than 800 hoofers on hand, Midsummer Night Swing (Lincoln Center, 62nd St between Amsterdam and Columbus Aves, 212-875-5766, lincolncenter.org) can appear more like a mosh pit than a cotillion. But there's order in the chaos, and whether the fare is salsa, two-step, swing, Charleston or tango, each evening begins at 6:30pm with a lesson for all levels of experience. The dance begins in earnest an hour later, with couples congregating at the front toward stage right, while singles gather stage left. Note that it's perfectly acceptable for women to ask men to dance. Tread lightly.

Midsummer Night Swing

793 Pay your respects to the legends of jazzy St. Albans

A handful of jazz greats have called St. Albans, Queens, home: Count Basie settled in at Adelaide Road and 175th Street in 1946 (his property boasting a front yard as long as a city block), Ella Fitzgerald was resident at 179-07 Murdock Avenue at 179th Street in the 1950s, and John Coltrane lived at 115-56 Mexico Street at Quencer Road. A mural depicting the borough's jazz powerhouses decorates the northern side of Linden Boulevard, under the LIRR.

794
Earn bucks as a temporary thespian

You've seen the Ricky Gervais show? Well, jobs as an extra are out there for the taking, no joke. They can be anything from modeling for print ads to appearing in commercials, and usually call for four to eight hours' work a day, for which you might earn $150-$200. "Last week, I got a call for a print job that was paying $1,200 for, like, a four- or five-hour job," says Extra Talent Agency rep Gabi Suau. "That was actually for an old man. So it depends. Right now, I need hipsters for $50 for a ten-hour day, which is, you know, going to be tricky to fill." On the bright side, you don't need a résumé, SAG card or, in fact, any experience at all. Go to extratalentagency.com, register as "actor," enter a short profile (hair color, eye color, ethnicity, height, weight) and snail mail a photo. Then wait for your not-so-close-up.
Extra Talent Agency *1133 Broadway, Suite 1201, between 25th and 26th Sts (212-807-8172/ extratalentagency.com).*

795
Get a beer and a back-rub

While biodynamic boosters and wheatgrass juice might go over well at girlier venues, you'll find that beer (Sixpoint's Brownstone and IPA) and liquor are the superfoods of choice at the midtown men's spa Truman's (120 E 56th St between Lexington and Park Aves, 212-759-5015). Drinks are served gratis with any service and can be enjoyed in the loungey reception area (where flat-screens display the latest game) or carried into the treatment stations. In a similar fashion, Body by Brooklyn (275 Park Ave at Washington Ave, Clinton Hill, Brooklyn, 718-923-9400) set apart a portion of its enormous 10,000-square-foot space to build a brightly lit bar and restaurant that's open to spa patrons and the general public alike. Drinks can be served before, after or even during a treatment, and customers are free to wander around in slippers and a robe between the spa and lounge areas.

796
Die for a Dior at FIT

The museum at the Fashion Institute of Technology houses one of the world's most important collections of clothing and textiles. Curated by the influential fashion historian Valerie Steele, it incorporates everything from extravagant costumes and designer dresses to sturdy denim work clothes.
Museum at FIT *Seventh Ave at 27th St (212-217-5800/fitnyc.edu/museum).*

797
Sample monkey glands

Are monkey glands really an aphrodisiac for men? Give them a chance at i-Shebeen Madiba (195 DeKalb Ave between Adelphi St and Carlton Ave, Fort Greene, Brooklyn, 718-855-9190), the city's only South African restaurant. Rickety wood tables are animated with a diverse crowd tucking into Durban Bunny Chow, ostrich carpaccio, Mozambique-style prawns, and baby-back ribs basted in a sweet monkey-gland sauce. Afro-pop and potent cocktails keep the joint jumping, but the glands' powers of arousal are hard to substantiate—menus don't serve love, so it's best to bring your own.

798
Watch women wrestle. In Jell-O

Think the days of female empowerment through combat were over? Think again: This tongue-in-cheek sports satire brings ready-made desserts, about 50 gallons of them each night, back into the ring where they belong. An introductory wrestling lesson starts things off at 6:30pm, while musical interludes from the likes of her Majesty, DJ Xerox and the Domestics keep things pumping all night long.
Arlene's Grocery *95 Stanton St between Ludlow and Orchard Sts (212-358-1633/jellowrestle.com).*

799-803

Shop for fruit and vegetables, direct from New York's farms

Thinking of turning locavore? *Rebecca Flint Marx* gives you a headstart on the comestibles.

Wyckoff Farmhouse Museum

Surrounded by verdant rows of Swiss chard, eggplant, garlic, beets, amaranth and mesclun, the Wyckoff Farmhouse Museum seems worlds away from its urban perch on Utica Avenue in East Flatbush, Brooklyn. The farm's 1.5 acres, wedged between two busy roads, are the stuff that the dreams of idealistic urban planners are made of—a lush, green space readily accessible to an inner-city community. But Wyckoff is no idle fantasy. Its farmhouse, which dates to 1652, may be a monument to a bygone way of life, but the organic produce harvested on its grounds has been a vital resource for the neighborhood since 2003, when the farmers' market was established (1-4pm Sun). During the summer and autumn, local high-school students learn about entrepreneurship by growing and selling the farm's 35 different vegetables (including collards, bitter melon and callaloo, favorites in this Caribbean neighborhood), 15 herbs and eight varieties of berry.
5816 Clarendon Rd at 59th St, East Flatbush, Brooklyn (718-629-5400).

Queens County Farm Museum

Occupying the city's largest swath of undisturbed farmland, the 47-acre museum farm has been operational for more than 200 years. Its apple orchard, livestock and 18th-century farmhouse have long made the site a field-trip favorite. During the late summer, the farm's chemical-free produce—like heirloom tomatoes, corn and peppers—is sold from its vegetable stand (10am-4pm Wed-Sun), and fresh eggs are available year-round. From summer 2008, wine from the farm's vineyard should be providing a more adult attraction. According to vineyard manager Gary Mitchell, the grapes—a blend of merlot, chardonnay, and cabernets sauvignon and franc—have flourished in the borough's loamy soil. Currently in their fourth season of growth, they'll be bottled next January. The concept of a city vineyard, much like the idea of a working farm in Queens, is sure to lure the curious and disbelieving. "There's a novelty factor," Mitchell acknowledges. "But we want to make a decent bottle of wine."
73-50 Little Neck Pkwy near Union Tpke, Floral Park, Queens (718-347-3276).

Taqwa Community Farm

In 1991, the land at the corner of 164th Street and Ogden Avenue in the Bronx neighborhood of Highbridge was a vacant lot littered with hypodermic needles, broken glass and the bodies of dead cats and dogs. Today, it's Highbridge's nearly two-acre answer to the Garden of Eden. Mulberry, fig, apple and cherry trees line the garden's perimeter, while a rose-covered trellis presides over carefully tended plots. Strolling among the pole beans, okra, eggplants, callaloo and collards, Bobby Watson explains how his father, Abu Talib, helped found the garden as a way to heal the community, which had been torn apart by drugs and crime. Approximately 100 families, many of them transplanted from the South, have plots, and many donate their produce to Taqwa's weekly youth-run farmers' market (9am-4pm Sat). The garden has become a de facto community center, providing both literal and figurative sustenance. "People come to volunteer, they come out of curiosity," Watson says. "People come just to come."
90 W 164th St between Ogden and Woodycrest Aves, Bronx (646-358-9254).

Hands & Heart Garden

One of the city's newest urban farms, the 22,000-square-foot site at the corner of New Lots and Alabama Avenues in East New York, Brooklyn, was officially unveiled in June 2007. A project of East New York Farms, it is home to more than 20 gardeners. While not all of its space has been cultivated thus far, the farm already boasts bounty that includes chard, kale, eggplant, okra, zucchini and peppers, much of this sold at the long-established East New York Farmers' Market (9am-2:30pm Sat). In an area where fresh, healthy food is often in short supply, the Hands & Heart Garden has become a symbol of community empowerment.

As councilman Charles Barron said at the garden's opening ceremony, "If local merchants don't take care of the food, we'll get it ourselves." *New Lots and Alabama Aves, East New York (718-649-7979). The market is on New Lots Ave between Barbey and Schenck Sts, East New York, Brooklyn (718-649-7979).*

Red Hook Community Farm

"Our farmers wear Phat Farm, not overalls," says Ian Marvy with a laugh. As he wanders through rows of vegetables, Marvy talks enthusiastically about neighborhood teens who have helped to make the Red Hook Community Farm's almost three acres the thriving space it is today. In 2003, the farm was an empty lot, before Added Value, the community-oriented nonprofit that Marvy helped found, began converting it into tillable soil in partnership with the city's Parks & Recreation Department. Now the farm is used as both a learning tool and a source of fresh, organic food. In addition to serving the community with two weekly, youth-run farmers' markets (10am-2pm Wed at the Red Hook Seniors Center, 6 Wolcott St at Dwight St; 9am-3pm Sat at Red Hook Farm itself), the farm also supplies local restaurants like 360 and the Good Fork with its produce; on a recent day,

crates of escarole, arugula and turnips were being packed up for delivery. Eventually, Marvy hopes to take the farm completely off the power grid, instead using solar power, biofuel and wind energy. In the meantime, he says that one of the farm's most important objectives is to work with the entire Red Hook community. "There are 11,000 people living here," he says as workmen hammer away at the Ikea store in a neighboring lot. "It's a realistic goal." *Columbia and Beard Sts, Red Hook, Brooklyn (718-855-5531).*

804 *Get a rockabilly haircut*

Specializing in 1940s and '50s haircuts ($15-$25) including WWII flyboy-style crew cuts and fades, Tomcats (130 India St between Franklin St and Manhattan Ave, Greenpoint, Brooklyn, 718-349-9666) has a laid-back, country vibe. Grab a cold beer from an authentic icebox in the cream-and-red space and relax to bluegrass while you wait for your shave ($25). Ask to be served by co-owner Joey Covington, who has been working as a barber across the country for 13 years and sports an Elvis-style pompadour.

Tomcats

805

Pick at french fries at Pommes Frites...

There are no better fries than at this 12-year-old East Village shack, which gives the side dish the spotlight it deserves. Owner-operators Suzanne Levinson and Omer Shorshi cook their taters twice before serving the golden-brown goodies straight up in a crisp paper cone. **Pommes Frites** *123 Second Ave between 7th and 8th Sts (212-674-1234/ pommesfrites.ws).*

806-808

...then nibble NYC's next best frites

Vol de Nuit

Both the frites and the wooden stand that they arrive in are handmade at red-lit Belgian beer haven Vol de Nuit. The vegetable-oil-fried russets (costing $4-$6) are slim, crisp-edged and always served piping hot. A side of thick, European-style aioli (50¢) is creamy, almost like frosting.
148 W 4th St between Sixth Ave and MacDougal St (212-979-2616).

Cookshop

The addictively crunchy, thin pommes frites (costing $5) served at Cookshop are dusted with a surprisingly complex conbination of spices (it's a mix that includes celery salt, shrimp powder, smoked paprika, cumin and coriander). Dip them in the house-made mayonnaise.
156 Tenth Ave at 20th St (212-924-4440).

Strip House

Though not quite a fry, the goose-fat potatoes ($11) at Strip House are a more than worthy alternative. Spuds are simmered in fat, mixed with rosemary and thyme, and baked, before being plunged into the deep fryer.
13 E 12th St between Fifth Ave and University Pl (212-328-0000).

809 Dress up as Björk

Fans of Iceland's most famous pop export reckon that chilling with their favorite avant-songstress is pretty unlikely, so Krista Madsen and Zofia Kazan do the next best thing: They dress up as the Nordic ice queen. The duo host an annual Army of Björk costume party every January at Stain (766 Grand St, 718-387-7840, stainbar.com), a raw but comfortable bar with deep couches, high ceilings, and a large outdoor garden. Ready your swan-wrapped dresses…

810-811

Teach the kids yoga

Once you've dropped your kids off for a class at Karma Kids Yoga (104 W 14th St between Sixth and Seventh Aves, 646-638-1444, karmakidsyoga.com), you can hang out in the parents area enjoying 45 minutes of peace while they sing, stretch and do animal poses. Classes cost $20-$30. Or, for more money but requiring less adult effort, you can hire one of the yogis from Next Generation Yoga (212-595-9306, nextgenerationyoga.com) to teach a private class right in your living room for $75-$125 per session. Chill out while the kids do traditional yoga poses and creative movement, and then join them at the end for the deep breathing and relaxation exercises, which feature an ultra-tranquil foot massage and lavender-scented eye pillows.

Army of Björk

812-820 *Catch a cab, every time*

Adam Rathe asks the drivers themselves how best to get a ride in the city's worst spots.

The Lower East Side on a Friday night

The mistake most people make, according to 11-year-veteran driver Ricky, is stumbling into the street and tossing their arm in the air. "Stand on the north side of Delancey," he says. "Catch an empty cab coming back from Williamsburg." Another tip: Trek to Allen Street, where traffic moves at a steady pace.

Fifth Avenue during rush hour

If you haven't got a driver waiting for you outside Bergdorf's, head a block uptown, near Central Park. "Fifth Avenue is the busiest street in town," says Ricky. "We like to cruise midtown, and mostly stay below 65th Street."

The Meatpacking District on a Saturday night

Luke Oil (63 Eighth Ave at 13th St, 212-645-9578), according to one cabbie with 20 years in the seat, is where you can find an empty taxi no matter how crazy the scene gets.

The Flatiron District

Where midtown and downtown meet, Fifth Avenue and Broadway converge to create a major traffic nightmare. Heading downtown will just drop you into the mess of Union Square, so cabbies suggest that you go north. "Cabs are more likely to be [traveling] between Fifth Avenue and Broadway," one driver says, so you can try catching them going crosstown above Madison Square Park while they're trying to avoid the same traffic you are.

The Upper West Side on a Friday night

People jet downtown for dinner, notes driver Muhammad Yasm, who's been on the road since 1989, so forget going south on Broadway. Head to West End Avenue, says Yasm. "And the lights are synced," he says. "I once went from 106th Street to 79th Street on one green light." Plus, there's a gas station tucked away on the glitzy corner of West End and 96th.

The gray area on a weeknight

The maps in the backseats of taxis don't even offer a name for the neighborhood from East 23rd Street to 34th Street between Madison and Lexington Avenues, so why would drivers ever think to cruise the 'hood? For the food—join them at Curry in a Hurry (119 Lexington Ave at 28th St, 212-683-0900), a favorite for a quick snack.

The Upper East Side during morning rush hour

Says Inda, a cabbie with two years on the road: Get yourself to York Avenue. Lots of cabs fuel up at the Shell station on East 96th Street and First Avenue, then head south looking for fares.

West Chelsea on a Saturday afternoon

Even if the plan is to just go gallery-hopping, make sure to wear your walking shoes. "No driver goes to Chelsea to find fares," says Bashir, who's been behind the wheel for ten years. "Your best bet is get a cab that just dropped someone off." The best place to do that is only a scary walk across the West Side Highway away. "Stand in front of Chelsea Piers," Bashir advises, since it's a steady dropoff location.

Alphabet City in the morning

"Never [try to] catch a cab off an avenue over here," says one driver, taking a break at cabbie canteen Punjabi (114 E Houston St at Ave A, 212-533-9048). "Walk down to Houston or up to 14th Street, where you'll catch cars coming off of the FDR." And what about Punjabi, where cabs are always lined up? "This is the best spot, because drivers always stop here to use the restroom!"

If you wanted, you could play drag-queen bingo—for prizes—nearly every night of the week. Sundays at 7pm, pay $5 to see Trai La Trash calling the numbers at Splash Bar (50 W 17th St between Fifth and Sixth Aves, 212-691-0073). A two-drink minimum gets you into the game at Mo Pitkin's House of Satisfaction (34 Ave A between Second and Third Sts, 212-777-5660) on Mondays at 9pm. On Tuesdays, join Kenny Dash for bingo at Climaxx (76 Christopher St between Seventh Ave South and Bleecker St, 212-929-9684), which was formerly Boots & Saddles. Bitchy Bingo with Yvonne Lamé and Ginger is a Wednesday night ritual at Lips (2 Bank St at Greenwich Ave, 212-675-7710)—here the game is free with dinner or drinks. Also gratis is Drag Queen Puppet Bingo at View Bar (232 Eighth Ave between 21st and 22nd Sts, 212-929-2243)—the puppet is the MC—on Fridays from 7:30pm to 10:30pm.

Lips

Big rub

Get a stranger to pummel your back? *Kate Lowenstein* ***heads to Chinatown to find out if it's really the right way to relax.***

There isn't a tension-free set of shoulders in New York City. And it doesn't help matters that relief from the knottiness usually costs over a hundred bucks—the idea of shelling out that much just makes us clench up all the more. But if you're willing to forgo Enya soundtracks and scented candles, there's a solution to be found on the cheap: There are about as many massage parlors in Chinatown as there are dumplings in a dim sum restaurant, and they all offer rubdowns at a fraction of the price of their uptown counterparts.

With a lightly padded wallet and heavily weighted shoulders, I hop on a train downtown and set out for Wu Lim Services Company (179 Grand Street at Baxter St). Set inside a "mall"—more like a grungy trio of shops—the operation offers ten-minute massages for $7 (or $42 for an hour). This place is a long way from Bliss Spa: The linoleum-tiled waiting room is furnished with nothing more than plastic chairs and a few yellowing posters with anatomical diagrams on them. A gaggle of Chinese women sit together talking loudly in Cantonese and eating out of Styrofoam containers. I get their attention and point to "Ten Minutes" on the wall menu (which includes the option of a foot massage for $3 more). After paying, I'm greeted by a wiry middle-aged man with a kind face who leads me into a dimly lit massage room with a neat row of five cots made up with white sheets. I lie stomach-down and my massage therapist proceeds to knead and thump, zeroing in on my especially tight trapezius muscles. His rhythmic manipulations are delivered with just the right amount of pressure and enliven my tired neck and shoulders. The allotted minutes zip by like seconds, and before I know it he's asking me if I want more time. I muster up enough self-control to say no, tip him $2 (about 20 percent is customary) and head on my way with newfound energy.

Certain blocks of Chinatown—especially those just above Canal Street between Lafayette and Chrystie Streets—look as through they are founded on subterranean operations hawking

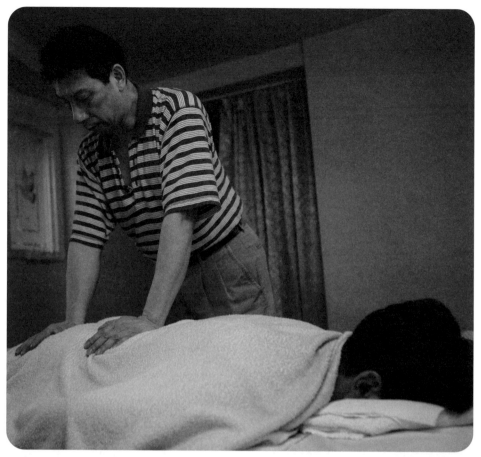

Qi Gong, Tui-Na and shiatsu. Qi Gong (pronounced "chee-gong") translates roughly to energy work, and is a general term for the practice of manipulating the body's flow of energy through a variety of methods including breathing, meditation and physical movement. Tui-Na refers to hands-on therapy traditionally used for healing, not just relaxation. And shiatsu employs acupressure techniques as well as assisted stretching. These three terms are used interchangeably on signs throughout the area—despite the differences in terminology, the routine at each place is markedly similar: customer lies on bed, therapist kneads for the allotted time. While the quality of the massage varies widely, the techniques all blend together.

Many savvy massage addicts credit Fishion Herb Center (107 Mott St between Canal and Hester Sts; $10 for 15 minutes) as the best place

"If you can forgo Enya and scented candles, there are almost as many massage parlors in Chinatown as there are dumplings in a dim sum restaurant."

in Chinatown for a rubdown. Indeed, there is an air of professionalism here—perhaps because the place is large and bustling, and notably free of the blaring TVs and dozing grandmothers found in many of the area's other massage parlors. I fork over a tenner and a tiny Chinese woman in her 50s or 60s points me to a private room—a rarity at these prices—and tells me to

strip. Lying face down on a paper towel (the disposable hygienic solution of choice at most places in the neighborhood), I can't help but note the dinginess of the simple space. The dust bunnies are quickly forgotten, however, when my therapist starts working into the gnarled muscles in my upper back. Tsking every time she comes upon a knot, she exerts fierce pressure that belies her age and size, peppering the 15 minutes of bliss with grimace-inducing dips into the especially tense points on my back. When she's done, she urges me in broken English to come back soon so she can finish releasing me from my knotty shackles. Enamored of her powerful digits and touched by her seemingly genuine concern, I promise that I will.

The rest of the day is a blur of white beds, paper towels and steel fingers. I stop at the darkened communal room of Back and Foot Rub (185 Mulberry St; $7 for ten minutes), the comparatively well-appointed Broome Sky Health Center (373 Broome St; 15 minutes $11) and the über-clean, super-friendly Howard Beauty Salon and Spa (34 Howard St), where I receive hot jasmine tea with my ten-minute massage ($10)—the only one for which I am seated on a stool, not prone on a bed.

At the end of my tour, my back as tenderized as a slab of Kobe beef, I wonder at the good deals I've found. After all, I've hardly missed the fluffy towels and New Age music of the pricey massage model. Is there possibly another reason why these downtown businesses don't charge even half of what other Manhattan massage parlors do?

Yes, there is: You'd be hard pressed to find a massage license anywhere in Chinatown. "Massage therapy in New York State is very regulated—you have to meet a lot of criteria to get licensed," says holistic chiropractor Jo Ann Weinrib, M.D., who warned me about the dangers of my downtown research. "There is no such regulation in these Chinatown businesses. They start pounding you and throwing your limbs around because they don't have the kind of education that a real massage therapist has. And if they break your neck you have no way to sue them because they don't have malpractice insurance."

While it may sound rather dubious to put yourself in the hands of an unlicensed practitioner, there is no shortage of New

"While it sounds rather dubious to put yourself in the hands of an unlicensed practitioner, there is no shortage of New Yorkers who see no problem with it."

Yorkers who see no problem with it. "It's an ancient Chinese tradition," says Sing Lin, a regular at Wu Lim Services Company, "and there's really nothing dangerous about it. If they're doing something that hurts, you just tell them to stop." A slightly more comforting proposition is that many of the Chinatown practitioners are just as experienced as licensed therapists, but have neither the money nor the English to get a license (which requires a $150 payment and proficiency in the language). "Most of our therapists are experienced, licensed acupuncturists and doctors in China," says Victor Liu, who works at Fishion. "They get to New York at the age of 60 and there's no way they're going through the process of getting a license."

Liu admits that it isn't unheard of for a customer to leave a session feeling worse than they did when they came in (of course, this isn't out of the question when you are paying big bucks for a massage either). When that happens, he says, Fishion will give the customer free services (massage, reflexology and acupuncture) until the problem is resolved. Which is probably better treatment than you'll find at a highfalutin spa.

What if a potential customer comes in and says that they only want a licensed therapist? Liu shrugs. "I tell them to go uptown and pay $150 for the same service." Um, no thanks. We'll take the risk.

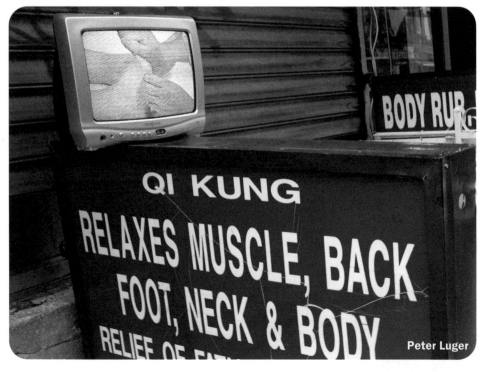

Peter Luger

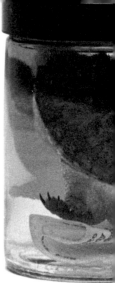

831

Visit the Staten Island Museum

Some of the city's coolest collections are just across the harbor. *Sabrina Rojas Weiss* ***explores this 125-year-old museum.***

It's unlikely the Staten Island Museum will ever cause that satisfying feeling of aching feet you experience after a day at the Met or Museum of Natural History. But a boat ride away from those hallowed marble floors and their throngs of tour groups, the modest red-brick institution is just big enough for a relaxed but still enlightening afternoon spent taking in the preserved specimens, municipal history and local artwork.

The museum's founders, a group of 14 botanists, entomologists, geologists and other scientists, began meeting at the home of prominent naturalist William T. Davis in 1881 to explore the island's natural history. In 1918, the current building in St. George, a mere two blocks from the Staten Island Ferry terminal, was constructed to hold the enclave's ever-growing displays of biodiversity. Today, the museum remains an intact model of 19th-century curating, where the diverse tastes of Victorian gentlemen played out in eclectic displays. Visitors can explore the fluorescent-mineral room, a wall of pinned insects, and a "wet collection" of antique jars filled with preserved snakes, frogs, lizards and a star-nosed mole.

"We don't have any species that are unique to Staten Island," explains director of science Ed Johnson. "But for a long time the human population was very small," which allowed for the unique study of a relatively undisturbed ecosystem.

It's not all pickled rattlers and glowing pebbles. A more civic-minded exhibit on the first floor celebrates the Staten Island Ferry's first century of service to the city. Photos and paintings documenting the transport's past hang next to signs, a giant compass and other ephemera. Three new murals depicting the daily life of the Lenape Indians, who inhabited the island until the 1670s, have been added to the museum's sizable exhibit documenting that people's culture.

But as charming as the St. George building may be, the museum has long outgrown the space. Hence, it is moving the bulk of its holdings to a building at Snug Harbor, a former merchant mariners' retirement complex that is now a cultural center and historic landmark district. Renovation of the structure is due to be completed in 2010. "What you see [in St. George] is the smallest tip of the iceberg," says Johnson. "One of the new buildings will be devoted to how humans impacted the island's flora and fauna. So people who visit from other communities can realize that even a small group of people can make a difference."

Staten Island Museum *75 Stuyvesant Pl at Wall St, New Brighton, Staten Island (718-727-1135).*

832

Access the Billy Rose collection and read Tennessee's letters

You'll be amazed at what your NYPL card gives you access to. Billy Rose's collection—five million documents strong—is the country's most comprehensive theatrical archive, featuring everything from recent TV scripts to 1700s Shakespearean playbills. The collection is also home to some shockingly intimate letters. Some of curator Bob Taylor's favorites include an exchange between Tennessee Williams and Cheryl Crawford, wherein Williams laments his alcoholism and how deeply it affected his writing (he would send a friend ahead to get him a drink to have on his way to the bar).

New York Public Library *40 Lincoln Center Plaza at 64th St (212-870-1639/nypl.org).*

833

Time it right for a roast beef, mozzarella and fried-eggplant hero at Defonte's

Play hooky from work to wolf down this weekday-lunchtime-only sub, a forearm-size roll stuffed with homemade roast beef, fried eggplant and fresh mozzarella. A small costs $7.75, a large $9.50. You want the large.

Defonte's Sandwich Shop *379 Columbia St at Luquer St, Red Hook, Brooklyn (718-625-8052).*

834 *Learn glassblowing*

Although it also provides facilities for experts, this glassblowing studio is a great place to try out the art for the first time, since founders John Pomp and Michiko Sakano offer one-day courses. They cost $300 for two people, and you

get three hours of tailored instruction, with tools and materials supplied. If you catch the bug, the studio also runs six-week courses. **one sixty glass** *160 Berry St at 5th St, Williamsburg, Brooklyn (718-486-9620/ onesixtyglass.com). Open 10am-6pm daily. 1135/statenislandmuseum.org).*

835

See a new show every time with TJ & Dave

Catch this regular improv duo at Barrow Street Theatre (27 Barrow St at Seventh Ave S, 212-239-6200, barrowstreettheatre.com) as they create a one-act play before your eyes. These guys swear the scenarios aren't predetermined and that in more than 100 performances, they've never repeated a character. Past subjects have included a South American sightseer witnessing a revolution, and clubbers trying to crash a VIP area.

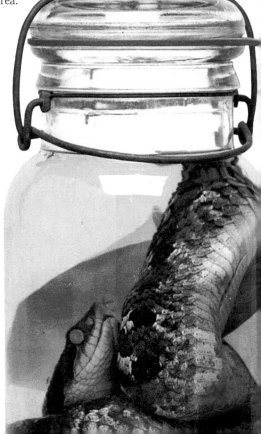

836 Sock it to the dancefloor at Studio B

What do old-school heroes like Afrika Bambaataa and Grandmaster Flash, baile funk monsters Bonde Do Role and prog-funk tyros Battles have in common? They've all guested at Studio B's weekly underground party Fun (myspace.com/funatstudiob), along with resident DJs Eamon Harkin and Rok One. Whatever your groove is—we also love the roller-skate mayhem of Down and Derby (downandderby.org)—you can expect a damn good time.
Studio B *259 Banker St between Calyer St and Meserole Ave, Greenpoint, Brooklyn (718-389-1880).*

837-839
Play golf indoors

Drive 495

The best place for golf training short of actually being on the course, this 15,000-square-foot private facility houses a gym, five simulators (loaded with around 40 different courses) and an upstairs lounge. Owner Don Saladino asserts that Drive495 is the only place in the city for a full 2-D and 3-D golf assessment—which comes with the $5,000 yearly membership fee. We're inclined to believe him; trainers at Drive495 break down your game to the point of not only giving swing tips, but also suggesting appropriate nutrition and non-golf-related exercises. And there aren't too many other options for hitting golf balls and enjoying a cocktail under the same roof.

495 Broadway between Broome and Spring Sts (212-334-9537/driveclubs.com).

Manhattan Athletic Club

You can play 18 holes on any of 20 different virtual courses via the simulator at the M.A.C. As a member ($165 per month), unlimited access costs $35 a month; otherwise it's $10 for every 15 minutes. Guests pay $35 a day plus $1 per minute. As with most quality simulators, electronic monitoring of club speed and head direction make for a surprisingly accurate translation of your real-life slice.

277 Park Ave, entrance on 48th St between Lexington and Park Aves (212-486-3477/macgym.com).

Chelsea Piers

This fitness behemoth proves, once again, that high-end training facilities abound if you're willing to foot the bill. A flat $45 rate will net indoor hackers an hour on either one of the two sims, which feature 52 championship-level courses—including Pebble Beach, the Old Course at St. Andrews and Pinehurst No.8. If you're still troubled by that near-impossible final hole at Oakmont, an hour with a Chelsea Piers teaching professional is available for $130-$160.

Pier 59, 18th St at the West Side Highway (212-336-6400/chelseapiers.com).

840
Study the World Trade Center Dossier

In just 5,000 square feet—very modest by any institutional standards, certainly so given the subject matter—the Skyscraper Museum (admission $2.50-$5) explains all about the high-rise buildings that made the city's iconic skyline. Most compelling, though, is the World Trade Center Dossier, a moving exhibit about the fallen towers and what will ultimately replace them.

Skyscraper Museum *39 Battery Pl between Little West St and 1st Pl (212-968-1961/skyscraper.org).*

841
Order dinner at Peter Luger without a menu

Is there another restaurant in the city where a menu is more of a formality? Sure, the waiter will hand you one when you sit down, but you don't need it. (What, you're having fish?) Nope, the only choice you'll need to make here is "steak for one" or "steak for two," because Luger serves only one cut: a porterhouse. No other restaurant quite does justice to the signature slab, seared at 800°F and offered up swimming in rich, spooned-on butter and fat that makes us sick—with love. Leave the menu-reading to first-timers.

Peter Luger *178 Broadway at Driggs Ave, Williamsburg, Brooklyn (718-387-7400).*

Sample the four types of broth available around the city.

Shio *at Setagaya*

Considered by many to be the most difficult broth to make, shio (salt) broths are typically clear and have high-class roots—in Japan, clarity is a sign of a well-made, expensive soup. The broth is largely based on vegetable scraps and is typically made without the kelp that causes murkiness in other ramens. Try it at Setagaya, a Tokyo-based chain that makes a satisfyingly salty shio ramen for $9.50.
141 First Ave between St. Marks Pl and 9th St (212-529-2740).

Shoyu *at Minca Ramen Factory*

Known to Americans as soy sauce, shoyu was discovered in the 17th century as the by-product of miso manufacturing. Shoyu ramen is made from a basic broth of kelp and bonito flakes, with mirin (a syrupy rice wine) to balance the soy. Minca Ramen Factory has a thick, nearly golden

shoyu broth with slightly chewy ha gotai noodles, which you can sample for $8.50.
536 E 5th St between Aves A and B (212-505-8001).

Miso *at Sapporo*

There are hundreds, if not thousands, of varieties of this fermented soybean paste. It is to Japan what wine and cheese are to Europeans: Each region has its own type of miso, and thus, each has its own miso ramen. With all the different colors of the paste available, you can typically expect a broth that is somewhere between pale yellow and dark reddish brown. The miso itself is tossed in at the very end of the cooking process, because its chemistry is such that the paste separates quite easily, which is why you often see soup bowls with murky clouds lurking at the bottom. And there's the distinctly sweet aroma

of miso, which stands a chance only if it is added at the last minute. Sapporo is well regarded for its miso broths, which start at $7.50.
152 W 49th St between Sixth and Seventh Aves (212-869-8972).

Tonkotsu *at Village Yokocho*
Lovers of animal fat, pay attention. This ramen is most easily understood as the sum of its words: *ton* = "pig," and *kotsu* = "bone." It is also the hardest to find done well in New York (fans are apt to head to the Mitsuwa Marketplace in New Jersey, for their fix). The tonkotsu at Village Yokocho, which is cooked for three to four days, can be ordered off the menu for $7.
8 Stuyvesant St between Second and Third Aves (212-598-3041).

846 *Hunt a coyote*
You're strolling through Central Park, near East Drive and 76th, when you happen to glance up at that rock outcrop and… yikes! What's that coyote doing up there? You're looking at *Still Hunt*, a lifelike and life-size bronze statue, which has been poised to pounce ever since the sculptor Edward Kemeys put it there in 1881.

847 *Wait for the hazelnut soufflé at Capsouto Frères*
Worth every second of the 20 minutes it takes to custom-make each one, the gossamer hazelnut soufflé at Capsouto Frères (451 Washington St at Watts St, 212-966-4900) has a dark, nutty aroma that balances the featherlight texture. Simply divine.

A few of my favorite **things**

848-852
Andrew Berman, *historical* *preservationist*

Walking over the Brooklyn, Manhattan, Williamsburg or Queensborough Bridges, in either direction, is worth it for the incredible views. It's rare that you get to see the perspective on the skyline shift over such a long plane—viewing the buildings through the filigree of the cables of the Brooklyn Bridge or the trusses of the Queensborough Bridge just makes it all the more dazzling. **One of the best places for freshly made falafel (they actually bake the falafel for individual orders) is Chickpea in the East Village (210 E 14th St, 212-228-3445). The food is healthy and fresh, and the restaurant is like a mini-Israeli community, filled with the buzz of Israeli expats who add an additional flavor to the experience.** I often go to one of the hookah bars on Steinway Street in Astoria (Egyptian Coffee Shop, 2509 Steinway St, Astoria, 718-777-5517) or Bay Ridge (Hookah Café, 7101 5th Ave, 646-515-2095). It's one of many ways you can turn a corner in New York and suddenly feel utterly transformed to a completely different place or time. **Going to Inwood Hill Park, at the north tip of Manhattan, I feel like I am a million miles away from the hubbub, even though I haven't left the borough. The forests, the lagoon off the Harlem River, the graceful arch of the Henry Hudson bridge, the Indian paths that criss-cross the park and the rock where Manhattan was purportedly bought from the Indians all give Inwood Hill a storybook quality that jaded New Yorkers rarely expect to find.** Watching the view of the skyline from my rooftop in Hell's Kitchen change on an almost daily basis. I've lived in the same apartment for 17 years, and more than two-thirds of what I can see has gone up since I moved in. It's like seeing the story of New York's growth written in front of me.

853

Admire New York's best building, bar none
Cliché, yes. But how could anyone resist the charms of the Chrysler Building? William Van Alen's Art Deco masterpiece was the world's tallest building for just a few months before the Empire State Building surpassed it. We still love the Chrysler better, especially from this vantage point on 42nd and Lexington.

854 Give Federal Hall a chance

There's a reason why those Japanese tourists flock here. Rather than avoid it, for a change why not join them? Our burg's first City Hall was built on this spot; after a little refurbishing it became the site of George Washington's inauguration and the first seat of the U.S. government. Long after the capital moved to Washington, D.C., the building was razed and the present structure was built—an 1842 Greek Revival gem that served as the country's first Custom House.

Federal Hall *26 Wall St at Nassau St (212-825-6888).*

855 Shop at an unusual railway station

It's just a strange little subterranean mall in Chinatown, to the right of an OTB parlor at 8 Chatham Square. But a quarter-century before the Chinese began to arrive here in the 1880s, Wing Fat Shopping is said to have been a "station" (stopping-off point) on the Underground Railroad.

856 See something arty at the Sunshine Cinema

This beautifully restored 1898 Yiddish theatre is one of the city's snazziest art houses: Well progammed, with comfy seats, good sound, a range of popcorn toppings… what more could a cinephile need? Tickets are $11.50 ($8 for seniors).

Landmark Sunshine Cinema *143 E Houston St between First and Second Aves (212-330-8182).*

857

Get your mugshot taken by the NYPD

The NYPD's museum covers the history of the force stretching over three centuries—fair enough, but the important thing is to persuade them to let you get your mugshot taken. Kids only? Tarnation. Guess you'll have to make do with gawping at Al Capone's submachine gun instead.

New York City Police Museum *100 Old Slip between South and Water Sts (212-480-3100/ nycpolicemuseum.org).*

858

Pick up a piece of Steve's key lime pie

Miami native Steve Tarpin has been making Steve's Authentic Key Lime Pies the same way for 25 years—with freshly squeezed key limes, milk direct from Wisconsin and genuine Graham Cracker crumbs. If you can find his unassuming storefront on Pier 41 in Red Hook, snag that frozen chocolate-dipped key lime pie novelty on a stick, the Swingle, or grab your own miniature pie. If you can't make it down there, they're happy to deliver or tell you which gourmet markets stock their pies.

Steve's Authentic Key Lime Pie *204 Van Dyke St at Pier 41 (888-450-5463/stevesauthentic.com).*

859

Order the prix fixe at Knife + Fork

Michelin-starred chef-owner Damien Brassel's $45, six-course tasting menu—three appetizers, a fish entrée, a meat main course and a dessert—may stretch your belly, but its inventive offerings can go dish for dish with any chichi à la carte meal. The denim-clad crowd and front-and-center beer taps give this East Village spot a pubby, anything-goes vibe, but appearances can be deceiving: If one of your group orders the prix fixe, so must the entire party. The strict ground rules didn't stop *Time Out New York* readers from voting this their favorite prix fixe in 2007. Where else do pickled white peach, caramel sauce and balsamic-poached fig meet a hunk of foie gras, and luscious venison finds a sweet soul mate in apple mash with a chocolate and raspberry reduction? The answer is nowhere. Who else would dare?

Knife + Fork *108 E 4th St between First and Second Aves (212-228-4885/knife-fork-nyc.com).*

860-866

Shop till you drop trou—in the city's most pleasingly designed retail restrooms

Addict
Continue your sartorial education in the john. At this fashion-forward trend hive, the latest issues of fashion mags are laid out next to fragrant candles and lush, vanilla-scented soaps.
20 E 12th St between Fifth Ave and University Pl (212-633-2672).

Buckler
Nods to cocaine abound in this washroom: A sign reading "Use the mirror, this position is bad for your back, besides it will get stuck in the lettering" bedecks the toilet seat, a history of cocaine has been hung up next to a list of nicknames for the narcotic (snow, charlie, K8, bump)—and then there's that swiveling mirror, which has been mounted on the wall for, er, touch-ups.
13 Gansevoort St between W 4th and Hudson Sts (212-255-1596).

Charles Nolan
"I'm very proud of my bathroom," says Charles Nolan of his shiny jet-black loo. And he has every reason to be. Exuberantly hued ribbons, which Nolan installed himself, arc from the ceiling—providing a nice counterpoint to the 35-square-foot room's glossy granite tiles, lacquered woodwork and mirror-flanking sconces.
30 Gansevoort St between Greenwich and Hudson Sts (888-996-6526).

Fendi
This Peter Marino-designed WC has the feel of an Italian bathhouse. Polished gray sanpietrini stone lies underfoot, Roman travertine marble shines forth from the walls, and a heavy door fashioned from calcified plaster panels ensures Vatican-like levels of peace and quiet.
677 Fifth Ave between 55th and 56th Sts (212-759-4646).

Marimekko
Not surprisingly, doing your business is a cheerful affair at this much-loved Finnish textiles shop, where splashy striped towels match the large turquoise, fuchsia and red poppy-print textiles on the walls.
1262 Third Ave at 73rd St (212-628-8400).

Patricia Field
The bathroom's 15-foot ceilings are strung with three cascading chandeliers, which—combined with an oversize mirror, holographic wallpaper, black porcelain fixtures and recessed neon lighting—create a distinctly clublike vibe.
302 Bowery between Houston and Bleecker Sts (212-966-4066).

Tracy Reese
"Marrakech on the Hudson" is the theme at this generously appointed, souklike space, where you'll find a walnut-and-mother-of-pearl sink, delicate crystal sconces and walls that have been hand-illustrated with a Moroccan bird-and-flora motif.
641 Hudson St between Horatio and Gansevoort Sts (212-807-0505).

867 Get a cup of joe at Joe

In fall 2006, burgeoning bean-lover's chain Joe—or, to give it its full title, "Joe, the art of coffee"—spawned its sleekest branch to date inside Soho's Alessi store. Although a slight departure from Joe's more down-to-earth Waverly Place and 13th Street spots, java cognoscenti have embraced this design-savvy, Italianate incarnation. Underneath the slick packaging, loyalists have found the espresso still ranks supreme. As at his other cafés, owner Jonathan Rubenstein has employed experienced baristas who proffer rich, nutty cups—with an expert foam for those who want it—from the glorious $14,000 La Marzocco machine. But here, the vaunted buzz juice is served in chic drinking vessels, which are also for sale.
Joe, the art of coffee *130 Greene St between Houston and Prince Sts (212-941-7330/joetheartofcoffee.com).*

868 Catch new acts at the Apollo

The city's home of R&B and soul is much cozier than it looks on *Showtime at the Apollo*. Famous as the launchpad for Ella Fitzgerald and Michael Jackson's stellar careers, Apollo continues to bring wannabe stars to the stage. Head down to spot the next James Brown.

Apollo Theater *253 W 125th St between Adam Clayton Powell Jr Blvd (Seventh Ave) and Frederick Douglass Blvd (Eighth Ave) (212-531-5305/apollotheater.com).*

869 Get to Great NY Noodletown in time for the baby pig on rice

Though it's always on the menu at this popular Chinatown spot, by 2pm any plates of this perfectly roasted pig ($7.95)—with crackly, sweet skin coating meat that barely clings to the bone—have vanished. Get there early.

Great NY Noodletown *28 Bowery at Bayard St (212-349-0923).*

870 Take your clothes off. For money

No matter what size or shape you are, you can earn 15 bucks an hour (two weeks in arrears) for just standing around. Yep, you'll be working as a "figurative" (nude) model for art students at the New York Academy of Art. If you're hired, you're basically privately contracted to work in one or more classes, which meet at various times throughout the week. You can't just show up because you like flaunting your naked bod, though. "We'd have to check out your references, make sure you're not, you know, somebody that would be causing any problems with the students here," says Frank Harrison of the NYAA. "We are a graduate school of fine art, we have to protect our students. You don't just walk in off the street."

New York Academy of Art *111 Franklin St between Church St and West Broadway (212-966-0300/nyaa.edu).*

871 Shop Polish in Greenpoint

The Polish community in Greenpoint isn't new, but it is being replenished by a new wave of immigration. Nowhere is this more evident than at West Nassau Meat Market, where folks line up for homemade kielbasa and hams, each offered in close to a dozen varieties—without a single sign to indicate what it is or how much it costs. "People know what they want and they know the price," says John Lubinski, whose family has owned the market since 1980. "And besides," he adds somewhat ruefully, "my father hasn't raised the prices in ten years." The *krajana* (lean, thick girth), *podwawelska* (barbecued) and *kabanos* (thin) *kielbasas* ($4/pound) are outstanding, as is the world-class Canadian bacon. Naturally, there's also a generous selection of mustards (sample the Kamis brand for under $2), cheeses, breads and brews on offer.

West Nassau Meat Market *915 Manhattan Ave between Greenpoint Ave and Kent St, Greenpoint, Brooklyn (718-389-6149).*

872 Visit the endangered New York State Pavilion

Every year, the World Monuments Fund (WMF) lists the world's 100 most endangered sites to help "safeguard the world's irreplaceable heritage." Most of the trouble spots on the 2008 list were in far-off lands like Peru (Machu Picchu) and Afghanistan (the Bamiyan Buddhas). What's surprised many, though, was the number of endangered structures on the list located in the U.S.—seven in total, including the Salk Institute, Frank Lloyd Wright's Florida Southern University Historic Campus and Route 66. One of them is right here in New York: the once-famous New York State Pavilion in Flushing, Queens, created for the 1964 World's Fair by renowned architect Philip Johnson. Hard to believe, but more than six million came to Corona Park to see the elliptical "Tent of Tomorrow" when it opened.

The WMF notes that, back in the day, the complex was one of the few World's Fair structures not panned by critics. In fact, they cite a *New York Times* architect review that called the piece "a runaway success, day or night... a sophisticated frivolity... seriously and beautifully constructed." Here's how the Fund describes the situation today: "An icon to some, an eyesore to others, this remarkable complex, including the 'Tent of Tomorrow,' is endangered by neglect and indifference as much as by rust." Harsh, but accurate.

The city has made numerous efforts to renovate the pavilion area over the past few decades—including a $24,000 partial reconstruction of the lower tower—but to date no plans to reuse the structure (with any significant amount of money attached) have materialized. So, is the former World's Fair structure worth saving? Hop on the No.7 train to Willets Point and judge for yourself.

873 *Visit the booth of subway sculptor Luis Torres*

MTA employee Luis Torres, 36, has created a token-booth sculpture garden out of used MetroCards at the 110th Street stop on the B and C lines. The statuettes—which Torres builds at his home in Spanish Harlem and transports piecemeal to work—represent NYC culture: everything from Lady Liberty to subway rats. Most of the art is origami, and Torres never uses glue: "I don't want to cheat. Just pressurize the cards, and it'll be okay." Up next? A three-foot-long Brooklyn Bridge and a full-scale, 5'10" MTA station agent. If all goes well, Torres anticipates an art show next year. Hear that, MoMA?

874 Stuff yourself with stuffed grape leaves at Bereket

Fragrant, moist, and studded with pine nuts and currants, these stout little delicacies at Bereket (187 E Houston St at Orchard St, 212-475-7700) are best consumed five at a time. Available 24 hours a day at $5 a plate, they also function as the ideal antidote to a 3am bellyful of LES booze.

875-879 Get a bra fitted by an expert

Bra Smyth

The staff at Bra Smyth's flagship Madison Avenue store offers more than 100 years of combined experience.
brasmyth.com; 2177 Broadway at 77th St (212-721-5111); 905 Madison Ave between 72nd and 73rd Sts (212-772-9400).

Linda's Bra Salon

This venerable shop carries hard-to-find sizes such as 44Bs, and Linda's four fitters go to a "bra school" refresher course once a month.
828 Lexington Ave between 63rd and 64th Sts (212-751-2727).

The Orchard Corset Center

Head fitter Peggy, granddaughter of a bra pattern-maker, can look at a person and know her exact size and what type of bra she should don without even reaching for a tape measure.
157 Orchard St between Rivington and Stanton Sts (212-674-0786).

Ripplu

Ripplu employs four trained fitters, and offers free alteration on all bras.
66 Madison Ave between 27th & 28th Sts (212-599-2223).

Town Shop

TS stocks a slew of well-known names such as Aubade, Wacoal and Lejaby, and employs eight to ten fitters daily.
2273 Broadway between 81st and 82nd Sts (212-787-2762).

880

Talk trash with OROE

Aside from the usual crowd of protesters, break-dancers and produce vendors that fill Union Square on any given Monday, keen observers will notice a Goodwill van parked at the north end of the park. From 8am to 6pm, a steady trickle of visitors stops by the vehicle, bearing clothing, fabrics and other textile donations. Material Mondays, as the weekly event is known, was started in 2007 by the Office of Recycling Outreach and Education (OROE): Since then, more than 31,000 pounds of jeans, T-shirts, bed linens, shoes and the like have been collected for eventual resale at Goodwill stores around the city. Its success sparked a sister program— Second Chance Saturdays, which takes place in Brooklyn's Grand Army Plaza—and plans are underway to add textile drives in other boroughs by the end of the year.

But clothing collection is just one of the ways that OROE encourages New Yorkers to reduce their overall output of garbage. A division of the nonprofit Council on the Environment of New York City, the group also oversees waste audits (which are designed to ensure apartment buildings comply with all existing regulations concerning trash-disposal), electronics-recycling events, community swap meets and a curbside campaign called "The Recycling Game," during which passersby are tested on their blue-bin expertise. "We try to put a face on recycling and fix people's misconceptions. We want to help them learn," says Christina Salvi, who is one of the recycling-outreach coordinators for the OROE.

OROE is always in need of volunteers, and getting involved easier than separating plastic and aluminum. Just attend a 90-minute training session (free pizza included) and register on the group's Listserv for details on upcoming events. "It can be frustrating to see how much isn't done—New Yorkers only recycle about half of what they could," says Salvi. "This is a very direct and personal way to correct the balance."

For details on specific OROE programs, call 212-788-7964, e-mail csalvi@cenyc.org or visit cenyc.org/recycling.

Entertainment center

So what if most of our favorite shows are filmed on the West Coast? Ben Walters grabs a portable TV and tours the sights of the city made famous by the tube.

It may be true that New York is a city made for the movies, but that doesn't mean the small screen shouldn't get a look-in. *Kojak, Seinfeld, Friends, Fame, Taxi, NYPD Blue…* they've all left their stamp on the city, each of them carving out its own little slice of New York lore. There's just one hitch: None of them was actually made here.

The trick lies in the different histories of the movie industry and the television industry. Needless to say, the entertainment business is firmly rooted in and around Los Angeles, California, and that's where the majority of its productions are based, in both film and TV. But while the past few decades have seen a rise in the number of features shot on location, in economic terms it remains overwhelmingly tempting for television series to stay fixed in L.A. Hence shows such as *Seinfeld* and *Fame*, despite being seen to represent an quintessentially N.Y.C. sensibility, were seldom shot in the city itself.

That said, a little establishing shot can go a long, long way—especially when the particular location-filmed exterior crops up a couple of times a week, week in, week out, year in, year out, sometimes for a decade or more. *Friends* fanatics, for instance, will instantly clock the apartment building in which most of the gang supposedly lived at the corner of Grove St and Bedford St in Greenwich Village. (If you head a bit further down the street, you'll also find 12-21 Grove, the apartment building where Ross and Ugly Naked Guy found themselves at home.) However, there's no point trying to track down the coffeeshop Central Perk: It only ever existed on a Hollywood sound stage.

Not far away, at 534 Hudson St, is the Dover Garage. This location was used as the setting for the sitcom *Taxi* and it is still a functioning cab garage. Up at Times Square, meanwhile, the former High School of Performing Arts—the place that launched a thousand toothy splits in *Fame*—is at 120 West 46th St. The

real school, however, has been part of the Fiorello H LaGuardia High School of Music & Art and Performing Arts, near the Lincoln Center, since 1984, and the *Fame* building now houses the Jacqueline Kennedy Onassis School of International Careers.

Like *Taxi* and *Fame*, *Seinfeld* and *NYPD Blue* were almost entirely shot in Los Angeles, but each of them has an iconic Manhattan location. The *Seinfeld* gang's favorite diner, Monk's, with its distinctive red-neon-on-blue signage, is in reality Tom's Restaurant at Broadway and 112th St, a few blocks down from Columbia University. (This eatery was

> "Shows such as Seinfeld *and* Fame, *despite representing a quintessentially* NYC *sensibility, were seldom shot in the city itself.*"

H&H Bagels

also the inspiration for Suzanne Vega's song "Tom's Diner," so you get double the pop-culture bang for your buck.) And the Ninth Precinct Station House at 321 East 5th St serves as the opening-credit base for the fictional 15th Precinct cops.

There are other shows which, although still shot on studio sets rather than on location, are based closer to home. *The Cosby Show*, for example, was filmed live in Brooklyn, where it was set (in Flatbush, to be precise), although the actual brownstone house presented as the Huxtables' home was in fact at 10 Leroy St in Greenwich Village. *Sesame Street*, meanwhile—whose longstanding set was explicitly modeled on a New York street and has latterly been the inspiration for the ribald musical pastiche *Avenue Q*—is filmed at the Kaufman Astoria Studios in Queens.

The cable television outfit HBO goes about things a little differently to the major studios. It can also claim credit for many of the best programs of the past decade—and, in a couple of them, the best use of authentic New York locations as part of the fabric of the show. Well, one of them—*The Sopranos*—is set just over the Hudson in New Jersey, but many

> *"Carrie Bradshaw supposedly lived at 245 East 73rd St. That address doesn't actually exist, but many of the nearby amenities featured in the show do, including H&H Bagels— 'the good bagels'."*

of its most characteristic spots are accessible to anyone with the time and the inclination. The Bada Bing strip club—which in fact trades under the even classier name of Satin Dolls—is in Lodi, NJ, at 230 Route 17 South. (If you want your souvenir without going the full monty, there's a Bada Bing booth at the front.) The Belleville Turnpike at North Arlington is home to the wee Pizzaland restaurant seen in the opening credits, while the New Skyway Diner in Kearny, at Central Ave and 2nd St, under the gloomy black bridge between Jersey City and Newark, is where Christopher Moltisanti was shot.

But there's really only one contender for the crown when it comes to New York on the small screen. Although HBO's *Sex and the City* made the leap to cinema in May 2008, it's the programme's drip-feeding of achingly hip real-life Manhattan haunts over its six years on television that gave viewers the feeling of being privy to the fabulousness of New York life. In the same way as have *Seinfeld* and *The Sopranos*, *Sex and the City* has spawned its own themed guided tours, but you can always make up your own itinerary. Carrie supposedly lived at 245 East 73rd St. That address doesn't actually exist, but many of the nearby amenities featured in the show do, including H&H Bagels ("the good bagels") and Zabar's. The stoop to Carrie's apartment as seen on the show can be found at 66 Perry Street in Greenwich Village, between Bleecker and West 4th. Not far away, at 401 Bleecker St, you can stuff your face with cupcakes at the Magnolia Bakery, but be prepared to wait in line. Sarah Jessica Parker lives nearby, so keep an eye out.

Oddly enough, it is a much-loved episode of *The Simpsons* that gives the landmarks of New York the most prominent television outing, even if it is in animated form. In "The City of New York vs. Homer Simpson," Springfield's first family arrive for a day-trip and have vastly different experiences. Marge and the kids tour Little Italy and Chinatown, visit the Statue of Liberty and Central Park, and watch a Broadway musical. Homer, meanwhile, spends his time in the city arguing with street-corner food vendors, transport officials and just about everybody he meets—something true Gothamites might relate to.

895

...or join the audience for a studio taping

The Daily Show with Jon Stewart

Tapings are at 5:30pm, Monday to Thursday. Reserve tickets at least three months ahead online, or call at 11:30am on the Friday before you'd like to attend to see if there's a cancellation. You must be at least 18 and have a photo ID.

513 W 54th St between 10th and 11th Aves (212-586-2477/comedycentral.com).

Late Night with Conan O'Brien

Tapings are at 5:30pm, Tuesday to Friday. Call at least three months in advance for tickets. A small number of same-day standby tickets are distributed at 9am (49th Street entrance), one ticket per person. You must be at least 16 and have a photo ID.

30 Rockefeller Plaza, Sixth Ave between 49th and 50th Sts (212-664-3056/nbc.com/conan).

Late Show with David Letterman

Seats can be hard to come by for Letterman tapings (5:30pm Monday to Thursday, with an extra show at 8pm on Thursday). Try requesting tickets for a specific date by filling out a form on the show's website. You may also be able to get a standby ticket by calling 212-247-6497 at 11am on the day of taping. You must be 18 and have a photo ID.

1697 Broadway between 53rd and 54th Sts (212-975-1003/lateshowaudience.com).

Saturday Night Live

Tickets are notoriously difficult to snag (either for the dress rehearsal at 8pm or the live show at 11:30pm) so don't get your hopes up. The season is assigned by lottery every autumn. Email snltickets@nbc.com in August, or try the standby ticket lottery on the day of the show, for which you have to line up by 7am under the NBC Studio marquee (50th St between Fifth and Sixth Aves). You must be at least 16 and have a photo ID.

30 Rockefeller Plaza, Sixth Ave between 49th and 50th Sts (212-664-3056/nbc.com/snl).

896 Spot the N.R.A.'s favorite Cupid

The Friedsam Memorial Carousel has been here, in Central Park near 64th Street, in one form or another since 1871—and a ride still only costs a buck-fifty. It's a masterpiece of 1900s folk art, with 58 of the largest handcarved horses ever constructed, and the original calliope still cranks out organ music. And the N.R.A.? We wonder whether they'd enjoy that somewhat psychotic frieze of Cupid shooting rabbits…

897 Tackle a java mee at Skyway Malaysian

Skyway's java mee is an immense, steaming bowl of egg noodles in a spicy dried-squid gravy—laden with potatoes, bean sprouts and shrimp—and topped with a shrimp pancake. It's the Chunky soup you never knew you wanted. Bargainous, too, at $4.95.
Skyway Malaysian *11 Allen St at Canal St (212-625-1163).*

898 Have a tot at the Brandy Library

This Tribeca bar, the only library we know where booze lines the walls, is beloved of the area's financial types. Its novella-size drink menu lists a glossary of around 430 brandies.
The Brandy Library *25 North Moore St at Varick St (212-226-5545/brandylibrary.com).*

899 Bite into a chocolate-chip walnut cookie at Levain Bakery

More landmass than mere cookie, this six-ounce colossus ($3.75) is an orgy of walnuts, chocolate and enough butter to grease the engine of a 747. Served warm and that perfect notch shy of raw, it is the very apogee of gooey and outrageous cookie goodness.
Levain Bakery *167 W 74th St at Amsterdam Ave (212-874-6080).*

900 Build a robot

In one corner, sleek and sophisticated million-dollar contraptions developed with a keen eye toward their marketability in the corporate arena. In the other, DIY tinkerers more interested in pushing creative boundaries and having fun. Guess which we prefer? Yep, David Greenbaum's type. In 2004, he opened Robot Village (robotvillage.com), a boutique-workshop on the Upper West Side where visitors can buy or build robots of varying complexity. "The store has been something of a lifelong dream. I grew up watching *Lost in Space* and thought everyone would have a robot by the year 2000," says Greenbaum. "Obviously, that hasn't happened, but I'm hoping we can get the public comfortable with robotics so that, down the line, maybe it will." Robot Village carries the usual robot toys and novelties, but it's the store's build-it-yourself kits that are the real draw. "The customers can take [the kits] home or we'll help them work on it here, at one of our workstations," says events coordinator Tom Hershner. To that end, Greenbaum holds bot-building classes, including an introductory seminar during which participants construct a robot with wheels, lights and infrared sensors that allow it to react to obstacles.

901 Witness the blessing of the animals

On the first Sunday in October, the Cathedral Church of St John the Divine (1047 Amsterdam Ave at 112th St, 212-316-7540, stjohndivine.org) hosts the Blessing of the Animals, a celebration of St Francis of Assisi and the animal kingdom. Following the Eucharist, the cathedral's doors swing open and large and exotic animals—including the occasional llama, boa constrictor or eagle—are brought in and led to the altar for their blessing. After the service, house pets have their turn on the cathedral lawn. Even if you don't have a pet, it's well worth stopping by just to watch a camel pass through the cathedral doors (surely easier than passing through the eye of a needle).

902
Get an old-fashioned shave at Freemans Sporting Club

This tiny yet bustling gentlemen's haven is hidden in the back of refined clothing shop Freemans Sporting Club (8 Rivington St between Bowery and Chrystie St, 212-673-3209). Outfitted with four stations, the minimalist spot is somewhat cramped, but an old-fashioned cut ($35) by expert shaver (and equally expert conversationalist) Ivan Ferdinand is worth the lack of elbow room.

903-912

Bite in to the city's best "fancy" burgers...

As the once-humble burger continues its ascent upmarket, Rose Palazzolo and Tracy Ziemer choose the best of the newfangled bunch, in order of merit.

Market Table

Our No.1 pick: Grilled and then finished off in a salamander (a type of broiler) with salt and pepper, this $12 treat arrives a perfectly cooked medium-rare, topped with house-made pickles, white cheddar, caramelized onions, lettuce and tomato in a garlicky bun. The flavors work in concert—a symphony of a burger.
54 Carmine St at Bedford St (212-255-2100).

Telepan

Part of the $28 prix-fixe lunch and brunch, Telepan's sandwich comes grilled to order

Bread (a bit too small for the fist-size burger—a minor downside).
72 W 69th St at Columbus Ave (212-580-4300).

Prune

The addition of ground lamb to the beef (from Pino's Prime Meats in SoHo) gives Prune's $12 burger a unique, gamey taste. A dainty six-ounce cooked-to-order patty is served without distraction: The presence of a single add-on, cheddar cheese, means the meat gets to shine. A large toasted Thomas' English muffin catches the burger's juices.
54 E 1st St between First and Second Aves (212-677-6221).

Back Forty

Described as a "steakburger" by chef-owner Peter Hoffman because of its blend of premium beefs, Back Forty's offering comes char-grilled and with a sprinkling of salt. Butter lettuce, sliced house-made pickles and red onion come atop the $10 burger; pay $2 extra for thick heritage bacon or a farmhouse cheddar that really got our saliva flowing. A thick Amy's Bread sesame seed bun sporting beautiful grill marks adds just enough texture and soaks up errant flavor flow.
190 Ave B at 12th St (212-388-1990).

Shorty's.32

Chef Josh Eden tops his lightly charred, expertly seasoned, medium-rare burgers with iceberg lettuce for its clean taste and crunch. Cheddar, blue cheese or Gruyère are the cheese

(we like it medium-rare), topped with Nueskes smoked bacon and a tangy Vermont cheddar that nicely complements the patty. Romaine lettuce, plum tomato and red onion fill out a toasted sesame seed bun from Amy's

options; a toasted and buttered cloudlike brioche roll from Tom Cat Bakery completes the $14 package.
199 Prince St between MacDougal and Sullivan Sts (212-375-8275).

67 Burger

Seven ounces of ground chuck mixed with tenderloin, this is the workhorse burger—reliable and tasty every time. Variety is king at 67: There are 14 signature burgers ($6.25-$9), plus eight cheeses and 15 toppings, including tapenade and crispy artichokes. A great seeded bun from Brooklyn's Pechter's Bakery stands up nicely to the overflowing toppings.
67 Lafayette Ave at Fulton St, Fort Greene, Brooklyn (718-797-7150).

Primehouse

This $14, ten-ounce behemoth comes broiled with a nice char; though the meat could be packed looser, it's still three-napkin juicy. The topping of Applewood smoked bacon with Maytag blue cheese could be a meal in itself. And a major plus: The pillow-soft pretzel bun is baked daily in Primehouse's bakery, ready to be toasted under the broiler before being served.
381 Park Ave South at 27th St (212-824-2600).

Resto

Resto's $13 burger is an ambitious blend of beef cheek with hanger steak and fatback, ground daily on-site. Panfried, the burger is available only one way: cooked through—no exceptions. The result is like meat-loaf. Gruyère, house-made mayo, Heinz pickles and red onion make an interesting topping combo, but we find the plain white bun, from Rockland Bakery, a bit lifeless.
111 E 29th St between Park and Lexington Aves (212-685-5585).

BLT Burger

The $11 signature burger comprises seven ounces of certified Black Angus sirloin, chuck, short rib and brisket from Pat LaFrieda, grilled to order with a good char. The burger's richness is helped along by the addition of sweet butter from Keller's Creamery in upstate New York. The Arnold's sesame-seed bun reminds us of those used in fast-food chains, and brings this burger down a notch.

BLT Burger

470 Sixth Ave between 11th and 12th Sts (212-243-8226).

Stand

The burger ($9-$11) takes a turn on the grill and comes medium-rare (unless otherwise requested)—and flowing with juices. Sundry topping choices include green-peppercorn sauce, onion marmalade and shredded lettuce. Don't overlook the ketchup—made in-house from more than 20 ingredients. There are also four different buns: brioche, plain, sesame, poppy seed, all coming from Reliable Bakery.
24 E 12th St between Fifth Ave and University Pl (212-488-5900).

913 *...or go for an old-school triple at Schnäk*

Schnäck wags a bloated finger in the face of the city's high-end burger joints. Load your bun with up to five godlessly greasy mini patties, and cement them with melted cheddar and aho, a bright-green garlic and jalapeño sauce ($7). Then watch your pulse.
Schnäk *122 Union St at Columbia St, Carroll Gardens, Brooklyn (718-855-2879).*

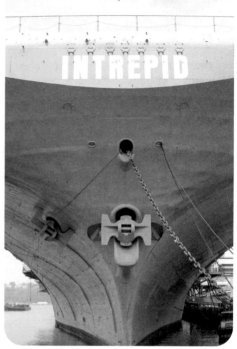

914

Eat at La Esquina— once you find it

Countless first-time visitors to Mexican hotspot La Esquina (114 Kenmare St between Cleveland Place and Lafayette St, 646-613-7100) stand on the corner of Lafayette and Kenmare gawking at the deli sign and wondering if they've written down the wrong address. But after watching dozens of people walk in through a door marked "employees only," it becomes clear that the restaurant lurks behind it. Follow them in and you'll be rewarded with such dishes as spicy sirloin with poblano chillies, Mayan shrimp coated in a chipotle glaze, and grilled fish with avocado salsa—somehow it all tastes better served amid exposed brick, wrought iron and wax-dripping candelabras.

915 *Get lucky for just a buck*

Ignore the glittering Buddhas, don't be seduced by the smell of incense… if you want to get a fortune slip at the oldest Buddhist temple on the East Coast you're going to have to make a $1 donation to their coffers.
Eastern States Buddhist Temple of America *64 Mott St between Bayard and Canal Sts (212-966-6229).*

916

Navigate Central Park by lamppost

When Henry Bacon designed the park's original lampposts in 1907, he affixed to each one a waist-high number that tells the nearest cross street. Lamppost 6725, for example, is near 67th Street. You'll never get lost again.

917

Take flight from the Intrepid

The *Intrepid*, a monstrously big former aircraft carrier, houses a sea, air and space museum. Which explains the A-12 Blackbird spy plane on the flight deck, and the presence of the world's fastest commercial airliner in the world—the *Intrepid*'s Concorde is the very one that made the fastest Atlantic crossing, in just 2 hours, 52 minutes and 59 seconds. Impressive, no doubt, but you want to be entertained: Time for the simulators. In the Navy Hall, you can climb into a tandem cockpit simulator and attempt to land an A-6 Intruder. It's free, too. Want to pull some Gs? In the Virtual Flight Zone, G-Force Encounter's suspended cockpit flings you about using the magic of hydraulics—not exactly free as a bird, but a great simulation of the real thing. The ship has been getting much-needed repairs in a New Jersey dry dock—prepare to welcome it back in November 2008.

Intrepid Sea-Air-Space Museum *USS Intrepid, Pier 86, 46th Street at the Hudson River (212-245-0072/intrepidmuseum.org).*

Shop for spices at Kalustyan's

Ask chefs where they find their rare exotic spices (not to mention oils, teas, nuts, seeds, and herbs) and they will inevitably mention Kalustyan's. This place isn't just the city's best source of spices, it's also one of the oldest, having opened in 1944. It's heaven for food lovers who need more than just parsley, sage, rosemary, and thyme—and just about the only place in the city where you can find certain ingredients. The website, for example, lists 1,322 spices, from aloo bhaji curry to za'atar Lebanese spice blend. Take that, Whole Foods.

Kalustyan's *123 Lexington Ave at 28th St (212-685-3451/kalustyans.com).*

A few of my favorite things

919-927

Bobbie Lloyd, cupcake baker

I love taking my kids to a movie at the Ziegfeld Theater (141 West 54th St, 212-307-1862, clearviewcinemas.com). Afterwards, we usually get lunch at Burger Joint at Le Parker Meridien (118 W 57th St, 212-245-5000) or head over to MoMA (11 West 53 St between Fifth and Sixth Aves, 212-708-9400, moma.org) to see some of the exhibits.

My family and I love to go on bike rides. We usually bike around Randall's Island or down the West Side Highway to Battery Park City (batteryparkcity.org) to catch the various festivals, art shows and concerts there.

For art, I love the Brooklyn Museum (200 Eastern Parkway, Brooklyn, 718-638-5000, brooklynmuseum.org). My family usually go there and then to Bubby's (1 Main St, Dumbo, 718-222-0666, bubbys.com) for lunch. It's a great spot for my kids: They hang out under the bridge and play while we wait for our food. At dusk, we walk back to Manhattan over the Brooklyn Bridge.

If I have dinner downtown, I always go to Little Italy for gelato afterward.

I love going to "Starry Nights" at the American Museum of Natural History (Central Park West and 79th St, 212-769-5100, amnh.org). It's a program that the museum puts on the first Friday of every month, where they play jazz and serve wine and tapas in the Rose Center.

In December, my family and I go to the Bronx Zoo (Bronx River Parkway at Fordham Rd, Bronx, 718-367-1010, bronxzoo.com) for the annual "Holiday of Lights" festival. It's free and always features entertainers like stilt walkers, as well fun arts and crafts activities for the kids. After, we go to Arthur Avenue for Italian food.

Bobbie Lloyd is head baker at Magnolia Bakery, which has two Manhattan sites; see magnoliacupcakes.com.

928

Bring quarters to Barcade
For stand-up thumb action, old-school gaming addicts flock to Barcade (388 Union Ave between Ainslie and Powers Sts, Williamsburg, Brooklyn, 718-302-6464). It's wall-to-wall with 25¢ games like 1943 and Super Mario.

929-933

Get high in a hotel

The Time Warner Center uptown might be little more than a glorified shopping mall, but even jaded New Yorkers can't deny that the location, overlooking Columbus Circle, provides some stellar views. One prime spot to enjoy them is from the comfort of a leather chair in the Lobby Lounge of the Mandarin Oriental Hotel (Time Warner Center, 80 Columbus Circle at 60th St, 212-805-8800), perched 35 floors above the southwest corner of Central Park. The drinks aren't exactly cheap (signature cocktails are $17 apiece), but the Fifth Avenue and Central Park South skylines, glittering through walls of windows, make those extra bucks worthwhile.

Plunge, the rooftop bar over at the Hotel Gansevoort (18 Ninth Ave at 13th St, 212-206-6700, hotelgansevoort.com) is where you'll find bikini-clad hotel guests—the bar has access to the adjacent pool. You, of course, will have to wear clothes if you want to make it through the posh lobby and up to the penthouse, but you can strip down once you get there and sunbathe, caipirinha, mojito or margarita in hand. Prices are again sky-high, but Plunge's $15 Mango Lime Rickey will at least have you tapping into the trendy soundtrack. At nearby Maritime Hotel (363 W 16th St between Eighth and Ninth Aves, 212-242-4300, themaritime hotel.com), the preppy striped banquettes at Cabanas give the place a yacht-ish vibe. This rooftop bar offers comfy alfresco couches, exotic drinks served by model-like cocktail waitresses and a canopy of paper lanterns to help set the mood.

Ava Lounge, at the Dream Hotel (210 W 55th St between Broadway and Seventh Ave, 212-247-2000, dreamny.com), is a chic, bi-level space offering gorgeous, nearly wraparound views across midtown, including an electric vista of Times Square. Equal parts safari, French Riviera and old-school Miami Beach, this spot is a superb perch (Broadway theatergoers should keep it in mind for pre- or post-show drinks).

Everybody knows that downtown is by far the coolest part of town, and it doesn't get any cooler than A-60, the rooftop bar at 60 Thompson (60 Thompson St between Broome and Spring Sts, 212-431-0400, 60thompson.com), where good-looking media types gather to celebrate their wonderfulness in a sleek, shimmering lounge with killer views. The snag? It is for hotel guests only. Still, if you're looking gorgeous and it's slightly off-hours, you might just be able to squeeze in.

934-937

Chew the city's best fried chicken

This deep-fried favorite, once synonymous with Colonel Sanders's original recipe, has gained new appeal, thanks to a popular Asian technique employed at several chicken joints in the city. These eateries skip the buttermilk bath and the heavy egg-and-flour dredging in favor of a seasoned bird that's lightly dusted with flour and dipped twice into 350-degree oil, leaving a smooth, brittle coating that the Chinese call "paper-thin skin." You can find this style of fried fowl made to order at Queens spot Unidentified Flying Chicken (71-22 Roosevelt Ave between 70th and 72nd Sts, Jackson Heights, Queens, 718-205-6662), new fast-food microjoint Bonbon Chicken (98 Chambers St between Broadway and Church St, 212-227-2375) and Forte Baden Baden (28 W 32nd St, second floor, between Fifth Ave and Broadway, 212-714-2266), which takes it a step further by roasting the chicken before dunking it in hot oil. The result is bite-size pieces of flesh with a supercrisp bronze coating, reinforced with fries or onion rings, a heap of deep-fried garlic cloves and hot sauce. If you still look to the South for your fix, new chicken stop Birdies (149 First Ave between 9th and 10th Sts, 212-529-2512) follows Grandma's recipe—not the Colonel's—using organic, hormone-free birds.

938

Attend the September Concert

Musicians at more than 80 venues across all five boroughs—including Central Park, Rockefeller Center, Washington Square Park, and McCarren Park—spread a message of peace and "fill the skies with music every September 11th". See septemberconcert.org for details of this year's performances.

939

Find a fedora at D/L Cerney

Specializing in timeless, original designs for stylish fellows, D/L Cerney (13 E 7th St between Second and Third Aves, 212-673-7033) features new and old clothing, none of it worn before. The highlight of the collection is the menswear from the 1940s to the '60s. Mint-condition must-haves include hats (such as some pristine fedoras), ties, cufflinks, costume jewelry and shoes.

940-942

Eat America's best cheesecake

That's right. We rate this number one, not just in Gotham but in the whole country. S&S has been producing cheesecakes (large $20; small $11) for 40 years in a hole-in-the-wall Bronx factory. The cake is rich but not heavy, sweet but not cloying, creamy but not artery-clogging: It's perfect and—sorry, America—inimitable. Buy it at S&S (222 W 238th St at Review Pl, Bronx, 718-549-3888) or the 238th Street delis, or by the slice at Peter Luger (178 Broadway at Driggs Ave, Williamsburg, Brooklyn, 718-387-7400) and Palm Too (840 2nd Ave between 44th and 45th Sts, 212-697-5198).

943 Take the tour at Radio City Music Hall

Few rooms scream "New York City!" like the gilded auditorium at Radio City Music Hall (1260 Sixth Ave at 50th St, 212-307-7171), headlined by (among others) Wilco, Alanis Morissette and Carole King. The popular hour-long behind-the-scenes tour brings the place to life with a stroll through the gorgeous Art Deco interior; a visit to the private apartments of showman Samuel Lionel "Roxy" Rothafel, who opened the hall in 1932; and a meeting with one of the high-kicking Radio City Rockettes. Tours ($17 adults, $10 children) run 11am-3pm daily.

944

Join the line for brunch at Clinton St Baking Company...

New Yorkers aren't usually keen on waiting patiently for things, but a late-morning (or midafternoon) table at the Clinton St Baking Company is clearly worth the line: Every Saturday and Sunday, a throng of brunchers line up to pack themselves into the wood-paneled restaurant's cozy quarters for a comfort-food feast. Out of the bustling kitchen come classics prepared with simple style. Pillowy banana-walnut pancakes ($11) are accompanied by an irresistibly warm, syrupy maple butter; eggs Benedict ($13) feature hearty slabs of ham just as moist and sweet as the buttermilk biscuits beneath them. Order the fried green tomatoes ($5) and you'll be rewarded with a satisfying crunch that confirms it: Good things really do come to those who wait. **Clinton St Baking Company** *4 Clinton St between Houston and Stanton Sts (646-602-6263/clintonstreetbaking.com).*

945-948

...or nosh without the wait at these speedy brunch spots

Sarabeth's. Popover Café. Balthazar. The list of city brunch spots where you'll endure hour-plus waits could go on and on. While it might be OK to make brunch your main weekend activity now and then, it doesn't always have to be an *event*—sometimes you just want to eat. No worries: We've scoured the city and found a handful of hot spots where a table is usually available.

Geronimo

Swarms of Gotham teens with plenty of time on their hands call the Yorkville and Carnegie Hill sections of the Upper East Side home, so it comes as no surprise that scoring a table for brunch in these parts tends to be hard. Geronimo, which is relatively new to the nabe, is an exception: We've been seated immediately on previous visits. The prix-fixe brunch menu includes a Mexican-style omelette and a Cobb salad. A Bloody Mary or margarita is included for the over-21 crowd. *1600 Third Ave between 89th and 90th Sts (212-369-0808).*

107 West

Nestled in that no-man's-land that exists between Columbia University and the Upper West Side, this Southwestern eatery thus far seems to have escaped the notice of the brunch-seeking hordes from both of its neighbours: students and families. Nearly all the entrées—from several variations on eggs Benedict to Southern-style French toast (dipped in cornflakes and served with sweet strawberry butter)—come with fruit salad and a heap of tiny home fries. *2787 Broadway at 107th St (212-864-1555/107west.com).*

Telephone Bar & Grill

Brunch here is offered prix fixe, and includes the likes of a hearty country breakfast with buckwheat pecan pancakes, eggs and bacon, or "green" eggs and ham (spinach, ham, scrambled eggs and cheddar cheese on an English muffin). And the name? Look out for the old-fashioned phone booth outside. *149 Second Ave between 9th and 10th Sts (212-529-5000/telebar.com).*

Vynl

A staple brunch spot in Hell's Kitchen for years, this retro diner recently opened a new location in the brunch epicenter of Manhattan, the Upper West Side. Snagging a seat in the midtown outpost is nearly impossible on weekends, but it's easier to get one uptown (at least, until locals catch on). Try the Vynl egg sandwich—a pile of scrambled eggs with cheddar cheese on a buttermilk biscuit—or creamy oatmeal (ask for the walnuts and dried cranberries to top). *507 Columbus Ave between 84th and 85th Sts (212-362-1107/vynl-nyc.com).*

949

Wake up and smell the lilac, cherry and magnolia

The serene 250 acres that make up the New York Botanical Garden are a magical respite from all the city's cars and concrete. There are some 50 gardens and plant collections, including the last 50 original acres of the forest that once covered all of New York City. In spring, the gardens are frothy with pastel blossoms, followed in the fall by vivid foliage in the oak and maple groves. Even on a rainy day there is no excuse to stay away: Stay warm and sheltered inside the striking Enid A Haupt Conservatory, a glass-walled greenhouse—the nation's largest—that was built in 1902; it now puts on seasonal exhibits, as well as hosting the World of Plants, a series of environmental galleries that will send you on an eco-tour through tropical rainforests, deserts and a palm-tree oasis.

New York Botanical Garden *Bronx River Pkwy at Fordham Rd (718-817-8700/nybg.org).*

950
Partake of the Feast of San Gennaro

On the orders of the Emperor Diocletian in A.D. 304, St. Gennaro was thrown to wild beasts, who refused to attack him. So the Romans beheaded him instead. Spare him a thought every September at Little Italy's Feast of San Gennaro (sangennaro.org), as you take in the scent of savory sausage and peppers or assess the difficulty of winning a cheap stuffed animal at a game of skill. Taking in the colorful characters, old-school hucksters and mouth-watering aromas is reward enough at this annual street fair, but the real lure here is the ten-block procession of a 100-year-old statue of the saint, which begins at the Most Precious Blood Church (109 Mulberry St between Canal and Hester Sts).

951 *Join the birders*

You might have thought NYC was a hostile environment for birders, but there are binocular joys aplenty for anyone with a MetroCard. It just so happens that Central Park is a hot spot for watching birds, with more than 200 species sighted here each year.

For millions of years, birds have been migrating annually from the tropics of South America and Central America, along what is known as the Atlantic flyway. Traveling north along the eastern coast of the United States, millions of birds make their way each year to summer breeding grounds as far away as Canada. Despite the urban sprawl, the birds are still programmed to fly over this area. Rare birds, like green herons, alight here because of something biologists call the "Central Park effect"—flying over they see a huge expanse of nothing but concrete and metal, except, of course, for the 843-acre green island that is Central Park.

The best months to catch unusual species are during the peak migration seasons—September and October in the fall, and April and May in the spring. Good spots in the park include the trees around the King of Poland statue (near Turtle Pond), which attract warblers, orioles, kingfishers, and robins, and the Jacqueline Kennedy Onassis Reservoir, home to about 100 birds at a time, likely including at least four kinds of gulls: great black-backed, herring, ring-billed, and laughing. The Ramble, a strip of the park between 72nd Street and 81st Street that is a notorious gay cruising spot, and the fairly dense, wooded area with streams and ponds at the north end of the park, above 103rd Street, are also perfect refuges for birds.

Loeb Boathouse is another must-visit for birders. On its oval wooden table you'll find the small, blue-bound, loose-leaf birders' journal, which details sightings of grosbeaks, falcons, egrets, more warblers and green herons, owls, even bald eagles. Among the luminaries who have written entries in it are former president Jimmy Carter—he spotted a red-tailed hawk.

Of all the birds you can see here, it turns out that the park celebrities are also red-tails: Pale Male and Lola, who have between them generated a surprising number of column inches, many of them relating to failed eviction attempt back in 2004. Their nest restored, they are still holed up just outside the park, on the 12th floor of a building at 927 Fifth Avenue (at East 74th Street), but can often be seen zooming above the Conservatory Water (the boat pond).

For birding details and tour information, call the American Museum of Natural History on 212-769-5100 or the New York City Audubon Society on 212-691-7483.

New York Botanical Garden

Football fortresses

You can get that hometown feel, says Katharine Rust, even when the big game is being screened in a New York bar.

It's 2:30pm on a Sunday in New York and I'm standing in a bar in Hell's Kitchen where hell has broken loose. Don't ask me the name of the man in the black and gold Rothlisberger jersey who has just erupted in tears and begun to jump up and down and hug me. I have no idea. But more importantly, it doesn't matter. The Pittsburg Steelers have just scored a touchdown and between throbbing strobe light, deafening cheers and "Who Let the Dogs Out" pounding from the speakers, I'm fairly certain I've forgotten my own name. (I'm sure the case of Miller Lite—half of which I'm wearing— has done its part as well.)

This is football season. For five months each year, fans around the country flock to bars to drink beer and cheer on their favorite group of padded warriors. If you live in a smaller city, chances are you're rooting for the local team— and you'll have no problem finding a place to do it. This, on the other hand, is New York and as per the Big Apple's amplified style, football season here takes on a slightly larger meaning.

For scores of non-native New Yorkers whose roots lie in towns throughout the nation, heading to their team's bar to watch the game every Sunday is akin to walking into their favorite hometown watering hole. Transfers to the city will even travel well out of their way (sometimes to a different borough) simply to stand alongside their brethren, unified in support of a single cause. Like the European immigrants of the 1800s, who congregated in cultural communities similar to their villages in the Old Country, city-dwelling football fans will do what it takes just to be among their own.

Fortunately, there's a bar for pretty much every team. At least that's what Todd Swedock, founder of the fan-based social networking website urbantailgate.com, would have you believe. He, along with friend and web-system programmer Chris Vander Poel, launched the site in the fall of 2006 in order to bring fans together to watch their team. Or, as the site's motto says, "The city is a big place. Everybody should have a bar they call home." Essentially,

Kettle of Fish

fans go on the site and create their own profile. From there they can find out where their team's bars are (some have several different spots), as well as meet other fans. Often, Swedock's job is to designate a pub as a home-base for a particular team.

"I'll get in touch with a bar and establish the game as a weekly event," he explains, "and the place will have drink specials in exchange for a packed bar." It's a pretty sweet deal for hardcore fans, as I had the fortunate opportunity to discover when I tagged along with Swedock to Red Sky (29th St, 212-447-1820, redskynyc. com), an urbantailgate.com-established Washington Redskins bar.

At first glance the spot—weirdly located between Madison and Park Ave South—seems fairly unassuming. That is, until you open the doors and are affronted by two floors packed with fans dressed in everything, from jerseys to Native American feathered headdresses, all in the Skins' signature ruby red. Ten-year-old kids cheer alongside their grandparents, while twenty-, thirty- and forty-somethings down $2 Bud Light draft beers. And all are screaming—from memory, natch—the

Redskins' fight song. According to one fan, the tune was a catalyst in the creation of the Skins' most hated rivalry with the Dallas Cowboys. When Redskins owners denied the Cowboys their entry into the NFL, Dallas's owners bought the rights to the song and would not permit the Skins' owners to use it unless they agreed to allow for a new team. This is the reason why fans now raise their voices in proud unity when they cheer, "Hail to the Redskins! Hail to victory! Braves on the war path! Fight for old D.C.!"

Of course, not all NY football fans have found their haven through social networking sites. One of the most well-known single-team bars, the West Village's Kettle of Fish (59 Christopher St, at Seventh Ave, 212-414-2278), is the New York home to one of the country's strongest fan-bases, that of the Green Bay Packers. Walking into "The Kettle" is like walking into any dive bar in Wisconsin. The joint is Packed (pun intended) with a versatile, multi-aged German and Scandinavian-looking crowd yelling fervently at the tiny TVs in the corner while downing Wisconsin staples, Sprecher beer and

Scruffy Duffy's

> *"For scores of non-native New Yorkers whose roots lie in towns throughout the nation, heading to their team's bar to watch the game every Sunday is akin to walking into their favorite hometown watering hole."*

Johnsonville Brats. When the Pack scores a touchdown, the crowd does a polka to the bar's favorite anthem, "I Love My Green Bay Packers!" When the other team scores a touchdown, the music comes on again, only on this occasion the song follows what every Packer fan constantly feels in his or her heart toward their mortal enemy (one of the greatest rivalries in American sports), "The Bears Still Suck." There's an anti-Minnesota Vikings ditty too, as well as, on the rare occasions the Pack faces the Dallas Cowboys, a slow country 'n' western tune with the chorus, "Mammas Don't Let Yer Babies Grow Up to Be Cowboys." "I've had my game day seat at the bar for seven years," says Packer fan and Wisconsin native, Steve O. "It's like a second home."

Indeed, even the supporters of completely different teams respect the lords of the Kettle. When I asked one guy who was sporting a Steeler's cap why he comes to Packer games, he was quick to demonstrate that he had the utmost respect for the fans. "During one Thursday night game against the Cowboys, I made sure to stay away in order to give room to true fans," he said. "Though I did sneak in to watch the last quarter."

Baltimore Ravens
Kate Kearney's *251 E 50th St between Second and Third Aves (212-935-2045).*

Buffalo Bills
Kelly's *9259 Fourth Ave between 92nd and 94th Sts, Bay Ridge, Brooklyn (718-745-9546/kellysnyc.com).*

Chicago Bears
Big Easy *1768 Second Ave between 92nd and 93rd Sts (212-348-0879/ bigeasynyc.com).*

Cleveland Browns
Blondies Sports *212 W 79th St between Amsterdam Ave and Broadway (212-362-4360/blondiessports.com).*

Dallas Cowboys
Stone Creek Bar & Lounge *140 E 27th St between Third and Lexington Aves (212-532-1037/stonecreeknyc.com).*

Denver Broncos
Butterfield 8 *5 E 38th St between Fifth and Madison Aves (212-679-0646).*

Indianapolis Colts
Coppersmith's *793 9th Ave at 53rd St (212-957-2994/coppersmithsbar.com).*

New England Patriots
Professor Thom's *219 Second Ave between 13th and 14th Sts (212-260-9480/professorthoms.com).*

Philadelphia Eagles
Town Tavern *134 W 3rd St (212-253-6955/towntavernnyc.com).*

San Diego Chargers
MJ Armstrong's *329 First Ave at 19th St (212-358-9946/mjarmstrongs.com).*

Seattle Seahawks
Crowe's Nest *1804 Second Ave between 93rd and 94th Sts (212-860-2300/ crowesnestnyc.com).*

Washington Redskins
Red Sky Bar & Lounge *47 E 29th St between Park and Madison Aves (212-447-1820/redskynyc.com).*

964 *Get in the line for a latte at Gorilla*

You think the wait at your local Starbucks is long? Think again. Extraordinarily strong espresso and rich lattes draw eternal lines—lines that are worth waiting in. Those seeking something less potent, try the Vermont-syrupy mild maple latte.

Gorilla Coffee *97 Fifth Ave at Park Pl, Park Slope, Brooklyn (718-230-3244).*

965 *Fence yourself fit*

Get a taste of life as it must be for the upper crust when you work out at West Side sports haven Chelsea Piers (Pier 60, 23rd St at the Hudson River, 212-336-6000, chelseapiers. com): The eight-person Basic Fencing class is a cardio workout with an emphasis on coordination, alignment and looking like you went to some fancy prep school. New membership costs $167 per month, plus a $200 initiation fee.

966
Enjoy slamming verse at the Bowery Poetry Club

"You and me and Kenny G / Blowing his horn and you're blowing me," serenades septuagenarian Bingo Gazingo during his Friday stints at the Bowery Poetry Club slam (308 Bowery between Bleecker and Houston Sts, 212-614-0505). The Flushing flophouse poet's 15 minutes of fame/infamy run from 6pm every week, and you can encourage his screamo (an inimical genre of punk and shouted vocals) while chugging PBRs. You can even make requests, maybe for his popular ballad "I Love You So Fucking Much, I Can't Shit."

Bowery Poetry Club

967 *Get pre-medieval on the Met's ass*

Years ago, a visit to the Metropolitan Museum of Art (1000 Fifth Ave at 82nd St, 212-535-7710, metmuseum.org) wasn't complete without a cafeteria lunch in the grand, dimly lit atrium around the big sunken pool—where the kids in E.L. Konigsburg's classic *From the Mixed-Up Files of Mrs Basil E Frankweiler* bathed. The pool was a post-war addition; McKim, Mead & White had designed the space, intended to evoke the garden of a Roman villa, for the display of sculpture.

Now a marble floor, similar to the purple stone in the Pantheon, has replaced the pool as part of the 15-year redesign and reinstallation of the museum's truly stellar Greek and Roman collections. Standing in the luminous double-story atrium with its newly raised glass roof, surrounded by monumental figures of Hercules and Dionysus, it's hard to imagine why the space was ever turned into a restaurant. Christopher Lightfoot, the Met's associate curator of Roman art, supervisor of the project with curator-in-charge Carlos Picon, says it was mainly because of increased tourism after the war. "At the time, the Greek and Roman period was not considered to be of prime importance," Lightfoot says. "The idea of the Roman Empire in 1950 wasn't one Western democracies wanted to promote."

Times change, and the Met's director, Philippe de Montebello, has clearly made the period a priority, devoting $220 million to reworking the wing. He moved his own office and others to create room for the new Hellenistic and Roman galleries on the ground floor, and the Etruscan galleries and Greek and Roman Study Collection on the mezzanine. The renovation yielded in excess of 30,000 square feet of new space, almost doubling the area devoted to classical art.

Most of the 5,300 or so objects on view had been in storage for decades: for example, the imposing pair of Hercules statues that flank the sculpture court. Elsewhere, the Met's holdings of Roman wall paintings—buried in the eruption of Vesuvius in A.D. 79 and excavated from two villas near Pompeii—are being shown together for the first time, and a frescoed bedroom, on view in the museum's main hall since the 1960s, now joins the rest of the group in the side galleries on the first floor.

Meanwhile, the contemporary role of antiquities is undergoing its own renovation of sorts, with ongoing controversies about whether museums have acquired works looted from Italy and Greece. De Montebello took the high road in 2006 by negotiating the return of 21 pieces in response to claims brought by the Italian Culture Ministry. But in late March 2007, another allegation, this one made by an Umbrian town without the backing of the Italian government, hit the news: The centrepiece of the new Etruscan galleries, a bronze chariot purchased in 1903 and recently restored, was sold illegally. Worse, recent news reports—unconfirmed as we went to suggested that the piece may, in fact, be fake.

Asked about the impact of such controversy, Lightfoot—standing in front of a vitrine filled with Hellenic silver, slated for return to Italy in 2010—insists "it hasn't affected us a great deal." He puts a positive spin on the subject, noting the museum's gratitude to the Italian government and European museums for loans. "It's nice to feel part of a wider community," he says. "I'm hoping people will see these displays and then want to go and visit Pompeii or the Colosseum in Rome. This is a great advert for their cultural heritage."

The Met

968 Swap clothes at The Dressing Room

Sure, it might appear like another LES lounge, thanks to a handsome wood bar that serves happy hour specials until 9pm every night, but stylist and designer Nikki Fontanella's quirky co-op-cum-watering-hole rewards the curious. Make a beeline past the mixologist and slip down the steps to the subterranean clothing exchange, where you can swap pre-loved loot for cash or a cocktails tab upstairs. If you've imbibed too much to make it safely down the stairs, you're still in luck: What you thought was an avant art display is actually racks of designs by ten indie labels, including Love Brigade and Suzette Sundae. The designers on offer rotate every four months.

The Dressing Room *75A Orchard St between Broome and Grand Sts (212-966-7330).*

969-973

Go fishing round the island...

Manhattan is an island, yeah? So it follows that there's good fishing to be had. Sure enough, blackfish can be fished all year, as well as striped bass, bluefish, snapper, weakfish, porgy, fluke, eel and blue crab in season (May to September). Remember: If you're anywhere south of the George Washington Bridge, you're required to throw back any catch less than 28 inches long. And, due to contaminants, the Department of Health and Mental Hygiene recommends not consuming more than half a pound of self-caught fish per month or more than six blue crabs per week; it also advises against eating eel altogether. Bad news over, here are our favorite five fishing spots.

Battery Park City, Pier A

During the day, Pier A is overrun with street vendors and tourists snapping pictures of the park's mini Statute of Liberty. By dusk, the gawkers have cleared out and the fishermen move in: Both rivers converge into a salty, fertile hot spot, making for great fishing. Many fishermen pull all-nighters, even though it's illegal to hang here after 1am.

Pier I, Riverside Park, South at 70th Street

People have been casting off the end of the pier since probably the 1800s, attracted by the plentiful bass. You've also a good chance of catching snappers and ling.

Riverbank State Park at 155th Street

Despite the fact that the park's built on a sewage treatment facility, it attracts fluke, blackfish and blue crab, depending on the tide. Fishermen wedge two-by-four between the rocks for chopping boards and benches.

Stuyvesant Cove

The bases of old piers, since torn down, attract fish to this brick-lined cove. Along with crabs and clams, you might also catch fluke, snapper and bluefish. (Note: A sign that the bluefish are out there is when the seagulls start diving—they're after scraps of bunker fish that the blues have just torn apart.)

107th Street Pier

Rods line the side of the cement pier, and old Spanish men sit on the edge of the pavilion, tapping along to salsa on a portable radio and passing around a tequila bottle wrapped in a paper bag. It's a good spot for blue crabs, striped bass, bluefish and snappers, sometimes even eels and snapping turtles.

974

...then cast a line in the middle of Manhattan

Visitors to Central Park's sprawling Harlem Meer can avail themselves of some brilliant catch-and-release fishing, courtesy of the Central Park Conservancy. Free rods and bait are available to help you land the likes of largemouth bass, catfish, bluegills and carp from the stocked ponds.

975-978

Bite your way through the city's best doughnuts

Alpha Donuts

Under the elevated 7 train this 24-hour greasy spoon slings eggs, Irish sausages and its featherlight namesakes. The selection is regularly decimated, so arrive early to order 90¢ homemade delights such as sugar crullers and the crumb-crowned, apple-jelly-stuffed yeast beauty—breakfast's answer to apple pie.
45-16 Queens Blvd between 45th and 46th Sts, Sunnyside, Queens (no phone).

The Donut Pub

Despite the neighboring Dunkin' Donuts, caffeine addicts and sugar jonesers beeline to this Kennedy-era institution (est. 1964) for their daily fix. Palm-size apple fritters, honey-dipped yeast doughnuts and Boston creams lacquered with chocolate icing are on offer any time of day or night.
203 W 14th St at Seventh Ave (212-929-0126).

Doughnut Plant

This nook on the Lower East Side has become an essential morning ritual for many sweets hounds, who are happy to line up for the chance to down Doughnut Plant's "100% natural" confections: Square yeast doughnuts are painted with a chunky peanut-butter glaze and injected with house-crafted seasonal jams, lavender flowers perfume cakes, and a ribbon of cream courses through a tres leches cake doughnut.
379 Grand St at Norfolk St (212-505-3700).

Peter Pan Bakery

You'll find doughy fritters, not Tinkerbell, at this Greenpoint standby. Dip lightly glazed raised doughnut into steaming coffee at the curved counter or box up a dozen still-warm chocolate cake rounds or black-raspberry jellies—just a select few of the 30-odd varieties that are baked here daily.
727 Manhattan Ave between Meserole and Norman Aves, Greenpoint, Brooklyn (718-389-3676).

979-987

Shop for a bespoke shirt

CEGO

Owner Carl Goldberg has been designing slim, sporty button-downs for nigh-on 25 years. Although some can get a little pricey, Goldberg offers a first shirt sample before you commit to a full order. He recommends calling ahead for an appointment. Prices range from $95 to $400 per shirt; five-shirt minimum for each order. *174 Fifth Ave, Suite 301, between 22nd and 23rd Sts (212-620-4512/cego.com).*

Duncan Quinn

Duncan Quinn has a design philosophy that is perhaps best captured by the various pictures of James Bond that adorn the walls. That is to say, if you wear expensive, custom clothes and resemble a secret agent, popularity is bound to follow. Prices range from $350 to $650 per shirt; four-shirt minimum for each order. *8 Spring St between Bowery and Elizabeth St (212-226-7030/duncanquinn.com).*

Hamilton Custom Shirtmakers

Don't mess with Texas. This Houston-based shirtmaker has been outfitting people since 1883. In New York, their fashionable cotton designs are sold through Barneys. Prices range from $300 to $450 per shirt; four-shirt minimum for each order. *Barneys New York, 660 Madison Ave at 61st St (212-833-2044/hamiltonshirts.com).*

La Rukico Hong Kong Custom Tailors

Mr Kelly—master tailor at this venerable shop—helps translate personal style into a sleek, custom fit. Prices range from $85 to $165 per shirt; three-shirt minimum for each order. Ask him about what it was like designing clothes in the disco era. *152 E 48th St between Lexington and Third Aves (212-832-0725/hongkongcustomtailor.com).*

Lord Willy's

This Nolita boutique's shirts—available in both long and short sleeves—are known for their fitted, British cut, spread collars and three-barrel cuffs, and look good with or without a tie. Be sure to stay on your best behavior; if owners Mr and Mrs Wilcox don't like you, they might decide you're not worth the trouble. Prices start at $250 per shirt; two-shirt minimum for each order. *223 Mott between Prince and Spring Sts (212-680-8888/lordwillys.com).*

Michael Andrew's Bespoke

Himself a lawyer, this shop's cofounder Michael Mantegna specializes in dressing bankers and fellow purveyors of even-handed jurisprudence. His showroom, which opened in 2007, is open by appointment only. Prices start at $145 per shirt; no minimum order. *20 Clinton St between E Houston and Stanton Sts (212-677-1755/michaelandrewsbespoke.com).*

Rothman's

This Union Square emporium specializes in affordable, locally manufactured pieces (most are made in Newark). The cuts are a bit boxier than some of the higher-end tailors, but that might work better on some rhomboid-shaped torsos. Prices starts at $95 per shirt; no minimum order. *200 Park Ave South at 17th St (212-777-7400/rothmansny.com).*

Seize sur Vingt

Myriad cuff styles, dozens of collar choices, a wide variety of buttons to choose from: It's all on offer at this wood-floored space. (They have off-the-rack shirts, too.) Prices range from $200 to $390 per shirt; initial five-shirt minimum, with single orders available after. *243 Elizabeth St between E Houston and Prince Sts (212-343-0476/16sur20.com).*

Turnbull & Asser

The consummate British tailor, this joint has made custom clothing for English royalty, Churchill and countless posh U.K. luminaries since 1885. Ever meticulous, they take more than 20 measurements to ensure the finest fit possible. Prices range from $325 to $475 per shirt; initial six-shirt minimum, then single orders are available. *42 E 57th St between Madison and Park Aves (212-752-5700/turnbullandasser.com).*

988

Celebrate US-made cheese at Anne Saxelby's dairy stall

Partially responsible for the final nail in the American-cheese-equals-Kraft-Singles coffin, Murray's Cheese vet Anne Saxelby introduced New Yorkers to the concept of the domestic artisanal dairy when she opened her Saxelby Cheesemongers stall back in summer 2006. The Essex Street Market destination (open every day except Sunday) has won national attention for focusing solely on USA curds along with butter, crème fraîche and other dairy goods. A large part of its success is due to the enthusiasm of its proprietor, who carries 35 fromages from farms reaching all the way to Iowa.

Saxelby Cheesemongers *Essex Street Market, Essex St between Delancey and Rivington Sts (212-228-8204/saxelbycheese.com).*

989 Race the crosstown bus

Try to walk five blocks faster than the glacially slow M23, which runs at an average speed of 4mph. If you're feeling energetic, try beating the second-pokiest bus, the M34, which runs at about 4.3mph. Build up to a calorie-busting race against the M5 on a midweek evening, as it zips along at 7.6mph.

990 Bowl in Billy-burg (at last)

We've fallen hard for the retro rates at The Gutter, Williamsburg's first new bowling alley in nearly half a century. Before 8pm, rented lace-ups are $2 and games are $6 on one of the eight 1970s-style lanes (snapped up from a Midwest factory). After tossing a frame, retreat to a lounge decorated with bowling trophies and ancient beer signs to enjoy one of the dozen killer microbrews on tap.

The Gutter *200 North 14th St between Berry St and Wythe Ave, Williamsburg, Brooklyn (718-387-3585).*

991

Browse the Oscar Wilde Bookshop

Not that you'd know it by counting the number of LGBT publishers and indie bookstores in existence, but queer lit is alive and well. For proof, slip into this tiny but packed-to-the-rafters bookstore, which turned 40 in 2007. Owner Kim Brinster may be surrounded by superstores, but her shelves—rich with everything from rarities and classics to hot-off-the-press fiction—show no sign of caving.

Oscar Wilde Bookshop *15 Christopher St at Gay St (212-255-8097/oscarwildebooks.com).*

992 Visit a Tibetan temple

Many New Yorkers seek refuge at the Jacques Marchais Museum of Tibetan Art (admission $5, free-$3 reductions), a reproduction of a Himalayan mountain temple with a formidable Buddhist altar, tranquil meditation gardens, and a small collection of Tibetan and Buddhist objects of interest. The museum also hosts meditation workshops and, in October each year, an excellent Tibetan cultural festival.
Jacques Marchais Museum of Tibetan Art *338 Lighthouse Ave off Richmond Rd, Staten Island (718-987-3500/tibetanmuseum.org).*

993 Take in a classical concert at lunch

Trinity Church and St Paul's Chapel (Broadway at Wall St, 212-602-0747, trinitywallstreet.org) host a "Concerts at One" series. For just a $2 donation, you can spend your lunchtime listening to, say, the Trinity Choir or the Proteus Ensemble. Better than KT Tunstall from a Starbucks speaker-system any day.

Trinity Church

994-996 Meet with brand-new flavors at a marvelous Momofuku

Original. Fun. At times, outstanding. The Momofuku mini-chain has taken David Chang from East Village rebel to awards-circuit veteran. He borrowed money from his dad to set up the original Noodle Bar when he was just 26, an age when even wunderkinds are still apprenticing as line cooks. His formula of bringing together a chic but electric informal setting and extraordinary flavour combinations was a huge success.

Then came spin-off Momofuku Ssäm Bar (207 Second Ave at 13th St, 212-254-3500), serving the titular Korean finger food Chang calls an "Asian burrito." Next Chang reopened his hopelessly busy flagship in larger premises a block north of the original (171 First Ave between 10th and 11th Sts, 212-777-7773), with another innovation: Tables, as foreign to the old Noodle Bar as reservations or a dress code. The new Noodle Bar doubled capacity to 55 seats, with no discernible reduction in quality. Most recently, he returned to the original Noodle Bar premises with Momofuku Ko (163 First Ave at 10th St, no phone), which adds another tweak to the plan: Reservations at this 12-seater chef's counter can only be made online at momofuku.com.

Expect floor-to-ceiling windows, light-wood paneling and a dining bar—as well as the usual Momofuku queue of scenesters awaiting a taste sensation: Perhaps cold smoked duck breast, slathered in swollen quince-flavored mustard seeds that pop in your mouth like fish roe, and a cinnamon-spiked sour cream that reminded us of tiramisu. Bizarre, and typically addictive.

997 Join the Prospect Park Moonlight Ride

Make sure you dress warmly for this monthly Saturday-night ride. Bring your wheels (bikes or skates) to the Grand Army Plaza entrance at 9pm for an hour-long scenic trek past a ravine, waterfalls and the illuminated boathouse. Go to times-up.org for more information.

998 Sample the soda fountain at Stand

Though oddball refreshments like rosemary-ade might scare the bejesus out of the folks in Pleasantville, they're perfectly suited to this progressive diner's NYU milieu. Stand's burgers are nothing to sniff at, but it's the long, distinctive list of house-made potables that thrills us with its reimagined retro favorites. After all, no '50s diner would make floats with strawberry gelato (from Il Lab, of course) crammed into a glass of Cel-Ray soda, or the deep-pink blackberry soda, dense with fruit pulp. Traditionalists, take note: The milk shakes do come in classic flavors like vanilla and chocolate malt. But why even go there when you can sample seasonal concoctions such as honey-lavender or fresh-mint flavor?

Stand *24 E 12th St between Fifth Ave and University Pl (212-488-5900).*

999 Borrow a book in Bryant Park

In the depths of the Depression, the New York Public Library did something wonderful: It established an outdoor library in Bryant Park (42nd St between Fifth and Sixth Aves), a library that lent books to whomsoever might want them, without demanding any kind of ID—you simply signed out your book, read it in the park that day, and signed it back in when you were done. Using custom-designed carts, volunteer librarians and donations from publishers, the park authorities have revived this fabulous idea. Drop by on a sunny day and bask in an uncommon demonstration of human trust.

1000 You've got to be exhausted. Have a rest

Sit down—maybe in the Rose Reading Room at the NYPL. Or in Sheep Meadow in Central Park. Or on the W out to Coney. Or on Dylan Thomas's stool in the White Horse Tavern. Or… oh boy, here we go again.

A-Z index

Note: number refers to page, not list entry.

Thematic index

Ad index

Please refer to relevant pages contact details

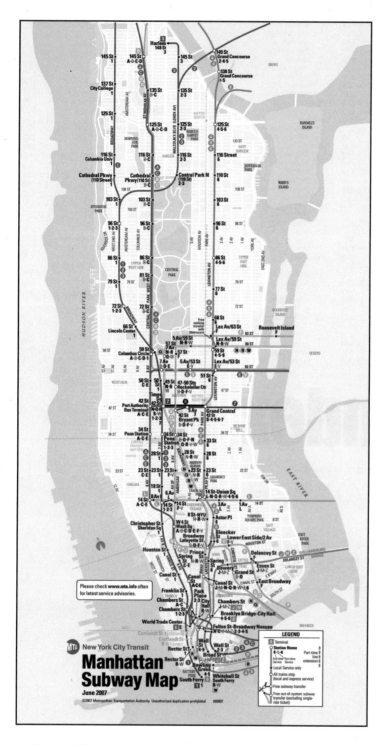